THE ROAD

Reading

Professor Théodore H. MacDonald, currently Director of Postgraduate Studies in Health at London's Brunel University and a consultant with the World Health Organisation, began his professional career nearly fifty years ago as a primary school teacher. Born in Quebec, Canada, Professor MacDonald holds undergraduate degrees in Music, Mathematics, Psychology, Physiology and Theology and doctorates in Mathematics, Physiology and Medicine, and has held chairs in Mathematics and Medicine as well as two chairs in Education. He has spent many years engaged in research on the psychological factors involved in acquiring reading and numeracy skills. In addition, he has practised as a GP both here and overseas.

Prior to taking up residence in the UK in 1987, he had extensive professional experience in a number of Third World nations, and has also held posts in the United States, Australia, Germany, France and Canada. Although his health-related research and teaching make stringent demands on his energies, he remains active on the education front. In frequent demand as a lecturer to parent groups and often requested to run INSET days in schools, he has been encouraged by numerous users of his successful 1982 book on the teaching of reading to bring out the present volume.

Théo and his wife, Chris, live in London and, now that their nine children have all left home, they are both kept in line by a level-headed black-and-white cat named Flower.

A selection of some other books by the same author

Elements of Mathematical Analysis
The Individual, Society and Health
Teach Your Pupil to Read
Teaching Primary School Mathematics
Teaching Secondary School Mathematics
Basic Mathematics, the Child and the Parent
The Literate Child
Perspectives on Illiteracy
Developments in Cuban Education
First Aid in Reading, Writing and Spelling
Hippocrates in Havana

for children
Hey! Ya Wanna Fight?

THE ROAD TO
Reading

Professor
Théodore H. MacDonald

AURUM PRESS

First published in Great Britain 1998
by Aurum Press Limited, 25 Bedford Avenue, London WC1B 3AT

A catalogue record for this book is available from the British Library.

ISBN 1 85410 583 3

Design by Roger Lightfoot
Typeset in 11/13 Palatino
by Action Typesetting Limited, Gloucester
Printed and bound in Great Britain
by MPG Books Ltd

To my grandchildren
this book is lovingly dedicated

Acknowledgments

Over the many joyful years I have spent teaching, numerous gracious people – children, teachers, parents – have contributed to making this book possible. To list them all by name would be out of the question, but to them all, nevertheless, I extend my heartfelt thanks.

With respect to the actual assembly of the book and its presentation, I must first record a monumental debt of thanks to my editor, Anica Alvarez. I have worked with many editors in my time, but none has been as patient or as thorough as she in the pursuit of educational integrity. The manuscript itself was typed by a young primary teacher trainee, Andrea Boyes. Her consistant thoroughness, accuracy and commitment speak well for her potential in her chosen profession.

Finally, but by no means of least importance in the execution of the work, I acknowledge the love, devotion and understanding of my wife, Chris.

To myself alone belongs the credit for any errors or imperfections in the text.

Théodore H. MacDonald
London, August 1998

Contents

Introduction

The Author's Purpose

What I have done in this book is to lay out a coherent, step-by-step system that you can follow in teaching your child to read and write. Under normal circumstances this can be done just prior to a child starting school or, if he* is already experiencing difficulty, alongside formal schooling. It is *not* intended to replace schooling, but to inspire a love of reading and to overcome such negative emotions as the fear of failure. Followed as intended, this method allows you to interact meaningfully with your child on a project which provides immense scope for the cultivation of intimacy, the inculcation of values and the creation of opportunities for that cherished sense of achievement. Because you value your child you will want to do whatever you can to enhance his development. Ideally, all children should be taught to read and write in this one-to-one way, because every child is unique and sensitive in ways that only his parents can be expected to know.

However, it is not a task to be assumed lightly. It *does* require work and commitment on your part and the child's, and a good bit of co-operation on the part of the entire family. But let us look at the positive side! In the deepest sense possible, it is intensely enjoyable. It is an enterprise like no other, for you are sharing ever so closely in the formation of your child's very

*Please note that I have used the masculine pronoun throughout. It avoids use of such artifices as 'he/she' and, as well, acknowledges the fact that about 80 per cent of children experiencing reading difficulties are boys. Naturally, great debate rages as to the reason for this, but the resolution of that issue is not the remit of this book! Although I use the masculine pronoun exclusively in the instructions, I have been careful to accord equal status to males and females in the material to be read by the child.

consciousness. The 'hard work' and 'commitment' aspects do not go on for long. Easily within one school year the job will be done. Of course, I don't guarantee that it will stop there! It has been my experience that parents and children grow to so value this kind of meaningful interaction that they tend to go on – sometimes to other school subjects, but more often to other, non-academic, life-enhancing activities.

While it is true that your goal will be achieved most quickly if you follow the routine precisely and completely, we are not all saints (in fact, I don't know any!) and doubtless sessions will be skipped and there may be fallow periods when you feel like giving up. But even if you follow the programme for only a month or two, the child will have already mastered many of the critical subskills. I am not recommending that you give up after so brief a time; but even if you did, the chances are that the child would have already learned enough to pick up the rest on a catch-as-catch-can basis at school. The results would not be anywhere near as good as if you had persisted, but your child would have been greatly advantaged by what you had done. The important thing to bear in mind is that this system does work if used sensibly.

The Child Must Come First

At this point, though, let me stress to any parent contemplating this undertaking the importance of keeping the enterprise posi- tive and esteem-enhancing.

Every session must be such that the child completes it valuing himself and the project even more than he had before embarking upon it. This will not happen if the parent is over- anxious and/or is overtly oriented towards competitive success for their child. For instance, try to keep it as a special project for you and your child. Don't use it as a means of getting him to 'perform' for other parents or to make him feel that he is 'better' than his playmates. Reading is best learned as a consciousness-enhancing skill, *not* as a competitive sport! Best results seem to be attained by parents and children who simply get on with it in good humour and purposeful intent. Frequent displays of anger or resentment on the part of either yourself or your child possibly suggest the need for a calm reevaluation of priorities and procedures.

The question invariably arises as to how your child's life at school might be affected by your efforts at home. For a great many reasons, schooling has not been as overwhelmingly successful in cultivating literacy as people have hoped it would be. Although reading is a basic skill, it is only one of many skills which schools are charged with teaching. In addition, we now expect the school to fulfil so many ancillary roles in our children's lives that there is even less time available for them to devote to strictly scholarly skills.

The professional preparation of school teachers involves a university degree course, but this has to cover an immense range of material. I, as a former professor of education and as one who is thoroughly familiar with the curriculum in such courses, know that only rarely is the teaching of reading taught as a specific skill and in a series of identifiable stages. What happens is that the trainees are told that there have been, and are, a number of possible approaches to the task – including phonics and whole-word recognition – and that the best routines seem to involve an eclectic mix of methods. Often the trainee teachers are given instructions in various aspects of educational psychology, but are not given enough specific instruction in methodologies of teaching reading for them to feel confident about it. The result is that they are obliged to simply fit in with whatever method prevails at whichever school they take up as their first post.

Indeed, two final-year, primary school teacher trainees, attending different highly regarded universities in London, were asked to read through the manuscript of this book and to comment on the programme presented. Both mentioned to me independently that reading this material constituted the first systematic instruction on the teaching of reading that they had experienced. In their entire training, it had not been dealt with. One even had no idea of how syllabication tied in with both word meaning and spelling!

The Basic Approach

The approach used in this book is strongly phonics oriented and is squarely based on the findings of a number of large-scale research projects. You will probably find that it is much more 'structural' and 'phonic' than anything your child's school teacher is offering. Indeed, I have met many qualified and intelligent primary school teachers who do not know the difference between long and short vowels (you will, if you use this book!), let alone when to use them, and who are decidedly hazy on elementary grammatical structures in English. Despite these differences, though, your home-based efforts need cause no friction with the methods used by your child's school. Even if the initial approaches differ, the method you are using so quickly develops an analytically sound approach to reading that it will within two or three months converge with and enhance the school programme. Basically, if your child learns to read before he starts school, the problem will not arise. If he is already attending school when you start, what you teach him out of this book will simply come as extra help in the phonics side of reading and spelling.

In my experience, few modern teachers react negatively when a parent mentions that he is, or has been, teaching a child at home. In the 1960s, this sort of thing was often a recipe for conflict, but that is not so now. Most contemporary primary school systems are sufficiently flexible as to allow scope for children with different home backgrounds in reading to work on slightly different material. Of course, best results are obtained in an atmosphere of co-operation.

So, is there a risk that your child will become bored at school if you take a hand in teaching this most important skill at home? This is a hoary old chestnut that for decades has served to warn parents away from the task, but it has no basis in fact. Even children who have been taught to read and write fluently before starting school are no more likely to be bored in a modern primary school than are children who haven't. Indeed, there is considerable evidence for the reverse, and the reasons are not hard to find. Modern primary teaching methods involve what I describe as a 'joyful and positive interaction with an array of exciting information and concepts'. The child who can already read and write will be able to engage with all of this even more effectively than would otherwise be the case. As mentioned earlier, time spent on the systematic teaching of reading as a skill in school is comparatively scant. The child who already has that skill may well feel enhanced by revisiting the fundamentals under the teacher's supervision, or, engage in it at a more sophisticated level. Boredom is a common enough curse in large group instruction situations, such as prevail in schools, but there is no evidence that a prior ability to enjoy books renders it more likely!

Therefore, have no fear. I invite you to embark on a voyage of self-discovery and an enriching relationship with your youngster. If you have never done this sort of thing before, I can guarantee that it holds in store for you and your child a host of treasures. Enjoy it.

Why Is Reading Important?

Books are frozen voices. As soon as I pick up a book, open it and begin to read, it speaks to me. Is there any experience quite like this one – so transporting and yet so easily accessible to anyone? An Arab saying has it that 'A book is a garden that fits in the pocket' (they must have either had small gardens or big pockets!) and a German adage tells us that 'A book is no more than a thick letter from a dear friend'. Neither of these analogies fully captures the pleasure of reading, but the fact that reading is an activity that has become internationally enshrined in proverbs gives some indication of its importance in people's lives.

We all recognise that reading and writing are fundamental skills, probably more basic than numeracy, for even to be in a situation in which calculation is required, some reading and writing are likely to have already been involved. But, of course, we don't read only to gain usable information. We read to excite ourselves, to experience the unexpected, to be challenged and moved; we read to explore feelings and possibilities that would otherwise be denied us. There are other media – such as radio and television – but only reading sets scenes while leaving one able to interpret them freely. It is this essentially 'private' aspect of reading which, I suggest, makes it the most enduringly popular of pastimes in the developed world. Indeed, literacy rates are widely used as one of the measures of the effectiveness of governments world-wide and of the very level of a country's development. My own research on the psychology of adult illiteracy has amply demonstrated that the ability to read is probably the most significant single factor (out of many) in determining a person's sense of autonomy and self-worth.

Is Reading a Difficult Skill to Acquire?

Since we are referring to such a crucial skill, a skill on which an individual's and a nation's liberty depends, a real concern must be the level of intellectual ability required to sustain it. If, for instance, it was shown that reading required a minimum IQ of 149 (only 1 per cent of the population exceed that!), we would have a serious social problem on our hands. It would imply that, with the best will in the world, the vast majority of people could never experience freedom as we know it. This is not idle speculation. I can think of a number of skills that I can never hope to get the hang of – certain sports, for instance, or portrait painting. Some skills really are not widely accessible and are the privilege of a gifted elite. Most of us can make a list of such skills which we can admire in others but realise that we cannot acquire.

However, fortunately, the capacity to learn to read and write is a wonderfully democratic endowment. I personally have taught people to read, and to gain pleasure from reading, who were so poorly endowed intellectually (an IQ of 60, in one case) that they have had to live in protected accommodation and to work – if at all – in sheltered workshops. I am referring to the sort of people who cannot understand the simplest of arithmetic and therefore have to have their shopping done for them and who cannot be allowed to cook their own food.

Why, then, you might ask, are there so many people who cannot read and write? Well, there are many answers to that question. For instance, we know of the condition called 'dyslexia' which makes it extremely difficult for even some highly intelligent people to make sense of print. Diagnosed early enough, though, even that condition can be effectively addressed in most cases. Also, we have a state school system which is so conspicuously deprived of resources (capital and human) that it is unable to give children the intensity of attention they need to effectively acquire literacy skills. Millions of young adults leave their secondary schools every year with just enough grasp of reading and writing to scrape by, but not enough to make the exercise of it an enjoyable pastime or a preferred method of communication. This is a disgrace, of course – and the blame does not lie primarily with the army of teachers at the front-line battling against fearful odds to cultivate these crucial skills.

Indeed, apportioning blame for this state of affairs has become something of a national indoor sport. In the larger scheme of things that is an important issue and its resolution even more important. However, it is likely that anyone who has read this far into the book has already adopted the view that the most effective contribution they can make is to do something about it personally.

The ability to read and write truly is a birthright and is something you no doubt wish your children to have. But hoping is one thing – actually achieving it is something else. My argument is that this most precious of basic skills is virtually guaranteed if you take the matter in hand yourself. Any number of studies has shown that children who are supported at home in acquiring good literacy skills make the most effective use of their formal schooling. This is so even if procedures and materials used by the parents differ from those used in the school, because both converge on and enhance literacy in the long run.

A Special Comment to Teachers

I will close this introduction with a comment to teachers. The method presented in this book also works well when used with learning-support classes and/or one-to-one work. The sequence of phonic analysis here presented is the most complete in print and also forms a sound basis for adult literacy programmes. For this latter category of student, of course, the reading material in the exercises would not always be the most appropriate.

The Title of the Book

A word about the title of this book is in order. About forty years ago, when I was camping in the Berkshire countryside, I came across a road sign:

ROAD TO READING

The thought crossed my mind that such a brilliant pun should not be wasted and I resolved that if I ever wrote a book on the teaching of reading, a better title would be difficult to find!

May you and your children enjoy using it as much as I have enjoyed writing it.

1

Using this method

Aims: Basic and General

The first and basic aim of this book is to show you how to teach a child to read 'from scratch'. This can be done if you follow the instructions exactly. The process is described precisely and has been thoroughly researched. I have been using and refining it for forty years and in that time have taught many teachers how to use it. In this book, the method is explained step by step so that ordinary parents who are not trained teachers can use it.

However, beyond the basic aim, the book's purpose is to indicate how you can insure that your child develops 'literacy'. We hear a lot about literacy – and illiteracy – but their meanings are not widely understood. In fact, there are several technical definitions of 'literacy'. As the term is used in this book, a 'literate person' is one who uses reading and writing spontaneously *as a means of communication*. It is not enough to be mechanically able to struggle through a page of print, calling each word out laboriously and to be able to write down one's name and address! A person can be trained to do both of those things and still not be able to communicate easily using those skills.

Thus, a child must be able to read in order to be literate, but that is not all there is to being literate.

In the process of teaching a child how to read, one can also teach him how to write. This book shows you how. Moreover, it also includes instructions on how to teach the child to *use* his writing effectively. Enough basic grammar is explained in Chapter Twenty-five to enable you and the child to give direction and coherence to his sentence structure. That chapter will not be relevant to the needs of every parent using the book (it was included with the needs of older children in mind – children who have already had trouble learning to read in primary schools and whose parents wish to take the task in hand themselves); however, you may find it of interest. You may also find of interest the detailed overview of this method and the research that supports it which are discussed in Chapter Three.

Length of Time Required

Often – and naturally – parents ask: How long will it take my child to go through this method? That depends on so many factors that it is really difficult to put a precise time span on it. We do know that it is *not* directly related to IQ, except at the extreme ends of the scale. But there are a great many more mundane factors to take into account: motivation of the child, amount of time devoted to each lesson, regularity of the lessons, etc. Whether or not the child sees you reading a lot for pleasure and stimulation is doubtless a major factor.

However, we can answer the question to some degree as far as *reading* is concerned. Let us assume that you give the child a lesson every day, beginning with twenty to thirty minutes per lesson, but gradually working up to an hour. Very roughly – because there are wide variations – we can say that in *about* six or seven months the child might well be reading fluently. Some children learn much more quickly than that, but I have had others take longer. It is important, though, to realise that reading, in one respect, is rather like driving. Once people can drive, they can drive! One day it just clicks, and while their confidence may grow with time, there is no way of telling, from watching them drive, how long it took them to pass the licence test. In fact, research done in California established that variations in driving skill and accident records have no connection at all with how long a driver took to qualify. The same is true of readers. Therefore, in teaching someone to read, don't be concerned about how long they take. The important thing is that you have taken the matter in hand and got started. Just methodically work through the exercises at the pace set by the child, systematically following the course.

As for *writing*, it is much more difficult to say how long it will take to teach someone this skill, as it varies even more greatly from person to person. This is discussed in greater detail in

Chapter Twenty-four.

Structuring the Lessons

As I mentioned in the Introduction, literacy brings with it much delight, but like many skills that we acquire for pleasure, achieving it nonetheless requires a seriousness of purpose. While we want the child to enjoy learning, it must be clear that you are not playing games. He must learn to concentrate and, in general, to enter into the spirit of the enterprise.

You, as the teacher, must be quietly insistent, cheerful, flexible and well organised. Remember to be positive throughout and not to force the child to go at a faster pace than is comfortable.

Organisation makes a tremendous difference to your effectiveness in teaching. Have a *fixed time* for the daily lesson, a time that you, the child and the rest of the family know is sacrosanct. It mustn't be chopped and changed around to suit extraneous demands. Likewise, have a *special place* where you do the lessons. There should be good light, comfortable, straight-backed chairs, a table and all of the required equipment to hand.

In the matter of equipment, you will need:

2 HB pencils
1 black, felt-tip pen
1 pencil sharpener
1 pack of index cards
several exercise books
1 rubber
1 folder to keep the child's work as he progresses through this book

The equipment must always be there and should be set aside *only* for the reading lessons. Once you allow it to be used by other people for other purposes, bits and pieces will go missing. Having to stop in mid-lesson to look for a rubber, or some such item, greatly diminishes the impact of the lesson.

Furthermore, neither you nor the child must be distracted during the lesson. One cannot expect a child's power of concentration to develop if the lessons are interrupted by conversations with other people or if the lesson is taking place within earshot of a television.

Preparing Yourself

To use this method well, make sure that you are thoroughly familiar with it. Before starting with a real, live child beside you, take a few hours to become acquainted with the book.

First, read Chapter Two *thoroughly*. If you are interested in the subtleties of this method or are an educational professional, do please read Chapter Three. However, if you are a parent who simply wants to teach your child to read, please feel free to skip that chapter. Next, read Chapters Four through Twenty-three. These cover the actual instruction in how to teach the child to read and will give you a grasp of the method to be used. It is important that you thoroughly familiarise yourself with the method before you begin, because, unless you do, your own confidence in using the method will suffer. Children are quick at detecting uncertainty in a teacher and respond adversely to it.

It is of interest to note that in Britain the 'a' sound, as in 'father', is generally given a slightly different inflection than is the case in other English-speaking countries. A great deal has not been made of this in the present text because children being taught from it will acquire the inflection used by their teacher or parent.

Finally, a word of warning. These exercises are specifically designed to be used *precisely* as indicated in the text. On no account should they be used out of sequence or without first paying meticulous attention to the lesson material relevant to each exercise. Any attempt to use these exercises otherwise than here indicated could seriously confuse a child and either cause him to develop reading problems and/or intensify those he already has.

Having said that, good luck and have fun.

2

First things first

A Two-sided Task

In this book you will be shown how you can teach a child to read and, moreover, how you can do it in such a way as to make him want to keep on reading for pleasure and profit throughout life. Thus, right from the very start, you *must* be equally concerned with two aspects:

1 The purely mechanical skill by which the child proves to himself and to you that he can turn lifeless print into spoken language.
2 The psychological issue: Is he happy doing it? Does it enhance him as a person or does it make him anxious and self-doubting?

As with the process of acquiring any skill, there will obviously be times when your child resents the necessity of spending time practising when he would rather be playing, but such incidents are usually episodic. However, if the child deeply dislikes his reading lessons and *always* fusses about them, don't persist in the hope that, if you can only drive the mechanics of reading into him, he will forget that he disliked the process and later come to enjoy books! That won't work. Moreover, if you find yourself always becoming irritable with your child, don't allow yourself to continue in that vein. Real and prolonged resistance on either side means that you must stop and reassess the situation.

Problems Which Can Arise

Some of the things which may be wrong are:

He is too young, either chronologically or psychologically

Age

It is difficult to state categorically *when* a child should be old enough to learn to read. Some may start at four or five and enjoy it, others shouldn't start even at six or seven. It is not related necessarily to intelligence and no hard and fast rule can be made. Generally, if the child enjoys having stories read to him, relives them in his imagination and plays them out, recalls them in conversation and can become emotionally involved with them, he will benefit from being taught to read.

Insecurity (and related emotional problems)

As a general rule, children love being read to. However, if a child feels insecure or in some sense doubts his parents' love for him, he may be reluctant to learn to read in case they then leave him on his own. I remember a case of a little seven-year-old girl who could read perfectly well and then suddenly got worse and worse until, in a matter of five months, she could barely read at all. What had happened? Her grandmother, who for years had read to her, said to the girl on her seventh birthday that she was a big girl now and didn't need to be read to any more. However, the little girl liked the intimacy of being read to. We are never too old for intimacy! An interesting clue arose when, on her seventh birthday, the child said, 'I want to stay six forever!' When I remembered this and put two and two together, the solution was simple: Grannie started to read bedtime stories again, and within weeks the little girl's reading picked up.

Children will let you know when they want you to stop reading to them. One of my children was twelve years old and was already reading complicated political books on his own before he stopped wanting stories read aloud to him.

Books aren't important to his parents

This implies, of course, that the parents and the household itself are not 'book oriented'. It is *very* unlikely that a child will find books emotionally relevant if his family doesn't.

When I was teaching primary school years ago, I had one bright, healthy and active six year old in my class who was making almost no progress in reading. He came from a 'good' home in terms of all the usual criteria: the family were affluent, they lived in a good, upper-middle-class area and often went on holiday to interesting and exciting places. His father and I both enjoyed fishing and often met socially. On one occasion I was invited to the house. The parents proudly showed me over their 'dream home'. It was replete with three TV sets, a sports/games room, a bar, sound equipment: every gadget imaginable – and some unimaginable! *But there wasn't a single book to be seen!*

Eventually, the conversation got around to their son's 'reading problem'.

'Do you ever read and talk about books?' I asked.

They replied in the negative, at the same time offering all sorts of reasons, as though they had to justify themselves.

'Oh hell,' said I, 'it's not a moral issue. If that's your lifestyle, and it's legal, you don't need to offer any excuses. But if your boy can see that *you* don't need books, why should he think that *he* does? I can teach him the mechanics – like someone teaching me the rules of cricket – but without practice he will never get good at it and the best motivation to practise something is finding pleasure in it. You two seem to get pleasure without reading, so why should he think differently?'

'But reading is so important,' said his father.

You bet your life reading is important! Whoever invented writing made a number of meaningless marks, each linked to a meaningless sound. But taken together they laid the foundations for a meaningful civilisation! The person who doesn't read and who doesn't enjoy reading is seriously disadvantaged, even socially. Huge areas of our common life are shut away from him and he moves about the periphery of things dreadfully unaware of so much, unable to fully participate. But if reading appears to be irrelevant to you, then it is likely that the child will find it to be irrelevant as well.

There is a health problem

Usually, the sorts of health problems that make it hard for a child to read are not obvious. They often don't interfere with his ability to play or socialise. So, to avoid difficulties down the line, before you start teaching your child, get him checked over by your doctor. Things to look out for are:

Amblyopia (lazy eye)

One eye doesn't work with the other to focus on detail. The condition is easily detected by a simple test, but is a nuisance to correct. Nevertheless, do see to it as early as possible because it becomes more difficult to correct as a child ages. Certainly, a child cannot learn to read comfortably with amblyopia, and to force reading upon him while he still has the condition can damage both his eyes *and* his self-esteem.

Eye-defects requiring spectacles

Until recently most people imagined that only older people ever needed glasses. This is not true. We now know that such conditions as myopia and astigmatism are not uncommon even among six year olds. Correction does require spectacles, but if the matter is seen to right away *and if the child is forced to wear his glasses as directed*, the condition often corrects itself within a year or so and the glasses can be dispensed with. If the child is allowed to lose his specs or to keep 'forgetting' to wear them, the condition will worsen and he will end up having to wear glasses for life. *Never* fool with a child's eyesight or allow him to do so. It is amazing how quickly simple, correctable eye conditions can become extremely serious if the doctor's advice is treated lightly.

Hearing problems

Reading involves turning little black marks on paper into spoken language. As such, it involves the child in being able to discriminate accurately between certain sounds. Even children of normal hearing often have difficulty discriminating between the 'm' sound and the 'n' sound until they are five or six years old. If a child's hearing is at all affected, he will have at least *some* trouble in reading. Most hearing problems can be corrected fairly easily.

There are various other medical conditions which can interfere with learning to read, but it is not necessary to go into them here. The important thing to remember is to make sure that the child has a medical check up before you embark on this adventure.

Other commitments

There is not enough time

What *does* your child do with his day? As discussed earlier, it is *imperative*, if the instruction is to have any chance of success, that you fix a specific time for the daily lesson. If his life is structured in such a way that his reading lesson must compete with time allocated to football practice, music lessons or television, then it is up to *you* to set the priorities.

Television is usually the devil in the piece! To avoid any resentment he might feel at being forced to give up viewing time, begin to restrict this *before* embarking on the lessons. That way, he will not equate learning to read with missing out on TV. In any case, any more than an hour or so of viewing time a day is probably too much, and an hour can easily be scheduled for after his lesson or before it. Monitor his viewing and you will probably find that most of what he is watching is unsuitable junk anyway.

Remember: the time is sacrosanct. Nothing must be allowed to interfere, even if you have to sit with your child in the car to get him away from domestic distractions!

Homework uses up all his free time

So far we have only considered the case of a child being taught to read at home. However, you may be helping a child with his reading because he is already having trouble at school. Almost invariably you will run up against the problem of homework. In reality, children in the early primary grades are not given that much homework, but – by definition – the child who has reading problems has more homework than do other children (because he rarely finishes his classroom work and has to 'finish it at home') and, of course, takes far longer to do it. I recall a child in 1955 (he is now a gynaecologist, so there was obviously nothing wrong with his intellect) who, although eight years old at the time, took three and a half hours to fill in six words ('catch', 'hatch', 'match', 'colour', 'set' and 'never') on a word-completion test assigned for homework! Even then, his sister ended up telling him how to spell each one of them. The child was virtually a 'non-reader' (although he quickly learned after two months' daily work in phonics at home) and disliked any task involving even the simplest reading so much that he dawdled endlessly. As I recollect it, the parents were determined (and rightly so) not to do his homework for him.

In situations even remotely similar to that one, the solution is to schedule in the homework alongside the child's other activities. In the first three years of school at least, homework is virtually never administered in excess of what a child can be expected to complete in less than an hour. If your child takes longer than that, then he needs supervising. This does *not* mean doing the homework for him – although the temptation can be almost overwhelming! What it *does* mean is that he must be compelled to stick with the task, to concentrate and not engage in any other activity until he has finished. If he cannot get it done in the hour, then he simply loses out on what he doesn't complete. This in itself serves the proper purpose of alerting the teacher to the child's difficulties. Homework that has been quickly and correctly done by virtue of the child having his dad or mum do it gives the teacher no useful feedback at all and only allows the child's unattended learning problems to worsen.

In any case, within a few weeks of systematic instruction, many of the child's reading problems will begin to disappear. This is not to say that the school is necessarily doing a bad job. Many factors can cause a child to have reading problems, only some of which come under the school's proper sphere of influence. The most usual problem is one of class size. The teacher may have twenty-nine other children to see to, all of them at different stages of development. No matter how well trained and capable the teacher is, even if the lessons have been well taught your child may not have been able to absorb them because the teacher had to aim the information at such a large number of children. In a situation like that, the parent has one distinct advantage: namely the one-to-one relationship with the pupil!

The Basic Technique

Despite the irregularities of English spelling, English is *basically* a phonically regular language. In fact, approximately 97 per cent of English words can be pronounced correctly by phonetic analysis of their spelling. Of course, much of the force of that comment is lost when one realises that:

1 Some of the rules of phonic analysis in English are rather obscure and replete with a welter of exceptions.
2 Included in the 97 per cent are all technical words (e.g. 'electromagnetic', 'haematoblastosis') and most non-technical long and rarely used words. The very common words, such as those relating to emotions, states of being, personal relationships, etc., contain a much higher proportion of non-phonic entities (e.g. 'are', 'be', 'have', 'cousin', 'father', 'rough', 'though').

If you think about it, this latter state of affairs (which is true to a degree in all alphabetical languages) is not unreasonable. The most common words – those that relate to the person and his possessions, relationships, states of being and fundamental activities – are the oldest. They are apt to reflect a long span of linguistic history, whereas sophisticated words and technical vocabulary came into the language much later – certainly after written forms of the language had been worked out and a comparatively stable set of conventions elaborated.

This can lead to some interesting anomalies. A child who has only had a few encounters with phonics might well be able to read 'antidisestablishmentarianism', 'optimistically' and 'retro-atavistic' and yet be baffled by 'the', 'so' and 'friend'. However, this does *not* militate against teaching phonics. In fact, acquiring a coherent and reliable set of phonic word-attack skills soon gives a child the confidence to tackle 'unknown' words, even non-phonic ones, with a high probability of success. For instance, consider a note which a five year old in one of my pre-school classes found on the road and brought to school. It was printed and said:

Derek –
Don't forget the van bumper. If you get stuck, I can be got at
547 9219.

I wrote the note up on the board. The children had only had
six weeks (twenty-seven days, exactly) of phonic instruction for
thirty minutes a day. 'Derek' came very quickly, in terms of the
children being able to say it without help from me. I explained
that 'Derek' was someone's name. 'Van', 'bumper', 'if', 'get',
'stuck', 'can', 'got' and 'at' all came soon after. 'The' had to be
taught as they did not know the phonic rule 'th' yet.

One child then said, 'Dawnt [rhyming with "gaunt"] far-get
the van bumper.' Almost immediately, the sentence 'clicked'
with most of the children, although a few of them repeated it
with 'Dawn't' and 'far-get' several times before the more
logical word sequence came to them. What was even more
interesting, none of them could say what a 'van bumper' was,
but they *could* gather that it was a thing that Derek must not
forget.

Two of the children knew what 'I' was and I let them tell the
others. 'Be', which they pronounced as in 'best', confounded
them. I therefore told them that one. Saying the number
presented no problems because of their very *lack* of sophistication! Slightly older children might have said, 'Five million, 479
thousand, two hundred and nineteen'; but not mine. They just
read out each digit and then realised that it was a phone
number.

Thus, with very minimal training in phonic analysis, those
young children could decipher a genuine adult communication. Their pride in the accomplishment was boundless.

Pleasure in Decoding

Whether you are teaching your child from scratch through a
carefully graded phonic approach or helping a struggling pupil
by systematically developing phonic analysis, you will notice
positive results within the first few days. One of the first such
results is an almost immeasurable confidence that *anything* can
be read – and indeed *any* printed word can thus be brought to
some kind of life, even if it is incorrectly pronounced! This is

quite different from the effect of introducing reading from a
'whole-word' or 'look–say' approach. Such an approach does
not give the child even the *impression* that he can decode words
he has never seen before. Along with this sense of power over
words comes the motivation to practice. Lists of words he has
never before seen – but which have been carefully selected by
you to reflect the phonics he already knows – are eagerly
attacked with both skill and confidence, which increase as he
moves down the list.

A lot of nonsense has been written and spoken about
'reading for meaning', to the effect that a child is not 'reading'
if he is simply 'barking at print'. What such comment fails to
appreciate is the elemental, almost mystical *pleasure* children
derive from being able to convert meaningless black marks into
predictable utterance. 'Meaning' is a relative term. 'Barking at
print' has meaning for the child because he can turn the black
marks into words. He has power over the system. To an adult
such an activity might be meaningless if he could not understand what the words were saying. But even that is doubtful.
For some time I taught New Testament Greek at university. As
the reader probably knows, the Greek alphabet is different
from our own and so is spoken Greek. To begin with, the
students (and they were all adults) had to learn the strange
alphabet and the sounds of the letters. Invariably, after that
first lecture, they derived immense pleasure from orally
reading Greek passages – either from the New Testament or
from other sources – even though they had no way of knowing
what the words meant. It was simply a revelling in the power
of breaking a code – and they were adults! 'Barking at print' *is*
meaningful and is the best basis for learning how to read.
Children will even approach lists of one-syllable sounds –

be   (as in <u>be</u>d)
de   (as in <u>de</u>nt)
fe   (as in <u>fe</u>d)
he   (as in <u>he</u>lp)
je   (as in <u>je</u>t)

– with zest and practise gladly, providing the strongest possible foundation for decoding print.

The method used in this book, then, is primarily phonic. I
have *very* rarely found it to fail (only once, in fact, in forty years

of using it!), but as I have said, it cannot be approached hastily or haphazardly. Follow the lessons meticulously and in order. Do not be in a hurry and do not exert undue pressure on yourself or your child. Make sure that each lesson is completely understood and fluently read before proceeding to the next one. Be calm, confident and of good cheer.

Learning to Read and Reading

Consider a skill such as riding a bicycle. Most children learn by attempting the actual task. This can be a bit messy, somewhat alarming for drivers, rough on the bicycle and an occasion for sundry bruises and abrasions. But in most cases it eventually works. The child actually learns how to ride a bicycle while he is doing so! Is there an easier way and does such an approach to learning work with a skill such as reading?

With respect to learning to ride a bicycle, an adult novice would be very ill-advised to learn the way that children do. He is heavier and much more likely to hurt himself badly in falling off, and he would certainly do more thorough job of damaging the bicycle! Such an adult would tend to approach the whole thing more analytically. He would carefully watch a few take-offs, he would try to get some feel of balance by sitting on a bike held upright by someone else; that is, he would precede bike-riding by a session or so learning how (and even why) it works. But children generally prefer the 'learning by doing' method.

Reading is rather like learning to play the piano. When children start music lessons, they want to be able to play immediately, so most music teachers start them off with a few simple tunes that can be played with the five fingers of the right hand; but the teacher knows that such an approach is not really teaching the child how to play the piano – it is only to secure his interest. Real teaching, and learning, can only begin when the child is motivated enough to put up with the necessary theory, mechanical drills and daily practice.

In some ways, reading is the same. The child can be given the illusion that he is reading by being taught to recognise the shapes of forty or so different words (roughly the equivalent of the 'five-finger tune'). As you may appreciate, this is not 'reading' as we know the term, but it can be done. If you try to go much beyond forty words which have to be recognised separately, the task becomes very laborious – rather like learning Chinese script. It took me ten months of hard work (ninety minutes a day of intense practice) to learn 1200 Chinese characters – and that was only *just* enough to read news bulletins, simplified summaries of research articles, etc.

But let us suppose that you are tempted to do it the Chinese way first. Find about forty words. Most of them will have to be nouns, of course, so that they can be portrayed pictorially. With each few that are memorised, make up sentences and to be read off the page. Using so few words, you will be highly restricted, of course, and the sentences you can make will hardly hold a child's interest for long:

Tim runs.
See Tim run.
Tim! Tim! Tim! Run! Run! Run!
Run, Tim. Run!

In a much shorter span of time, the child could be taught phonics to a level sufficient to enable him to read material that really interests him with no serious restrictions on the number of words he can use. Moreover, several research studies have shown that to commence reading instruction with whole-word methods actually makes it *more* difficult for the child to use phonics afterwards. What may work as a gentle introduction to piano playing without harm may not work so well with the teaching of reading!

In my personal experience, I have always found it best to start directly with phonics, even though this means for some days the child is only learning to respond fluently to phonic letter combinations, very few of which are actual words. However, when he does get started on reading, he is able to move forward quickly and accurately. In addition, I have always concurrently taught children (and illiterate adults) to write, which very much enhances their capacity to spell correctly.

I well remember that, with one of my own children, I varied this procedure. When he was three, I was teaching his elder sister, aged five, how to read by the tried and true phonics-first approach. He listened in from time to time, picked up a few phonic rules – though not many – and came to recognise many of the whole words that she was reading. In fact, she used to teach them to him when they played school. Therefore, when he came to learn to read, I more or less just gave him a 'lick and a promise', assuming with his sight vocabulary and his facility in reading easy readers that he just needed a bit of phonics thrown in. I left the rest up to the schools. The result is that, unlike all eight of his siblings, he didn't maintain a taste for reading, and writing and spelling have remained terrible chores for him.

It is far more difficult to correct such a situation with older children because they have to be willing to go right back to the beginning, which presents a number of psychological problems.

The point of mentioning all of this is that, as soon as you start teaching your child, he will almost invariably want immediately to begin reading whole stories and words that 'mean something'. To some degree you may have to give in – for instance, he will want to see his name printed – but you should resist the idea of teaching him whole words as an approach to reading. Let the mechanical phonic drills be a pleasure in themselves.

On a practical note, it is a good idea at first to keep the daily instruction down to no more than thirty minutes or so – although most children will then practise on their own for longer than that. The activity should be gratifying, not stressful.

In closing this preliminary discussion, the importance of *reading stories aloud* to your child must not be forgotten. This is even *more* critical during the first few weeks of phonic work because it contrasts nicely with the necessary emphasis on mechanical drill. In that context, too, avoid asking the child to decipher words in the middle of a story that you are reading aloud to him. This interrupts the flow and the atmosphere created by the story itself and by your reading of it. Reading aloud to your child can be one of the most intimate occasions of the day. If he thinks that you are going to suddenly demand a reading task from him part-way through, this greatly reduces his capacity to enjoy the story and to derive all the positive psychological benefits from your contact with him. Thus, especially at first, keep the phonics drill quite separate from your bedtime story reading sessions.

What Should the Child Be Reading?

Long before the child has been through this complete book with you, he will doubtless be reading material not contained in it. At appropriate places in the text, the suggestion is made that you encourage this and explicitly provide for it. However, I avoid making prescriptive suggestions as to precisely *what* this extraneous reading material should be as there is now a huge array of stimulating and amusing books which a child might use in his initial forays into reading for pleasure and probably no one book or set of books will be best for any two children.

Before that issue becomes pressing, a good idea is to visit your local library on your own and see what interesting books are to be had. Some series are so popular that parents feel that if their child is not turned on by these books, then there must be something wrong with the child! The Dr Seuss books tend to fall into this category. They might be your child's cup of tea, but they might not. Another set of books which still enjoy great esteem are the Ladybird series of little readers. These make available all of the 'traditional' folk tales, such as *Cinderella* and *The Three Bears*, at two different reading levels. At level one, the print is larger and the number of words used is fewer, while at level two, the narrative is less constrained by a restricted vocabulary. But again, not all children will go for them. Indeed, one cannot even assume that our children will like these stories just because we did.

When one of my daughters was seven, someone gave her a beautifully illustrated copy of *The Wind in the Willows*. The book was a pleasure to look at and handle, even without reading it. What did my little Philistine do? She wrote a thank you letter for it, but never read past page five. When I asked her what she thought of it, her answer was: 'It's a stupid story. I don't like it. But don't tell Aunty I said so!'

The lesson to be learned is not to be stampeded by other people's judgements of what your child should or should not like. You are probably in a much better position to judge that, and even you will often get it wrong.

After a few experiences with books selected by yourself, take the child to the library and let him browse. Even he will sometimes get it wrong and pick a book he can't get into. If so, don't make an issue of it. Simply let him return it and get another.

3

A detailed overview of this method

Introduction

This chapter is *not* required reading for a parent who simply wants to go about the process of teaching a child to read. It is included *only* for those who may have some academic interest in the matter or who, as professional teachers, for instance, may be interested in the general rationale for the procedures advocated in this book. Therefore, people whose aim is the purely practical one of teaching a child to read and who do not wish to investigate the academic background to the issue will miss nothing if they simply skip this chapter and go on to the next one.

It is important to note at the outset, as every primary school teacher knows, there is no one best method of teaching children to read. Indeed, studies done on good readers show that they eclectically adopt a whole range of word-attack skills – phonics, whole-word recognition, use of syntactic and semantic clues, guessing, etc. – and bring these to bear smoothly and effortlessly in extracting meaning from print. However, research has shown – as shall be briefly detailed later in this chapter – that although reading involves several subskills, the *sequence* of attaining these skills is of enormous importance in determining whether or not a child becomes a fluent reader.

For instance, all good readers have a 'sight' vocabulary, a list of words which they recognise in written form instantly without the necessity of decoding. In an adult, especially an academic, such a list is huge. Starting in the 1940s in the United States, a movement arose, and soon gathered a very enthusiastic following, which advocated getting children started on reading by having them learn a core of sight words first, so that they could have the positive psychological reinforcement of reading a little book (or a series of them) right through without any preliminary training in structural analysis or alphabetics and spelling. Until then, the emphasis had been on beginning with letter–sound bonds (each letter given one sound) and the rote spelling of words. It was found that this earlier approach created immense anxiety in many young children and effectively put them off reading altogether. The whole-word recognition system seemed, by contrast, to point a way out of this because (properly mediated) it engaged the enthusiasm of young children immediately and conferred on them a sense of mastery.

If that technique is followed, some children, through copying their sight words on paper, gradually work out enough of the rudiments of phonics to see how the system works. English (unlike Spanish or Italian) is not the best language with which to do this, however, for the relationship between letters and sounds is somewhat inconsistent in English. The situation is amusingly illustrated by the observation that 'fish' could be spelt 'ghoti': 'gh' as in 'tough', 'o' as in 'women' and 'ti' as in 'station'. (The perceptive reader will quickly recognise the fallacy in such an analogy used as an argument against the use of phonics, but the author did see it seriously put forward by a lecturer in a California teacher-training college as late as 1966!)[*]

Defects of the Look–Say Method

The fundamental problem with emphasising acquisition of a sight vocabulary as an initial teaching method was not so much that it simply deferred the real task of reading until later, but that it made that task almost insuperably difficult for both child and teacher when it finally was addressed. Why was this so?

---

[*]This amusing example was *reputed* to have been put forward by George Bernard Shaw, who had a bee in his bonnet about alphabet reform. The perceptive adult will know from experience that English, due to the fact that it derives from so many linguistic roots, reflects certain anomalies in its spellings. However, these are irregularities in the main. For instance, 'gh' *does* sound like 'f' in some words – 'tough', 'rough', etc. – but never at the beginning of a word, and sometimes not even at the end of one: 'although'. Moreover, these minor clusters of irregularities do not constitute a serious rebuttal to the proposition that phonic analysis does work on most words.

Hindsight is a wonderful thing and those first enthusiastic exponents of the look–say method can hardly be blamed for not being able to predict the problem, which was, simply, that the process of learning to recognise whole words by their general shape and then trying to remember them in different groupings caused most children to use guessing as a priority in attacking new words. Once the serious business of systematically applying an analytical word-attack skill, such as phonics, was introduced, many children had already developed the habit of guessing when uncertain. This new discipline, coming after such licence, not only suddenly made reading rather disagreeable and tedious, when it had been such fun before, but also made a chaos of attempts to teach children to spell.

Given that, one might well ask: Why not continue with whole-word recognition? The answer is that one can easily learn to discriminate between, say, forty word shapes – enough words to make up the text of a very thin 'reader', though even then with lots of unnatural repetition. Some look–say reading schemes go beyond a very basic forty words to, say, 150 – enough to fill three readers with rather inane stories. By that point, trying to keep track of 150 shapes is definitely imposing a rather severe test on memory, and, although 150 words sounds rather a lot, it falls short of the working vocabulary of even a five year old classified as operating under what is euphemistically known as a 'restricted code'. Disadvantaged five year olds from the inner city characteristically use and understand three or four *thousand* words at *least* in day-to-day conversation!

Obviously, a technique for teaching reading that does not come anywhere near to allowing a child to recognise his own utterances in print is rather seriously defective.

Advantages of a Phonics-first Approach

Of course, look–say and phonics are not the only alternatives, but a similar analysis of other word-attack routines easily shows that, by themselves, they are neither ideal as initial teaching methods nor can they carry the process far without having to invoke other subskills. One advantage of phonics is that one can go such a long way with it as a subskill in its own right on the basis of a few easily learned rules. As one becomes more and more sophisticated in the use of it, one can gradually add a few more sight-words – in the case of phonics, words that fall outside the phonic skills already learned or that are even totally phonically unfriendly – and the child's reading skill will (ordinarily) develop apace. Another clear advantage of phonics is that the process of phonic analysis gradually becomes more rapid, so that it is not long before many of the words which the child is accustomed to working out by phonics slip into his growing sight vocabulary.

But overwhelmingly, the strongest argument for phonics as an initial teaching method (and this is well borne out by the research described at the end of this chapter) is that it allows the child to develop simultaneously the skills of decoding (reading) and encoding (writing). In addition, it provides a system which is always understandable, even if the spelling is not conventional. Thus, a child might wish to write: 'I like to read and write about soldiers and their battles' and render it as: 'I like to reed and rite about sojers and their battells'. This, despite the plethora of spelling errors, is completely under-standable. Any teacher who has struggled with the attempted encodings of children taught initially by the look–say system will appreciate the difference!

For instance, a five year old whose reading lessons had initially emphasised word recognition once gave me a picture. Under the picture – which itself gave away very few clues (a perfectly normal state of affairs with five year olds!) – was a line of writing:

Makar gtg To refttosn

One has to be very careful in situations like this, because the worst thing is to discourage the child from attempting to write, so the conversation went something like:

Me: 'Oh, thank you. What a clever boy! Tell me about the picture.'
Child: 'Me dad took me and the dog and all.'

Vainly I struggled with the writing to see if I could pick up any of what he was saying in it so that I could then pretend to read it out. I was defeated, but in a moment of inspiration, I said, 'I bet the hamster can't read what you wrote. Go and tell him what it says!'

The translation? 'Mark goes to the firestation.'

I have the drawing in front of me as I write this and I can say that the author (and artist) is now an accomplished chief librarian at Georgetown University in Washington D.C., so his unpromising beginnings with written English clearly did not bespeak any lack of intelligence! What it does suggest is that the child recognised in printed form his own name, 'to', 'the' and 'firestation', and these words excited him so much he just had to try to reproduce them. But he had no clues – not even a bit of a code to help him work out what each word must start with. If the reader looks at what he wrote, it will be seen that he got the relative lengths of the words right. Thus, 'firestation' is the longest phrase that he wanted to write, and so is 'refttosn' in what he did write.

For a child to write down things that even the people who know and love him cannot translate into speech must in time become a serious impediment to learning. Phonics, on the other hand, despite the spelling (which should not be excessively pushed in the initial stages as long as what is written makes sense), gives the child an *immense* sense of power over the process. The importance of this in developing a child's sense of confidence and worth cannot be overstated.

Before giving an overview of phonics, and showing thereby that it invokes much more than the mastery of letter–sound relationships, it is crucial to briefly comment on the psychological aspects of reading.

Psychological Aspects of Reading

All learning activity carries with it the possibility of failure, but most children learning most disciplines are not too worried by the prospect of not being able to master something first time round. For instance, with some school subjects, commonly mathematics, large numbers of people quite cheerfully do badly at it and seem to emerge from the experience without immense psychological harm having been done to them. Likewise, most people who start off optimistically on a musical instrument and discover they have less than prodigious natural ability, will just as cheerfully give it up before they get very far.

But reading, writing and speaking – the language skills – are different.

We have probably all met confident, accomplished, professional people who unblushingly make such comments as: 'I can't add two and two and get the same answer twice in a row' or: 'I'm so tone deaf, I can't tell the difference between *God Save the Queen* and Beethoven's Fifth Symphony'. We can admit most of our failings and laugh at them. But how often have you heard someone cheerfully admit to being illiterate? About 12 per cent of British adults are illiterate and in my work I have met many of them. They are not all dyslexic nor are they all mentally impaired. How can it be, then, that a skill which most people acquire without difficulty causes such problems for a sizeable minority?

An important part of the answer lies with the psychology of self-esteem. In a sense, one can think of some skills as being external to or separate from one's sense of inner integrity, while other skills are very much linked to the person's sense of self. For instance, most people don't really care if they become effective swimmers. They will go through the routines, attend the relevant lessons, practise while the teacher is at the poolside, etc., but if it does not pan out – well, no big deal. For such people we could really call swimming an external skill: it's nice to have if you can get the hang of it, but no great loss if you can't. Obviously, what a person regards as an external or internal skill will vary with other circumstances, such as age, etc., so that while a given skill may not seem rather important at age seven, it might be of earth-shaking importance at age thirty-seven.

Reading and self-esteem

Again, no teacher must forget the communication aspect of language, whether spoken or written. Language, of course, starts off as spoken – both in the development of an individual child and in the development of cultures. When the child is very young, one of its most intimate experiences should surely be that of being cuddled and read to at the same time. That creates such a strong, supportive, positive association that it is difficult to underestimate its psychological value. By being read to, the child experiences words in the deepest aesthetic sense – words not as ciphers only but as embodying emotion and tenderness. The desire to re-create that sense of protection and shared pleasure is probably the strongest single incentive for wanting to learn to read. It is also a strong argument for the parent being a child's first reading teacher.

Numerous studies have shown that children who have been read to at home are far more likely to develop into effective readers than those who have not – whatever method of reading instruction is used. That is why, when one is actually teaching a child the phonic code, one should take into account these other psychological factors.

At various points throughout this text I indicate strategies for broadening out and encouraging the child to read material other than the sparse and mechanical exercises provided here. The exercises in this book have an important place in developing a smooth command over the code itself, but at all times the teacher must remember that the most important objective is to meet the needs of children seeking to *use* the code.

The child is more important than the skill

The ability to use language is certainly a skill which can be learned, but it is more than that. It is, perhaps more than any other accomplishment, inextricably tied in with a person's sense of being. For instance, speaking is not merely an oral code-making activity – it is a projection of that person. If the way a child speaks is ridiculed or is otherwise not accepted, he does not think, 'I'm all right, it's just that I can't talk conventionally.' Indeed not! He is much more likely to think, 'I'm no good.' The same is true of all the literacy skills. Careless criticism of inadequate performance in that area can cause deep psychological harm to a child's sense of self-esteem. A basic rule in teaching a child to read and write is that the sessions must be structured so that he is almost always successful. Failure to perform adequately must never dominate a session, at most it should be a transitory event in an otherwise positive feedback situation: 'Sometimes you turn your "b"s and "d"s around. Let's do a bit of practice on that so that they come out as well as the rest of your work!' As any teacher knows, the use of sarcasm, threats, invidious comparisons and humiliation constitute bullying and have no place in any kind of teaching of any subject, but in the language arts it is particularly unforgivable because it assaults a child's very sense of himself.

Similar considerations should warn the teacher against an overly mechanistic approach to the teaching of reading. The child is not likely to lose sight of the fact that reading is pleasurable – in other words, it is a skill with some purpose outside of itself – but a teacher might easily forget that. One can get so carried away with the intrinsic interest and logic of the 'rules' – spelling and that sort of thing – that one can forget to give the child something interesting to do with it. When I was a young boy, the priest who taught us Latin used to take a few of us aside twice a week to teach us Greek. Initially, our motivation was intense: here was a different alphabet and a highly esoteric-sounding language. But our enthusiasm soon died away because the good Father was fascinated with the purely 'architectural' splendour of ancient Greek grammar. Unlike his Latin classes, in which he illustrated his lessons by getting us involved in long, complicated conspiracies associated with the in-fighting in the Roman Empire, in Greek he taught nothing but grammar. Indeed, the text he used was an ugly, little, green book called *Essential Greek Grammar* and among ourselves we used to discuss how it could possibly be 'essential' as we could see no earthly use for it! It was only years later that I realised that the book's title referred to the fact that it covered the 'essence' of Greek grammar only and was not concerned with its application beyond that! The experience put us all off Greek. It was only by the merest chance that I came across a collection of Greek myths and legends later in life and found them so absorbing that I was then motivated to use what I had been taught out of the *Essentials* to make sense of them.

Using reading skill for pleasure

Thus, long before the child has acquired sufficient phonic skill to be able to read widely, he will want to be able to read books and stories. This calls for some flexibility on the part of the teacher. It is no good saying, 'No, you can't for another six months.' We have come a long way from the days when I was a child and each of the books in the library had either a pink or a blue sticker on it – pink for girls, blue for boys – and one was forbidden to read books bearing the wrong colour sticker! But, even in modern primary schools, I have heard children being told that a book they have chosen is too old or young for them. A much more acceptable approach is to let the child choose any book he wants. To start off you may have to tell the child almost every word. If it really is too far out of the child's grasp for whatever reason, he will soon get bored and simply ask to be allowed to choose another book. Once it is clear that the book picked by a given child is likely to sustain his interest, then it is wise to glance through it when the child isn't there to find all the words that are going to be problematic.

As far as possible, children should not be made to feel that their choice of books has an approval rating. Often, accomplished readers will go through a phase of reading little storybooks that, to us, appear far too juvenile for them. But as we have seen, reading is a very 'psychological' process. Reading such books may be reassuring to a child (or an adult!) who might be feeling insecure about some other aspect of life.

What Do We Mean by 'Phonics'?

As mentioned earlier, I have found that, even today (or possibly particularly today), many teacher-training programmes do not actually instruct student teachers how to teach reading from scratch. There is often discussion about it – about various methods for encouraging it, etc. – but little explicit and systematic instruction in how to go about it. The graduates of such programmes are expected to (and largely do) fit in with whatever teaching system their first assigned school uses. As recently as 1994, I was talking to a group of final-year primary education students just prior to their graduation. I was amazed to discover that none of them was sure what long and short vowels were! They couldn't be blamed, of course. Not only had no lecture actually dealt with the subject, but they could not see why it might be useful to know about them.

A view widely held about phonics is that it is a process of sounding out words based on established letter–sound relationships. If that is what phonic instruction is confined to, it will be found that it does not work on many English words. But phonics far transcends such a limiting remit. If the reader of this chapter now looks through the rest of the book, it will be seen that acquisition of the full range of phonic analysis follows a systematic sequence of simple routines. As far I have been able to ascertain, no other account of English phonics is as complete as the one embodied in this text. Although various readings schemes claim to cover phonics 'incidentally' or 'as one word-attack skill among others', I have never run across one that addresses phonics as comprehensively as I do in this book. First, though, a brief overview of the main features of phonic analysis might be useful.

The alphabet and 'sounding out'

The basic tool in phonic analysis is the alphabet. As indicated later in this book, this can be learned first as a series of sounds – in which case the sequence of letters need not be conventional – or one can simply teach a child to recite the alphabet and to recognise each letter shape by name. Done that way, it makes best sense to follow the conventional letter sequence. Even at this rudimentary stage, a bit of humour can liven things up:

Q: Why is the letter 'V' terrifying?
A: Because it always comes after you.

I have encountered no research study which indicates the superiority of one or other of these approaches to learning the letters, but since most children pick up the alphabet from jingles on television, etc. long before they learn to read, there is probably a strong argument for teaching them the sequence first and then the sounds after.

Various studies have identified the most common phonograms.[*] For instance, three letters ('e', 't' and 'a') account for 32 per cent of the total letters used in English words. Add three more letters ('e', 't', 'a', 'n', 'o' and 'i'), and these six account for about 50 per cent; eleven letters ('e', 't', 'a', 'n', 'o', 'i', 's', 'r', 'h', 'd' and 'c') account for 75 per cent. The ten most commonly used words make up more than 25 per cent of the words used altogether, while only 100 words account for about 50 per cent

---

[*]A sequence of written symbols having the same sound in a variety of different words, for example 'ough' in 'bought', 'ought' and 'brought'.

of all the English words used by the average English-speaking person!

While it is fairly easy to assign unambiguous sound-values to individual vowels, this is difficult to do with consonants. Indeed, even the word 'consonant' suggests that the sound is not pure: 'con' (with), 'sonant' (sounding) – with another sound. Thus, how does one attach a sound-value to the consonant 'l'? First of all, it differs according to whether it comes at the beginning of a word ('lips') or at the end ('gull'). An approximation of an initial sound for 'l' might be 'le', with the 'e' de-emphasised so as to easily merge with the next vowel sound in the word, as in 'lamp', 'lend', 'list', 'lost', etc. An approximation of a terminal sound for 'l' might be rendered as 'ul', as in 'mental', 'gerbil', 'spell', 'doll' and 'bubble'. Both of these phenomena are rendered less problematic if we move away from individual sounds to liaisons of consonants with vowels ('la', 'le', 'li', 'lo', 'lu') and vowels with consonants ('al', 'el', 'il', 'ol', 'ul'). Such is one of the systematic approaches employed in this text.

Blending and phonograms

A major hurdle in teaching children to use phonics involves the 'blending' of sounds. We want to move the child on from reading 'cat' as 'kuh–a–tuh' to the point at which the 'ca' is sounded as 'kah' immediately with a quick 't' sound following. It is a process which this author has been found to be very much expedited by the child sounding out, then developing an instantaneous recognition of all the consonant–vowel blends, e.g. 'ra', 're', 'ri', 'ro', 'ru', 'sa', 'se', 'si', etc., before words are encountered. An even stronger foundation can be laid if one also teaches the child to respond quickly and unambiguously (and correctly!) to the vowel–consonant blends. When these two steps have been thoroughly mastered, blending presents few difficulties and a sound basis for fluent reading has been laid.

There are further hiccups, of course, even before one runs into the rules for long and short vowels. For example, two- and three-consonant phonograms need to be systematically drilled before a child can be expected to sound out words like 'stem' or 'sprig'. The most common two-letter initial-consonant phonograms are: 'st', 'sh', 'ch', 'th', 'cr', 'tr', 'sp', 'br', 'gr', 'cl', 'wh', 'sl', 'dr', 'fr', 'bl', 'pl', 'fl', 'sw', 'pr', 'wh', 'sm', 'sn', 'gl' and 'tw'. Of course, 'th' can be 'soft' ('the', 'them', 'then') or 'hard' ('thank', 'thin', 'thought'). Then one needs to address final-consonant phonograms, the most common of which are: 'nd', 'ng', 'll', 'ck', 'st', 'nt', 'ss', 'sh', 'ld', 'ch', 'th', 'nk', 'ft', 'mp' and 'ct'. Initial-consonant phonograms are best mastered in combination with each of the five vowels: 'sta', 'ste', 'sti', 'sto', 'stu', etc., and the same is true of the final-consonant phonograms: 'and', 'end', 'ind', 'ond', 'und', etc.

If one were only teaching reading as a mechanical phonic-decoding activity, there is much more that could be done along these lines, but since the purpose is primarily to assist reading, one must soon turn one's attention to the question of long and short vowel sounds, because they are basic to so much ordinary vocabulary. A good starting point is the rule of terminal 'e', as in: can/cane, pin/pine, pet/Pete, rob/robe, tub/tube, etc. When these have been thoroughly mastered, other ways of making long vowel sounds can be considered: 'ai', 'ay', 'oi', 'oy', 'oo', 'oe', 'ou', 'ow', 'aw', etc.

Once a child has learned this much, especially if he has learned to write as well as to read such phonemes,* he can (and should be) reading quite widely outside of routine phonic exercises. The actual sequence of phonic instruction followed in this book has proven to me to be the best, but no meticulous empirical research has been done on it.

Irrespective of sequence, though, a really key phonic skill involves the understanding of syllabication** and the accurate recognition of syllables in words. This involves an appreciation of open and closed syllables and of the idea that a syllable is defined in terms of having a single vowel sound, which, needless to say, is *not* necessarily the same thing as a single vowel! Obviously, the most common prefixes and suffixes also need to be explored and their spellings mastered.

---

*One of the set of speech sounds in any given language that serve to distinguish one word from another, for example 'ph'.
**The process of dividing a word into its constituent syllables.

What Research Tells Us

There are strong arguments for systematically laying out and explaining the whole arsenal of phonic word-attack skills then drilling children until they are proficient in the use of these skills. The basis on which such a claim can be made has been unambiguously established not only in my mind and through my own experience, but through the results of a number of rather convincing longitudinal studies. This chapter will close with a summary of some of these findings.

There has been a plethora of empirical experiments – principally in Britain and the United States – designed to ascertain the relative efficacies of phonics and look–say as initial methods in the teaching of reading, but the really fascinating thing about it is that all but one have indicated that a phonics-first method produces the best results. In 1991, Her Majesty's Inspectorate in Britain issued a report* which, among other things, made the point that various teaching methods work, *provided that any method includes systematic instruction in phonics.*

As far back as 1913 (when look–say reading schemes were first becoming popular), Professor C.W. Valentine of the University of St Andrews, Scotland carried out the following experiment. He took a paragraph of descriptive prose from Robert Louis Stevenson's *Kidnapped* and rendered it in Greek letters. He then gave two groups of twenty-four students each two minutes in which to decipher it. One group had only been coached in the phonic values of the Greek letters but had not ever been shown any complete words written in Greek. The other group had been coached for an equal length of time to recognise the actual words in the passage – in their Greek letter form – but with no instruction in the phonic values of individual letters. The first group performed exactly twice as well as the first.** From then until 1945 there was a steady stream of experiments in the United States and Britain, the results of which were reported in a book by Rudolf Flesch, *Why Can't Johnny Read?* (1955), all of which came to the same conclusion.

Despite this evidence, though, and despite the lack of any

*HMI Report No. 10/91 'The Teaching and Learning of Reading in Primary School', 9 January 1991.
**As reported in the *Journal of Experimental Pedagogy*, 1913.

empirical evidence indicating that look–say was a better initial teaching method, such research made little impact on classroom practice. Look–say prevailed. Phonics gradually became marginalised and some school districts in the United States actually banned it as being psychologically retrogressive.

However, in 1955 the trend in the United States began to reverse. The appearance of Flesch's book probably made an impact, but there were additional factors causing public unease about teaching methods, not the least of which was the fact that in October 1957 the then USSR beat the United States into space with Sputnik. By that time the Americans were aggressively revamping their entire primary school curriculum and teaching methods, partly in response to a number of scathing attacks which had been made on their poor record in the teaching of reading. (Be that as it may, just as the Americans were beginning to question the de-emphasis on phonic skills which had been the dominant trend in their schools since 1925, British primary schools began to embrace it!)

In April 1965, Dr Louise Gurren of New York University and Mrs Hughes of the American Reading Reform Foundation published an article in the *Journal of Educational Research* entitled 'Intensive Phonics vs Gradual Phonics in Beginning Reading: A Review'. It listed thirty-six studies and concluded:

1 Rigorous controlled research clearly favours the teaching of formal phonic analysis from the start of reading instruction.
2 Such teaching enhances comprehension generally as well as success in decoding individual words.
3 Children who have had systematic phonic instruction from the outset show a superiority in the language arts from age nine upwards.

Perhaps the most noteworthy analysis, though, was that published in 1967 by Professor Jeanne Chall of the Harvard University Graduate School of Education in a book entitled *Learning to Read – The Great Debate*. She reviewed eighty-five studies and her conclusions, on page 307, were as follows:

My review of the research from the laboratory, the classroom and the clinic points to the need for a correction in beginning reading instructional methods. Most school children in the United States are taught to read by what I have termed a meaning-emphasis method. Yet, the research from 1912 to 1965 indicated that a code-emphasis method – i.e. one that views beginning reading as essentially different from mature reading and emphasises learning of the printed code for the spoken language – produces better results, at least up to the point where sufficient evidence seems to be available, the end of third grade.

The results are better, not only in terms of the mechanical aspects of literacy alone, as was once supposed, but also in terms of the ultimate goal of reading instruction – comprehension – and possibly even speed of reading. The long-existing fear that an initial code-emphasis produces readers who do not read for meaning or with enjoyment is unfounded. On the contrary, the evidence indicated that better results in terms of reading for meaning are achieved with the programs that emphasise code at the start than with the programs that stress meaning at the beginning.

Another comprehensive analysis of the accumulating research evidence was done in 1973 by Professor Robert Dykstra, Chairman of the Education Department at the University of Minnesota. It appeared in the book *Teaching Reading* edited by Walcutt, Lamport and McCracken. In it he reviewed fifty-nine studies and, summarising the evidence, on page 397, he states:

Reviewing the research comparing (1) phonic and look–say instruction programs, (2) intrinsic and systematic approaches to helping children learn the code, and (3) code-emphasis and meaning-emphasis basal programs; leads to the conclusion that children get off to a faster start in reading if they are given early direct systematic instruction in the alphabetic code. The evidence clearly demonstrates that children who receive early intensive instruction in phonics develop superior word-recognition skills in the early stages of reading and tend to maintain their superiority at least through the third grade ...

We can summarise the results of sixty years of research dealing with beginning reading instruction by stating that early systematic instruction in phonics provides the child with the skills necessary to become an independent reader at an earlier age than is likely if phonics instruction is delayed and less systematic. As a consequence of his early success in 'learning to read' the child can more quickly go about the job of 'reading to learn'.

Before going further with this evidence, however, let us examine the one important experiment, done more than 110 years ago (and in German rather than English), which seemed to suggest that initial training in whole-word recognition is a more effective way of teaching children to read. The experiment was done by the renowned psychologist Dr James McKeen Cattell in 1885 at the University of Leipzig in Germany. He tested readers with a tachistoscope, an instrument that can be arranged to reveal a word on a screen for a predetermined very brief interval of time. His results showed that fluent readers could read whole words more quickly than it took them to recognise individual letters. But his logic was flawed in assuming that this implied that it would be better to start children off with whole words rather than phonics. His subjects were all already accomplished readers! In other words, he assumed that beginning readers read in the same way that fluent readers do. Amazingly, despite this obvious – and fundamental – flaw in his logic, this research has been quoted time and time again to vindicate the look–say method.

Finally, in 1965 Dr Harry Levin and Dr Gabrielle Marchbanks at Cornell University tested the whole-word method more rigorously. They took fifty kindergarten children and fifty first-graders and asked them to pick from a group of nonsense words the one most like another nonsense word already shown to them. Most of the children did *not* go by the general shape (configuration) of the word, but by the first letter of it. In 1970, Dr Joanna Williams, Ellen Blumberg and David Williams repeated the experiment. On this occasion three groups were tested: kindergarten children, first-graders and adults. The kindergarteners never used configuration as a clue, the first-graders only occasionally did so (about 4 per cent of the time) and the adults did so with only 10 per cent of the words. Dr Williams summed up the group's research by asserting:

> In view of these and other findings, there seems to be no justification for developing instructional methods or materials based on the use of configuration as the primary clue ... It is worth noting that the most widely used reading method over the past thirty years (the 'look–say' or 'whole-word' method) has stressed identification of words on the basis of configuration.

Many more subsequent research studies could be cited, but by the 1970s – in American educational circles – the phonics-first method gradually dominated. In 1979, a comprehensive three-volume work called *Theory and Practice of Early Reading*, edited by Lauren Resnick (of the University of Pittsburgh) and Phyllis Weaver (of Harvard University) was published. It contained fifty-nine papers by scholars involved in the debate, including papers by Kenneth and Yetta Goodman and Frank Smith. These three are well-known opponents of the phonics-first approach. Three other papers in the anthology take the same line. Thus, while six papers were anti, the remaining fifty-three papers endorsed the phonics-first approach. In summing up these articles and their findings, Dr Resnick writes that: 'As a matter of routine practice we must include systematic, code-oriented instruction (i.e. phonics) no matter what else we do'. Her stand, of course, is virtually identical to that taken in England in 1991 by HMI quoted earlier in this chapter.

I would like to draw this chapter to a close by quoting from three other contributors to *Theory and Practice of Early Reading*, as follows:

> Instructional procedures should inform children early on that the printed word is a model of the component phonemes (sounds) and their particular succession in the spoken word ... The instruction should not, as it often does, mislead children into assuming that the printed word is an ideographic symbol, a notion that will have to be corrected later and, apparently for some children, with great difficulty. Procedures that initiate children into the mystique of reading by drawing their attention to the visual configuration ('remember this shape, it has a "tail"') and its associated meaning ('the one with the tail means monkey') without alerting them to the relevance of the sound structure of the word may lead them into a blind alley. Their ability to memorise the shapes and associated meanings of a handful of words may lull them and their parents into the comfortable belief that they can read, but it may leave them stranded at that stage, functional illiterates with no keys to unlock new words.
>
> Dr Isabelle Y. Liberman and Dr Donald Shankweiler,
> University of Connecticut

> I had an opportunity to discuss what was needed to improve the teaching of reading with Tom Sticht, John Guthrie, Harry Singer and Dennis Fisher. There was consensus that at the present time a sufficient amount is known about practical aspects of reading so that all children, even those at risk (the lowest 15 per cent on the IQ scale) can be taught to read. The problem, then, is not a

lack of knowledge about how to teach reading. The problem is ...
not very different from the problems of changing the smoking
habits of the American public. Presently we know that smoking
is dangerous to health. Despite this knowledge, many people are
unable to change their smoking habits, and many others take up
this harmful habit. The task of changing smoking habits is probably more formidable than changing the reading practices of
school systems...With the recognition by taxpayers and educators alike that the school must be accountable in some sense for
the products of its system, we may well be moving toward an era
in which schools will be doing a more efficient job of teaching
reading.

Dr Jay Samuels, University of Minnesota

And finally – and rather resoundingly:

Near failure-proof methods for teaching all children to read are
already available. Continued failure of schools to employ these
(phonics-first) programs is at best negligent and at worst mali-
cious.

Dr Barbara Bateman, University of Oregon

I have refrained from quoting in detail my own research findings on the epistemological bases of reading skill acquisition,
based on work in the United States and Australia. Suffice to say,
it heavily supports the argument that phonics-first is the most
cognitively effective approach to the teaching of reading to children.

4

Planning the sessions

Introduction

I cannot stress often enough that there can be few set expecta-
tions as to how quickly a child of a given age can or should
learn. As a society we are perhaps too pre-occupied with that.
Literacy is one gift that is indispensable and likewise it is one
that virtually every child can receive (barring serious develop-
mental problems). It is every child's *right* to be literate.
Therefore, we must make sure of it without concerning
ourselves as to whether he is learning more slowly or quickly
than anyone else! As well, different children have different abil-
ities. Your child may have no problem with long and short
vowels, but take ages to cope with soft 'c' and 'g', while another
child may be just the reverse.

Teaching your child to read and write is *not* a competition; it
is the conferral of a birthright.

Therefore, I am reluctant to suggest a timetable for the
sessions in case it creates anxiety where none should exist.
However, the following suggested Programme of Lessons gives
a rough guide to what many users of this method have found.
I refer to Lesson 1, Lesson 2, etc. and not days of the week
because individual parents will vary in whether they have a
session daily or only on weekdays and, as I have said, each
child will learn at a different pace.

My practice has always been to have one session every day,
regardless of the day of the week or the time of the year. A session
does not make a serious inroad into either your free time or the
child's, and yet daily sessions provide continuity and build up
confidence more quickly. Again, while the sessions should be
thought of as 'serious', they should never be regarded as disagreeable and therefore regarded as 'unfairly' inflicted on holi-

days! For instance, children learn all sorts of interesting things from their parents, such as how to get dressed, how to ride a bike, etc. We don't forsake learning those things on holidays. Why should literacy – the child's passport to freedom, dignity and self-expression – be different?

In the programme that follows, your child may not need the preliminary stages of the alphabetics, for instance. Therefore, use the guide eclectically. But one thing I would urge is: don't be in a hurry. There are no Brownie points for getting through the stuff in record time! No two children are identical and there is little reason to suppose that the programme suggested here will *exactly* coincide with the length of time required by your child for each stage of the process.

Suggested programme of sessions

Although you will already have read the introductory chapters, and perhaps even some of the later chapters, I would draw your attention to the importance of reading (and even reread-ing) the appropriate chapters before embarking upon the corresponding lessons. Some of what I discuss is common sense, but I also discuss potential problems and how to resolve them. Moreover, as I stated earlier, it is your responsibility to be prepared.

Chapter Five: Getting started

Reread Chapter Two and read Chapter Five.

Lesson 1	Preliminary work.
Lesson 2	Preliminary work and alphabet.
Lessons 3–7	Alphabet.
Lesson 8	Short vowels.
Lesson 9	Short vowels and some consonants.
Lesson 10	More consonants: Exercises 1–6.
Lessons 11–13	Consonants: Exercises 7–19.
Lesson 14	Review.
Lesson 15–16	Capital letters: Exercises 20–38.
Lesson 17	The 'qu' sound: Exercises 39 and 40.
Lesson 18	The 'x' sound: Exercise 41.
Lesson 19	Vowel–consonant blends: Exercises 42–58.

Chapter Six: One-syllable words and simple sentences

Read Chapter Six.

Lesson 20	Single-syllable words with the short 'a' sound: Exercise 59, lines 1–5.
Lesson 21	More single-syllable words with the short 'a' sound: Exercise 59, lines 6–11.
Lesson 22	Single-syllable words with the short 'e' sound: Exercise 60, lines 1–5.
Lesson 23	More single-syllable words with the short 'e' sound: Exercise 60, lines 6–10.
Lessons 24–30	Single-syllable words with the short 'i', 'o' and 'u' sounds: Exercises 61–63. Working on the basis of a daily session, it generally takes about a week to get through this material comfortably and securely.
Lesson 31	Reading passage: Exercise 64.
Lesson 32	Reading passage: Exercise 65.
Lessons 33–36	More reading passages: Exercises 66–68, at the rate of one per day, with the exception of Exercise 68, which may require two days. Keep the cursive practice going. By now almost all of the child's writing should be cursive.

Chapter Seven: Longer single-syllable words

Read Chapter Seven.

Lesson 37	Double consonants: Exercises 69–71. Generally, these are all learned in the same session; in the dictation section, allow for some good cursive writing practice.
Lessons 38–39	Two-consonant word beginnings: Exercises 72 and 73.
Lesson 40	Three-consonant word beginnings: Exercise 74.
Lessons 41–42	Review of two- and three-consonant beginnings: Exercises 75–77.
Lessons 43–45	Two-consonant word endings and review: Exercises 78–80.
Lesson 46	The 'ck' ending: Exercise 81.
Lesson 47	Reading practice: Exercise 82.

Chapter Eight: Words of more than one syllable

Read Chapter Eight.

Lesson 48	Explaining syllables.
Lesson 49	Explaining vowels.
Lesson 50	Explaining consonants.
Lesson 51	Two-syllable words: Exercise 83.
Lesson 52	The 'nk' ending: Exercises 84 and 85.

Chapter Nine: Some useful beginnings and endings

Read Chapter Nine. While working on this chapter, you should include some oral reading from stories the child likes you to read to him. Select a small section and – *before the lesson* – lightly underline in pencil all of the words which the child will not be able to work out. This is so you can tell him those words as he comes to them. If there are not too many, you might find that he will guess at them and get them right.

Lesson 53	The 'sh' sound: Exercise 86 *only*. Remember to do some reading aloud and dictation.
Lesson 54	The 'ch' sound: Exercise 87.
Lesson 55	The 'th' sound: Exercise 88.
Lesson 56	The 'ng' sound: Exercise 89.
Lesson 57	The 'ing' ending: Exercises 90–92.

Chapter Ten: More beginnings and endings

Read Chapter Ten.

Lesson 58	'Y' endings: Exercises 93–95.
Lesson 59	The 'w' and 'wh' sounds: Exercises 96 and 97.
Lesson 60	The 'er' sound: Exercises 98 and 99.
Lesson 61	The 'ir' and 'ur' sounds: Exercises 100–102.
Lesson 62	The 'ar' sound: Exercises 103 and 104.
Lesson 63	The 'or' sound: Exercises 105 and 106.
Lesson 64	The terminal 'le' sound: Exercises 107 and 108.
Lesson 65	The 'all' sound: Exercises 109 and 110.

Chapter Eleven: Four important blends with 'i' and 'y'

Read Chapter Eleven.

Lesson 66	The 'ay' and 'ai' sounds: Exercises 111 and 112.

Lesson 67   More sight words and reading practice: Exercise 113.

Lesson 68   The 'oy' and 'oi' sounds: Exercises 114 and 115.

Chapter Twelve: Short and long vowels

Read Chapter Twelve.

Lesson 69   Short and long 'a': Exercises 116 and 117.
Lesson 70   Short and long 'i': Exercises 118 and 119.
Lesson 71   Short and long 'o': Exercises 120 and 121.
Lesson 72   Short and long 'u': Exercises 122 and 123.
Lesson 73   Short and long 'e': Exercises 124 and 125.

Chapter Thirteen: More work on syllables

Read Chapter Thirteen.

Lesson 74   Compound words: Exercise 126.
Lesson 75   Open and closed syllables: Exercise 127.
Lesson 76   Doubling a consonant: Exercise 128.
Lesson 77   Two unalike consonants: Exercises 129 and 130.

Chapter Fourteen: The 'ou', 'ow', 'oo' and 'ol' sounds

Read Chapter Fourteen.

Lesson 78   The 'ou' sound: Exercises 131 and 132.
Lesson 79   The 'ow' sound: Exercises 133 and 134.
Lesson 80   More 'ou' and 'ow' sounds: Exercises 135 and 136.
Lesson 81   The 'ou' sound and review: Exercise 137.
Lesson 82   More 'oo' sounds: Exercises 138 and 139.
Lesson 83   The 'ol' sound: Exercises 140 and 141.

Chapter Fifteen: The various 'ea' sounds

Read Chapter Fifteen.

Lesson 84   The most common 'ea' sound: Exercises 142 and 143.
Lesson 85   'Ea' as in 'learn': Exercise 144.
Lesson 86   'Ea' as in 'break' and 'death': Exercises 145 and 146.

Chapter Sixteen: The sounds in 'kind', 'wild', 'load' and 'few'

Read Chapter Sixteen.

Lesson 87   The 'ind' and 'ild' sounds: Exercises 147 and 148.
Lesson 88   Variations on the long vowel sound of 'o': Exercises 149 and 150.
Lesson 89   The long vowel sound of 'u' in disguise: Exercises 151 and 152.

Chapter Seventeen: Plurals with 'y' and further work on short and long vowels

Read Chapter Seventeen.

Lesson 90   Plurals of words ending in 'y': Exercise 153.
Lesson 91   Short or long vowels with words ending in 'y': Exercise 154.
Lesson 92   Words ending in 'ed': Exercises 155 and 156.

Chapter Eighteen: Hard and soft 'c' and 'g' can deceive unless you believe!

Read Chapter Eighteen.

Lesson 93   Hard and soft 'c': Exercises 157 and 158.
Lesson 94   Hard and soft 'g': Exercises 159 and 160.
Lesson 95   Words with 'ie' and 'ei': Exercises 161 and 162.
Lesson 96   Review: Exercise 163.

Chapter Nineteen: More common sounds

Read Chapter Nineteen.

Lesson 97   The 'tion' ending: Exercises 164 and 165.
Lesson 98   The 'ous' sound at the end of words: Exercise 166.
Lesson 99   Other 'sh' and 'ch' sounds: Exercises 167 and 168.
Lesson 100   Three awkward combinations: Exercises 169 and 170.

Chapter Twenty: The 'ph' and 'gh' sounds and the fourth 'y' sound

Read Chapter Twenty.

Lesson 101   The 'ph' sound: Exercise 171.

Lesson 102   The 'gh' sound: Exercise 172.
Lesson 103   The fourth 'y' sound and review: Exercises 173–175.

Chapter Twenty-one: Some word families

Read Chapter Twenty-one.

Lesson 104   The 'thought' family: Exercise 176.
Lesson 105   The 'taught' family: Exercise 177.
Lesson 106   The 'work' family: Exercise 178.
Lesson 107   The 'high' family: Exercise 179.
Lesson 108   The 'air' family: Exercise 180.
Lesson 109   The 'father' family: Exercise 181.
Lesson 110   The 'busy' family: Exercise 182.
Lesson 111   The 'Australia' family: Exercise 183.
Lesson 112   The 'suit' family: Exercise 184.
Lesson 113   The 'active' family: Exercises 185 and 186.

Chapter Twenty-two: Silent letters

Read Chapter Twenty-two.

Lesson 114   The silent 'k': Exercise 187.
Lesson 115   The silent 'g': Exercise 188.
Lesson 116   The silent 'w': Exercise 189.
Lesson 117   The silent 'b': Exercise 190.
Lesson 118   The silent 'l': Exercise 191.
Lesson 119   The silent 'h': Exercise 192.
Lesson 120   The silent 't': Exercise 193.
Lesson 121   The silent 'gh': Exercise 194.
Lesson 122   Review of various silent letters: Exercise 195.

Chapter Twenty-three: Prefixes, suffixes and polysyllabic words

Read Chapter Twenty-three.

Lessons 123–125   Prefixes: Exercise 196.
Lessons 126–129   Suffixes: Exercise 197.
Lessons 130–136   Syllabication rules: Exercises 199–204.
Lesson 137   Polysyllabic words: Exercise 205.

Chapter Twenty-four: The writing side of literacy

Read Chapter Twenty-four.

Lesson 138	Sequences of simple sentences: Exercises 206 and 207.
Lesson 139	Writing using his own words.
Lesson 140	Writing in response to your questions: Exercise 208.
Lesson 141	Asking the questions himself.
Lesson 142	Writing as personal expression.
Lesson 143	Formal instruction in sentence construction: Exercises 209 and 210.
Lesson 144	The paragraph.
Lesson 145	Written responses to picture sequences.
Lesson 146	Extended writing from personal experience.
Lesson 147	The structure of a simple theme.

5

Getting started

The Alphabet

There are a variety of ways of presenting the letters of the alphabet. Sometimes they are shown one-at-a-time (both capital and lower case) and taught by name. If three or four letters are presented a day with a daily review of the ones already learned, the child will know the letters of the alphabet in a week or so. Then he can be taught one sound for each letter (never mind the exceptions and variations at this point) at the same rate, so that – with daily review of past work – by the end of two or three weeks, the child will know every letter (in capital and lower case form) and a sound value for each. At other times the *sounds* of the letters are taught first, rather than their alphabetic names. You may choose to do it that way. However, in the approach which you are now reading, I have set out the programme as though you are going to teach the *names* of the letters first. Whichever method you choose to use, once the letters and sounds have been learned, the rest of the programme will apply equally to all students.

Lesson 1: Preliminary work

Introduce the child to a complete set of magnetised plastic lower-case letters – all twenty-six of them – but don't name them. Let him mount them on a fridge door or an equally convenient surface. If you don't have a magnetised surface, a table top will do. The only thing you must insist on, on this first day, is that each letter be the right way up and right way round. (On some sets of plastic letters, there are little markers showing which part is the top, bottom, left and right but it doesn't matter whether your set has these or not.) Don't worry about letter *order* at the moment. Let the child play with the letters, but you *must* be there, giving him your undivided attention. After about twenty minutes, put them away. This must remain a treat. Tell him that he can do it again tomorrow.

When it comes to teaching your child the alphabet, avoid the common little alphabet songs. Best results are always obtained by simply learning to recite the letters in sequence. The following seven days of lessons will see that accomplished.

Lesson 2: Preliminary work and alphabet

Can the child place all twenty-six letters the right way up and with the correct left–right orientation? If so, start acquainting him with the *names* (not the sounds) of the letters in the right order. Remember: avoid the songs. Teach him the first group of four – 'a', 'b', 'c', 'd' – then stop and make sure that he can:

1 Say the group of four.
2 Recognise them when you put them in sequence.
3 Recognise them out of sequence.
4 Recognise them when you draw them on paper.

He may confuse 'b' and 'd'. If that happens, spend a few minutes practising these two letters. A good form of practice is to have the child learn to 'draw' each with a wet fingertip: lick your finger and print the letter on some surface where it shows up. Then, let the child do the same.

Lesson 3: Alphabet

Ask him to pick 'a' out of the set. Now 'b'. Now 'c'. Now 'd'. Shuffle the letters back into the pile and ask him to do it again. Now, introduce 'e' and 'f' by *name* only. Teach him the sequence 'a', 'b', 'c', 'd', 'e', 'f'. Let him pick out these letters from the shuffled pile.

Next, write them out on a piece of paper and point to individual letters at random. Keep doing this until the child can call out each letter's name unambiguously.

Review: Dump all the letters in a pile on the table and see how quickly the child can place all the 26 letters right way up and right way round – 'a', 'b', 'c', 'd', 'e' and 'f' should be in the right order, after that it doesn't matter.

Lesson 4: Alphabet

Review 'a', 'b', 'c', 'd', 'e', 'f'.

Next, teach the child 'g', 'h', 'i', 'j', 'k' from the plastic letters. When he can say the name of each of them unambiguously and pick them out upon request, make sure that he can:

1 Recite 'a', 'b', 'c', 'd', 'e', 'f', 'g', 'h', 'i', 'j', 'k'.
2 Pick all these letters out.
3 Recognise them in your printing.
4 Draw 'a' and 'e' with his fingertip, and possibly 'b' and 'd', if he has learned to do so.

Lesson 5: Alphabet

Review 'a', 'b', 'c', 'd', 'e', 'f', 'g', 'h', 'i', 'j', 'k'.

The child should be able to pick each of these letters out of the pile quickly and then place them in the correct sequence. Now, teach him the name of the next six lower-case letters: 'l', 'm', 'n', 'o', 'p', 'q'. Make sure these are learned thoroughly as with the previous clusters of letters. Confusion may arise with: 'b', 'd', 'p' and 'q'. If it does, the only solution is to practise those four letters separately and to print them, as discussed before. By the end of this session the child should know how to arrange the letters 'a' through 'q' in the correct sequence.

Review the drawing of 'a' and 'e' and of 'b', 'd', 'p' and 'q' if these have caused difficulty.

Lesson 6: Alphabet

Review letters 'a' though 'q', making sure that the child can quickly put them in the correct sequence and also can recognise them individually and out of sequence.

Teach the child to print 'i' and 'o'. Now, review the letters that he has learned to write: 'a', 'e', 'i' and 'o', and possibly 'b', 'd', 'p' and 'q'.

New letters: Teach him the names of 'r', 's', 't', 'u', 'v'. Make sure that he can tell them apart and quickly select them on request: 'n' and 'u' are often confused, so be sure he knows the difference in their position and place in the sequence of letters.

Now, review letters 'a' through 'u'.

Lesson 7: Alphabet

Make sure the child can recite the alphabet up to 'u'. Teach him to print the letter 'u'. He should now be able to print 'a', 'e', 'i', 'o' and 'u'.

Teach him the names of the last five letters: 'v', 'w', 'x', 'y' and 'z'.

When these have been thoroughly mastered, mix them in with the other letters. He should now be able to recite the entire alphabet. Remember: avoid singing or using various common rhyming verses for the alphabet.

Vowels

Now we get down to business!

Lesson 8: Short vowels

Teach the child the *short* sounds of the vowels: 'a', 'e', 'i', 'o', 'u'. This takes *lots* of patience and practice.

Remember, the *names* are:

ay
ee
eye
oh
you

But the short *sounds* are:

a   (as in apple)
e   (as in egg)
i   (as in Indian)
o   (as in octopus)
u   (as in umbrella)

Remember, keep drilling the *short sounds* for the vowels only – over and over again – until the child can make the appropriate sound for: 'a', 'e', 'i', 'o' and 'u' in *any* order.

Now, to make sure it has stuck, practise printing the letters (see 'Writing the Letters' at the end of this chapter). Start off by saying, 'Print "a" and say what it sounds like.' Do that with each of the five vowels until they are perfect.

Next, have the child print the letter that begins the words 'elephant', 'umbrella', 'ant', 'excellent', 'odd', 'Inca', 'aspic', 'idiot', 'every', 'operate', 'ask', 'uncle'. In each case, speak clearly, really mouthing the first sound.

Consonants

The consonants can now be presented, but a little thought will show you that here we run into a problem. You will notice that the vowels can each be assigned a 'pure' sound. That is, you can open your mouth and give forth *one sound* for, say, 'a' without having to start it off with another sound. That is impossible with the consonants. Try it with 'r' for 'rabbit' – try to say the 'r' sound in isolation.

You cannot do it. Either you will say 'ruh', in which case you are adding 'uh', even if you are whispering, or you will say 'er', in which case you are adding a bit of a vowel sound to bring out the 'r'.

This is not a *serious* problem, but you must be aware of it. For each consonant, give the rendering involving an aspirated 'uh' at the end, but minimise the 'uh' sound. Figures 1–26 at the back of the book are designed to help the children learn the sounds.

Lesson 9: Short vowels and some consonants

The emphasis here is on connecting the visual and printed shape of the vowels with their short sounds. Review Lesson 8 and add the following exercise. Ask the child to name the letter that begins 'in', 'Oz', 'empty', 'axle' and 'upset'.

Next, begin to learn the sounds of the consonants, starting with 'b', 'd' and 'p'. It is a good strategy to start with these letters because, as we have discussed, children sometimes confuse these shapes in writing *and* reading, so the more systematic practice they have in telling them apart, the better. Point to each of the letters and emphasis the difference in shape and sound.

Then, show the child how to *blend* the sound of the consonants with *each* of the vowel sounds, using *short* vowel sounds only:

ba   (as in <u>ba</u>t)
be   (as in <u>be</u>g)
bi   (as in <u>bi</u>g)
bo   (as in <u>bo</u>ther)
bu   (as in <u>bu</u>s)

Say, 'Look at "<u>ba</u>"'. Point to the 'b' and have the child sound it out, then slide your finger along to the 'a' and have him give the sound of that.

His effort will sound something like: '<u>buhaaaa</u>'.

Aim for smoother and smoother blending, eventually getting him to see that the sound is 'ba' as in 'bat'. Then, have him *print* the sound combinations 'ba' as he *says* it.

Do exactly the same with the rest of the list. (Avoid the mistake of pronouncing 'be' as 'bee', as in 'What do you want to be?' Don't forget that he has not learned the long vowel sounds yet.)

When you have got that far, do some oral spelling: 'How do you spell the sound "ba", like in band?', etc. It will take a lot of practice before the child can combine the two sounds, but work at it until he has the idea.

Follow the same procedure with:

ca   (as in <u>ca</u>t)
ce   (as in <u>ke</u>pt – give 'c' the *hard* sound)
ci   (as in <u>ki</u>t – give the 'c' the *hard* sound)
co   (as in <u>co</u>p)
cu   (as in <u>cu</u>t)

Lesson 10: More consonants

Review all work from Lesson 9, then use the same method for the consonant 'd':

da   (as in <u>da</u>d)
de   (as in <u>de</u>n)
di   (as in <u>di</u>p)
do   (as in <u>do</u>g, *not* as in 'I'll do it')
du   (as in <u>du</u>g)

Give him some practice printing these sound combinations in random order as you call them out. Some more useful words are: 'dam', 'desk', 'dish', 'dog', 'duck', 'daft', 'den', 'dig', 'dosh', 'dump', 'dash', 'dell', 'Dick' and 'dull'.

Now, introduce three more consonants: 'f', 'g' and 'h' – again by *name* and *sound*. Go through exactly the same drills and sound blends.

fa	(as in <u>fa</u>t)
fe	(as in <u>fe</u>d)
fi	(as in <u>fi</u>g)
fo	(as in <u>fo</u>g)
fu	(as in <u>fu</u>n)
ga	(as in g<u>a</u>s)
ge	(as in <u>ge</u>t, *hard* sound of 'g' only)
gi	(as in <u>gi</u>ll, *hard* sound of 'g' only)
go	(as in g<u>o</u>t, *not* as in 'Go away')
gu	(as in g<u>u</u>n)
ha	(as in <u>ha</u>t)
he	(as in <u>he</u>n, *not* as in 'He went away'!)
hi	(as in <u>hi</u>m)
ho	(as in <u>ho</u>p)
hu	(as in <u>hu</u>t)

Have the child print all of these blends. Then, mix them in with the ones he has done before and have him print any that you call out at random.

Now, direct the child's attention to Exercises 1–6. He should be able to read these through quickly as you point your finger to each one. It would also help if you printed these exercises neatly on cards for the child to use at his own discretion. You will often find that a child treasures these cards, wandering about sounding out the combinations as a play activity.

Exercise 1: Lower-case 'b'

ba   be   bi   bo   bu

Exercise 2: Lower-case 'c'

ca   ce   ci   co   cu

Exercise 3: Lower-case 'd'

da   de   di   do   du

Exercise 4: Lower-case 'f'

fa   fe   fi   fo   fu

Exercise 5: Lower-case 'g'

ga   ge   gi   go   gu

Exercise 6: Lower-case 'h'

ha   he   hi   ho   hu

Lesson 11: Consonants

Introduce a few more consonants – whatever the traffic will
bear – up to and including 'p', but do not crowd the child. Go
as slowly as he requires. Sometimes this might require learning
only one new letter a day, or possibly none on some days, while
old material is being reviewed. The sound values should be as
follows:

ja   (as in jam)
je   (as in jet)
ji   (as in Jim)
jo   (as in job)
ju   (as in jump)
ka   (as in karate)
ke   (as in kept)
ki   (as in kit)
ko   (as in cot)
ku   (as in cud)
la   (as in lamb)
le   (as in lend)
li   (as in lip)
lo   (as in log)

lu   (as in <u>lu</u>ck)
ma   (as in <u>ma</u>t)
me   (as in <u>me</u>n, *not* as in 'Give it to me')
mi   (as in <u>mi</u>tt)
mo   (as in <u>mo</u>p)
mu   (as in <u>mu</u>d)
na   (as in <u>na</u>g)
ne   (as in <u>Ne</u>d)
ni   (as in <u>ni</u>p)
no   (as in <u>no</u>d, *not* as in 'I have no toys')
nu   (as in <u>nu</u>t)
pa   (as in <u>pa</u>t)
pe   (as in <u>pe</u>t)
pi   (as in <u>pi</u>n)
po   (as in <u>po</u>t)
pu   (as in <u>pu</u>nt)

Then, dictate random selections from Exercises 1–12 for the child to print. Remember: printing is laborious and uncomfortable. You should not expect the child to print from dictation for more than ten minutes. Now, do some oral spelling, as described in Lesson 9.

Exercise 7: Lower-case 'j'

ja   **je**   **ji**   **jo**   **ju**

Exercise 8: Lower-case 'k'

ka   **ke**   **ki**   **ko**   **ku**

Exercise 9: Lower-case 'l'

la   **le**   **li**   **lo**   **lu**

Exercise 10: Lower-case 'm'

ma   **me**   **mi**   **mo**   **mu**

Exercise 11: Lower-case 'n'

na　　　**ne**　　　**ni**　　　**no**　　　**nu**

Exercise 12: Lower-case 'p'

pa　　　**pe**　　　**pi**　　　**po**　　　**pu**

Lesson 12: Consonants

Introduce the consonants 'r', 's', 't' and 'v' using the same method described above. Teach the child to print them and give their sounds.

ra　(as in <u>r</u>at)
re　(as in <u>r</u>ent)
ri　(as in <u>r</u>ip)
ro　(as in <u>r</u>ot)
ru　(as in <u>r</u>ut)
sa　(as in <u>s</u>ap)
se　(as in <u>s</u>et)
si　(as in <u>s</u>in)
so　(as in <u>s</u>oft, *not* as in 'I told you so')
su　(as in <u>s</u>un)
ta　(as in <u>t</u>ap)
te　(as in <u>t</u>en)
ti　(as in <u>t</u>ip)
to　(as in <u>t</u>op, *not* as in 'Go to bed')
tu　(as in <u>t</u>ug)
va　(as in <u>v</u>at)
ve　(as in <u>v</u>et)
vi　(as in <u>v</u>im)
vo　(as in <u>v</u>omit)
vu　(as in <u>v</u>ulgar)

Now, have the child read Exercises 13–16, first in sequence, then randomly. Then, do dictation from those exercises, with a few from Exercises 1–12 thrown in. Finally, do some oral spelling of selected sounds from these exercises.

Exercise 13: Lower-case 'r'

ra   re   ri   ro   ru

Exercise 14: Lower-case 's'

sa   se   si   so   su

Exercise 15: Lower-case 't'

ta   te   ti   to   tu

Exercise 16: Lower-case 'v'

va   ve   vi   vo   vu

Lesson 13:

Introduce the remaining consonants – 'w', 'y' and 'z' – using the same method.

    wa   (as in <u>wa</u>g)
    we   (as in <u>we</u>t, *not* as in 'We came here')
    wi   (as in <u>wi</u>g)
    wo   (as in <u>wo</u>g)
    wu   (as in <u>one</u>)
    ya   (as in <u>ya</u>k)
    ye   (as in <u>ye</u>s, *not* as in 'Come all ye faithful')
    yi   (as in <u>Yi</u>ddish)
    yo   (as in <u>yo</u>nder, *not* as in 'I have a yo-yo')
    yu   (as in <u>yu</u>m)
    za   (as in <u>za</u>p)
    ze   (as in <u>ze</u>st)
    zi   (as in <u>zi</u>g-zag)
    zo   (as in <u>zo</u>mbie)
    zu   (as to rhyme with <u>fun</u>)

As each set of new consonants is introduced, be sure that the child does the corresponding Exercises 17–19.

Exercise 17: Lower-case 'w'

wa   we   wi   wo   wu

Exercise 18: Lower-case 'y'

ya   ye   yi   yo   yu

Exercise 19: Lower-case 'z'

za   ze   zi   zo   zu

Lesson 14: Review

This is a review day. Ask the child to print out the entire alphabet and time him. He will make lots of mistakes and the progress will be slow. When he has completed the alphabet, give him a fresh sheet of paper and ask him to do it again. Remember, he is dictating each letter to himself, and this represents much more of a challenge than you dictating to him. However, each successive time he does it, he will get faster and faster – do encourage him as it gives a child great satisfaction if he can beat his previous time.

Lessons 15 and 16: Capital letters

Teach the child to recognise, name and sound each of the capital letters in the same way you did the lower-case letters. Simply explain that every letter has a *capital* (or 'big' form) and a *lower-case* (or 'small') form. The figures at the back of the book are designed to help you do this. As he learns each letter, work on Exercises 20–38. Do each at least three times, aiming to break his previous speed records.

Exercise 20: Capital 'b'

Ba   Be   Bi   Bo   Bu

Exercise 21: Capital 'c'

Ca   Ce   Ci   Co   Cu

Exercise 22: Capital 'd'

Da   De   Di   Do   Du

Exercise 23: Capital 'f'

Fa   Fe   Fi   Fo   Fu

Exercise 24: Capital 'g'

Ga   Ge   Gi   Go   Gu

Exercise 25: Capital 'h'

Ha   He   Hi   Ho   Hu

Exercise 26: Capital 'j'

Ja   Je   Ji   Jo   Ju

Exercise 27: Capital 'k'

Ka   Ke   Ki   Ko   Ku

Exercise 28: Capital 'l'

La   Le   Li   Lo   Lu

Exercise 29: Capital 'm'

Ma   Me   Mi   Mo   Mu

Exercise 30: Capital 'n'

Na   Ne   Ni   No   Nu

Exercise 31: Capital 'p'

Pa   Pe   Pi   Po   Pu

Exercise 32: Capital 'r'

Ra   Re   Ri   Ro   Ru

Exercise 33: Capital 's'

Sa   Se   Si   So   Su

Exercise 34: Capital 't'

Ta   Te   Ti   To   Tu

Exercise 35: Capital 'v'

Va   Ve   Vi   Vo   Vu

Exercise 36: Capital 'w'

Wa   We   Wi   Wo   Wu

Exercise 37: Capital 'y'

Ya   Ye   Yi   Yo   Yu

Exercise 38: Capital 'z'

Za   Ze   Zi   Zo   Zu

Review any difficulties encountered on previous days and do some written work with the blends each day.

Lesson 17: The 'qu' sound

You can now introduce the letter 'q' *name*. Explain that it only has a *sound* when used with 'u' as in 'qu' (consult Figure 18). Have him print that 'qu' combination a few times, naming the sound 'kwuh' as he does so and using lower-case letters only. Then again introduce the blending with four of the vowels:

　qua　(as in <u>qua</u>ck)
　que　(as in <u>que</u>st)
　qui　(as in <u>qui</u>t)
　quo　(as in <u>quo</u>tient)

Do Exercises 39 and 40 with the child. Dictate those sound blends to him for his day's printing work, along with some of the previous material.

Exercise 39: Lower-case 'q'

qua　　　que　　　qui　　　quo

Exercise 40: Capital 'q'

Qua　　　Que　　　Qui　　　Quo

Also, do some oral spelling: ask the child, 'How does "quack" start off? What about "question"? "Quiet"? "Quaff"?' For today's dictation, review work from the previous exercises. Some of each day's material must be reviewed so that every few days every combination is reviewed at least once.

Lesson 18: The 'x' sound

While the word 'xylophone' can be mentioned, the value of x *after* a vowel is more important:

　ax　　(as in <u>ax</u>e)
　ex　　(as in <u>ex</u>it)

ix   (as in s<u>ix</u>)
ox   (as in b<u>ox</u>)
ux   (as in H<u>ux</u>ley)

Have the child do Exercise 41, the associated printing and some review.

Exercise 41: Lower-case 'x'

ax   ex   ix   ox   ux

Lesson 19: Vowel–consonant blends

In the next chapter we shall go on to words, but before doing so a few more mechanical drills on vowel–consonant blends are in order. This time we will concentrate on blends in which the vowel comes first. This is very important because a child who is taught carelessly is very likely to persist in making such mistakes as: 'on' for 'no' and 'was' for 'saw'. Explain the blend 'ab', as you did with 'ba'. Then, go through Exercises 42–58.

ab   (as in <u>ab</u>sent)
eb   (as in w<u>eb</u>)
ib   (as in <u>Ib</u>sen)
ob   (as in <u>ob</u>vious)
ub   (as in t<u>ub</u>)
ac   (as in l<u>ac</u>k)
ec   (as in n<u>ec</u>k)
ic   (as in f<u>ic</u>tion)
oc   (as in d<u>oc</u>k)
uc   (as in m<u>uc</u>k)
ad   (as in <u>ad</u>d)
ed   (as in <u>ed</u>ucate)
id   (as in <u>id</u>iot)
od   (as in G<u>od</u>)
ud   (as in m<u>ud</u>)
af   (as in <u>af</u>t)
ef   (as in <u>ef</u>fect)
if   (as in <u>if</u>)
of   (as in <u>of</u>fice, *not* as in 'None of it')
uf   (as in r<u>uf</u>f)

ag   (as in r<u>ag</u>)
eg   (as in b<u>eg</u>)
ig   (as in p<u>ig</u>)
og   (as in j<u>og</u>)
ug   (as in t<u>ug</u>)
aj   (as in <u>aj</u>ar)
ak   (as in t<u>ack</u>)
ek   (as in tr<u>ek</u>)
ik   (as in l<u>ick</u>)
ok   (as in l<u>ock</u>)
uk   (as in l<u>uck</u>)
al   (as in <u>al</u>low)
el   (as in <u>el</u>bow)
il   (as in <u>il</u>l)
ol   (as in f<u>ol</u>low)
ul   (as in d<u>ull</u>)
am   (as in j<u>am</u>)
em   (as in h<u>em</u>)
im   (as in r<u>im</u>)
om   (as in r<u>om</u>p)
um   (as in l<u>um</u>p)
an   (as in b<u>an</u>)
en   (as in t<u>en</u>)
in   (as in b<u>in</u>)
on   (as in <u>on</u>)
un   (as in <u>un</u>tidy)
ap   (as in <u>ap</u>pear)
ep   (as in p<u>ep</u>)
ip   (as in d<u>ip</u>)
op   (as in m<u>op</u>)
up   (as in <u>up</u>)
as   (as in <u>as</u>semble)
es   (as in <u>es</u>cort)
is   (as in <u>is</u>sue)
os   (as in <u>os</u>sify)
us   (as in <u>us</u>)
at   (as in <u>at</u>)
et   (as in m<u>et</u>)
it   (as in <u>it</u>)
ot   (as in <u>ot</u>ter)
ut   (as in <u>ut</u>ter)

av (as in <u>av</u>enue)
ev (as in <u>ev</u>ery)
iv (as in l<u>iv</u>er)
ov (as in h<u>ov</u>er)
uv (as in l<u>ov</u>e)
az (as in ja<u>zz</u>)
ez (as in f<u>ez</u>)
iz (as in di<u>zz</u>y)
oz (as in <u>Oz</u>)
uz (as in b<u>uzz</u>)

The child should be given ample practice printing some of these every day until he can do random sets of them easily. 'Aj' has been included in this list, but the other 'j' blends have not, this is because it is the only short vowel blend which occurs with any regularity. Also, none of the 'r' blends have been listed here, as they will be taught as special phonemes later in the book. Neither omission should affect your instruction of Exercises 48 or 54.

Exercise 42: Blends with 'b'

ab	eb	ib	ob	ub
Ab	Eb	Ib	Ob	Ub

Exercise 43: Blends with 'c'

ac	ec	ic	oc	uc
Ac	Ec	Ic	Oc	Uc

Exercise 44: Blends with 'd'

ad	ed	id	od	ud
Ad	Ed	Id	Od	Ud

Exercise 45: Blends with 'f'

af	ef	if	of	uf
Af	Ef	If	Of	Uf

Exercise 46: Blends with 'g'

ag	eg	ig	og	ug
Ag	Eg	Ig	Og	Ug

Exercise 47: Review of blends

ac	ef	id	ob	ug
Ac	Ef	Id	Ob	Ug

Exercise 48: Blends with 'j'

aj	ej	ij	oj	uj
Aj	Ej	Ij	Oj	Uj

Exercise 49: Blends with 'k'

ak	ek	ik	ok	uk
Ak	Ek	Ik	Ok	Uk

Exercise 50: Blends with 'l'

al	el	il	ol	ul
Al	El	Il	Ol	Ul

Exercise 51: Blends with 'm'

am	em	im	om	um
Am	Em	Im	Om	Um

Exercise 52: Blends with 'n'

an	en	in	on	un
An	En	In	On	Un

Exercise 53: Blends with 'p'

ap	ep	ip	op	up
Ap	Ep	Ip	Op	Up

Exercise 54: Blends with 'r'

ar	er	ir	or	ur
Ar	Er	Ir	Or	Ur

Exercise 55: Blends with 's'

as	es	is	os	us
As	Es	Is	Os	Us

Exercise 56: Blends with 't'

at	et	it	ot	ut
At	Et	It	Ot	Ut

Exercise 57: Blends with 'v'

av	ev	iv	ov	uv
Av	Ev	Iv	Ov	Uv

Exercise 58: Blends with 'z'

az	ez	iz	oz	uz
Az	Ez	Iz	Oz	Uz

Writing the Letters

As I mentioned earlier, I have always found it best to move from printing to cursive writing as quickly as possible, usually when the child is beginning to write complete sentences (see Figures 29–31). However, some children prefer to print for a little longer, especially if they are below school age. For further discussion of this topic, see Chapter Twenty-six.

The very *best* way to start off is to purchase ordinary school exercise books with lined pages. Then, go through them with a black biro and ruler, drawing in every *second* line. In this way the original lines will appear relatively light and run halfway through each space (see Figures 27 and 28). At this stage, do not worry too much about neatness, as long as his lettering is clearly recognisable. But, do not let him print too small: his printing should be of a size comfortable for him to execute without leaning too close to the paper, tensing his wrist or straining himself unduly. He should do his work with a good HB pencil in good light and seated properly beside you at a table. Do not let him use a ballpoint pen because it slides too easily over the paper.

When a letter has a body and a tail, the child can be taught to use the light-coloured lines as a guide. Eventually he will get so that he can estimate the size of his letters accurately and do his writing on ordinary lined paper. However, this takes some weeks to develop, so do not make the child feel pressured.

Until he can do this 'estimating' comfortably and feels confident about it, simply keep buying exercise books and ruling
alternate lines!

Start off with the lower-case letters. Print the shape:

$$a$$

with the dotted form beside it. The child should first draw over
the dotted form with you holding his hand and guiding it. It
should be done in *two* movements:

Needless to say, he will have to do it ten or fifteen times, each
time on a new 'dotted form' (drawn by yourself) before he gets
it done correctly. Then he can try it – as often as he likes – by
himself without any dotted guide. The same procedure should
be followed for the lower-case forms of each of the other
vowels. It is important to teach the child to make the
constituent shapes of each letter in the order shown: ① means
to do that stroke first, then stroke ② and so forth. It is worth
spending a few days getting this right, even though with the
reading itself you might be getting further ahead.

Then, go back and do them all over again, this time using the
capital forms. To make the point, be sure to draw each capital
about twice as tall as the body of its corresponding lower-case
letters.

While you are teaching him to make each vowel shape, keep
emphasising both the *sound* of the letter *and* the *name* of the
letter. For instance, while pointing to 'a', ask him:

'What is the *name* of that letter?'
'What does it *sound* like?'

In this way, the child gets a double drill of both the names and
sounds of all the letters.

Whether the child is still printing or has moved onto cursive writing by the time he is writing whole sentences, you are going to have to face the problem of teaching him to leave a space between words – a bigger space than he leaves between individual letters in a single word. One way of doing this is to train him – at first – to separate words by the breadth of two fingers. This makes for slow work in the beginning, but if it is done conscientiously for the first few days, you will notice that the child soon will be able to space the words by eye alone and will not need to keep using his fingers.

You will find that the child will usually do a lot of lettering on his own. For this, he should feel free to use any paper he wishes and any instrument (*except* a ballpoint pen) – and as such effort is spontaneous, it obviously should not be supervised.

Congratulations – you and your child have just completed the first stage on the road to reading!

6

One-syllable words and simple sentences

One-syllable Words

If the child has mastered thoroughly all of the material referred to in the previous chapter and can read and print the work in Exercises 1–58, he is ready to begin reading words by phonics. At this point we start reading and printing complete words. Go as slowly as the child requires and remember that each day's work should involve:

1 Reading from the exercises.
2 Dictation from the exercises.
3 Oral spelling from the exercises.

Three-letter words, with a vowel in the middle and a consonant at either end, involve two sound blendings. So, for instance, 'Max' would first be pronounced 'Muh–a–x', then 'Ma–x', and finally 'Max'.

With enough practice on the previous exercises, this should not be a major problem, simply guide the child's finger in moving across the first couple of rows of words, working letter by letter, sound by sound. Do not move onto a new word until the child can sound out the previous word correctly. He should become fairly adept at it by the time he has finished Exercise 59.

At this point you may be strongly tempted to teach a bit more than is indicated. For instance, why stop at three letters? Surely such words as 'pots' or 'maps' would be deciphered easily enough. This may be true, but I have found that *generally* it is best to move slowly and thoroughly at first. At a certain point, usually after the rule of terminal 'e' has been learned, the child seems to take off on his own and it takes a lot to slow him down. Prior to that 'reading explosion' taking place, though, it is well worth a *little* monotony to do the job properly. The foundations are vital.

Once the child begins to read words and sentences, there is also the temptation to teach a few whole words in order to create more realistic sentences. For instance, such comments as: 'Nan has a rag' are not the most stimulating or natural form of conversation in the world! However, be patient. If you persist with the phonics-first approach, the child will quickly enough develop such facility at decoding words that you can then afford to introduce exceptions without interfering with his developing word-attack skills and his capacity to spell intelligently.

Lesson 20: Single-syllable words with the short 'a' sound

Begin by having the child read through the whole exercise using the method described above. When the child has finished reading the exercise right through, have him read the first line again.

Then, have him print the words on the first line as you dictate them one at a time. This may present difficulties at first. Encourage the child to repeat the word you have given him several times, slowing down his rate of saying it so that he can eventually isolate the separate sounds. Then, have him re-read the same line again, aiming for error-free fluency. Treat each line similarly. Do this for the first five lines.

Exercise 59: Some single-syllable words with short 'a' sound

man	tap	at	am
Sam	ran	nab	nap
rap	cap	cab	sat
pan	pat	lap	rat
hat	fat	mat	tan
ram	mac	cam	gag
rag	pal	lab	bat

van	nag	lag	mad
dam	tag	gas	ham
Hal	hag	has	pad
am	as	lad	at

Lesson 21: More single-syllable words with the short 'a' sound

Using the same technique as in Lesson 20, work through lines 6–11 and do some dictation and oral spelling. Remember, there is no rush. Only move on when you are sure the child is ready.

Lesson 22: Single-syllable words with the short 'e' sound

Do lines 1–5 from Exercise 60, and review a few lines from Exercise 59 so the child learns to distinguish between the short sounds of 'a' and 'e'.

Exercise 60: Some single-syllable words with short 'e' sound

bet	get	jet	let
met	wet	set	yet
yes	net	vet	den
Ben	hen	pen	bed
fed	led	Ned	red
Ted	Ed	end	wed
Jed	beg	keg	leg
Meg	peg	hem	hep
pep	Lem	Wes	web
bed	den	wet	pet

Lesson 23: More single-syllable words with the short 'e' sound

Using exactly the same procedure, finish Exercise 60, reviewing some of the lines from Exercise 59.

Lessons 24–30: Single-syllable words with the short 'i', 'o' and 'u' sounds

Presuming one is having daily lessons, it generally takes about a week to get through the material in Exercises 61–63 comfortably and securely. Use the method described in previous lessons and make sure the child is secure in all knowledge before moving on.

Exercise 61: Some single-syllable words with short 'i' sound

big	fig	pig	dig
wig	jig	win	rig
in	wit	tin	nit
nip	pin	fin	bin
sin	din	did	kin
dim	hid	bid	kid
lid	Sid	fit	lip
bit	hit	kit	lit
pit	Tim	sit	nib
rib	bib	fib	him
Jim	rim	vim	jib
hip	rip	sip	tip

Exercise 62: Some single-syllable words with short 'o' sound

pot	lot	hot	cod
cot	dot	got	mop
not	sot	jot	tot
sop	top	pop	hop
cop	fog	lop	fop
Bob	cob	job	mob
sob	rob	Dom	fob
gob	hob	lob	cog
jog	log	Mom	sod
hod	rod	pod	nod
God	dog	on	Don
con	yon	Ron	tog

Exercise 63: Some single-syllable words with short 'u' sound

cut	but	rut	tug
rug	bun	nub	nut
gun	fun	pun	run
sun	gut	Gus	bud
mud	cud	dud	yum
sum	hum	gum	rum
tub	sub	rub	hub
cub	dub	dun	bug
pug	mug	lug	jug

hug	dug	pup	sup
pus	hut	jut	up
nun	us	bus	rub

Reading Sentences

With Exercises 64 through 68 great care must be taken. In these exercises, we introduce sentences. Even though these sentences may seem trivial, if not downright tedious, to an adult, they can be delightful to a child. And, if approached with a sense of humour, the sentences can be amusing in their own right, as the restrictions put upon them by being confined to the use of a narrow range of phonic skills can produce some interesting results!

As each sentence is worked out, have the child repeat it until he can read it *with expression*. That is of paramount importance. So much oral reading done in public is colourless and totally lacking in life. You can prevent your child from ever developing such bad reading habits by cultivating tone and expression at the outset.

The sentences also embody certain conventions which can be pointed out to the child. First, point out to him that sentences have to begin with a capital letter. Insist on this when he is printing out sentences that you dictate to him. Second, indicate that people's names begin with a capital letter. Likewise, insist on that when he is putting sentences down on paper. Third, introduce a little punctuation. Have the child observe the *full stop*, the *question mark* and the *comma*. As a rule of thumb he should begin to learn – you will have to keep on reminding him for months before it sticks – that a sentence must have a full stop at the end, unless it is a question. In the latter case, it has a question mark. We will not introduce the exclamation mark until later. The comma simply indicates a pause. It makes it possible to read the sentence with expression.

Now, let us consider the procedure for handling these exercises. Never attempt more than one of these exercises (64–68) on any one day. After the child has read through all the sentences in an exercise, smoothly and with good expression, turn your attention to writing. In most cases, unless the child is very fond of writing and can print at a fair speed, it is unnecessary to have your child write out every sentence in the exercise. One or two – dictated by you to him as he writes – are sufficient. Without getting angry or reproachful about it, insist on the capital letters and the correct punctuation at the end of the sentence. At present he has only two terminal punctuation marks to choose from – full stop or question mark. If a question mark is called for, help him remember to use it by giving a very strong inflection to your dictation of the sentence. Make sure it *sounds* like a question. He can be reminded when a comma is called for, but this is not as critical.

From now on, every lesson should include:

1 Reading aloud.
2 Writing from dictation (gradually all in cursive).
3 Practising new spelling rules.

Lesson 31: Reading passage

You will be lucky to get Exercise 64 done completely in one day. Have the child read it aloud, maybe two or three times, until he can do so fluently. Then, dictate each sentence to him for him to write. As the weeks pass, if you start teaching him today, he will gradually move from printing to cursive writing. See the discussion below and in Chapter Twenty-six for help with this task. Ideally, you should allow about ten minutes per session for learning to write in cursive script until it has been mastered.

Exercise 64: Reading passage

A man ran.

Dan ran.

A fat cat ran.

Can Nan pat a cat?

A fat cat ran at a fat rat in a bag.

Lesson 32: Reading passage

Following the same pattern, do Exercise 65. Have the child read it two or three times, or until he is fluent. Then, you dictate to him while he writes it. When he makes a mistake, correct it immediately by crossing through the offending word and writing it afresh. On each day, be sure to review mistakes he has made previously until he gets the words right without trouble. Practise cursive writing from Figure 32. If the child needs to write a capital letter when he is using cursive script, simply let him print the capital sufficiently close to the rest of the word for it not to be seen as separated. Eventually, he will learn to write the capitals in cursive (see Figure 33), though he will not necessarily learn to write capitals as shown there.

Exercise 65: Reading passage

Dan had a big ham.

A tin can hit a van.

Sal had a big pig.

A bad man hid a pig in a big bag.

If Hal can hit a pig, his cat can bag a rat.

Lessons 33–36: More reading passages

Work on Exercises 66–68, at the rate of one a day, with the exception of Exercise 68, which may require two days. Keep the cursive writing practice going. By now, almost all of the child's writing should be cursive.

Exercise 66: Reading passage

A fat man sat in a bus.

A fat cat had a big nap in a sub.

Can a fat man run in a bus?

Gus had a fig, but Sal had a nut.

A big fat bug sat on a map and had a nap.

Exercise 67: Reading passage

Sam hit it.

Ben can get ten buns.

Did Dan bat yet?

His Dad let him get a cap gun.

Ten men and a dog can sit in a big bus.

If a pup can sit up, it can beg.

Yes, a pup can beg and a pup can run.

Can a bat hit a pup on his leg?

Exercise 68: Reading passage

If Bob can get a job, Bob can get a dog.

Bob got a job and got a cat.

Is his cat as fat as a dog?

A bad man can rob a cat, but a cat can hit him and nip him.

Mum got Ted a red cap. It did not fit him, but it did fit Jim.

A bad pup got mud on a rug, but Nan got a wet rag and can mop it up.

Written Work

From this stage on, in particular, it is valuable to keep track of all of his written work, especially work done during daily dictation. He should be able to look back over his work from time to time so that he can see his progress. On the top of each sheet of writing practice, record the date on which it was done.

By now his printing should be quite secure and there is considerable merit in moving onto cursive ('running' or 'joined-up') writing. Once it is learned, it is neater, faster and *much* less tiring than is printing. You will want to read Chapter Twenty-six carefully before beginning.

A comment should be made at this point about mistakes. While the child should not be made to feel guilty about mistakes – we all make them! – you should stress the need for care and attention. As mentioned previously, his work sessions should take place under optimum psychological conditions. He should be relaxed and his hands should be clean. If a mistake is made – say he writes 'lep' for 'lap' – do not erase it with a rubber. Instead, have him neatly cross it through and write the correction beside it, thus:

In this way, both you and he can note the fact if he makes the same kind of mistake repeatedly. (A rubber should be available, but only for him to erase minor errors, such as in the shape of a letter or something of that order, and correct them.)

Casual Reading

Because he is now reading sentences and some whole words, the child will suddenly begin to take note of writing around him. Notices on the street and in shops are likely to catch his attention. This can really slow things up on a trip to the supermarket as he keeps stopping you to demonstrate that he can decipher some word on a cat food packet or whatever! Advertising billboards are another source of tremendous interest for the beginning reader. You will also find, if you have not already realised it, that most vulgarities are phonically regular and are read with great glee – and generally in a loud voice in public!

Tiresome as all of this can sometimes become, it is an important stage of reading development and should not be discouraged. The results can often be amusing. Once, while I was on a tram in Melbourne with my four-year-old daughter, I saw her studying a government notice on the tram wall. It said, 'If you think you have V.D., you can get help!' Almost with dread, I wondered what she would say. I wasn't in suspense for long, as she piped up for all to hear: 'Daddy, do you have V.D.? Because, if so, you can get help!'

Making Progress

Your child has now been learning for a month or so, if you have been doing a daily session, and already he has made great strides. He knows the rudiments of how the system works and can both encode and decode. There are many conventions and spelling rules that he has not yet learned, but he can probably write any word he chooses in a fashion that is understandable to someone reading it.

Congratulations! You should both celebrate!

7

Longer single-syllable words

Double Letters

Once a child has achieved fluency with the material up through Exercise 68, he will experience no difficulty with double 'l', double 's' and double 'f' at the ends of words. Exercises 69–71 cover these endings and should be gone over carefully with the child. At first, say nothing about the double letter. See what he says! The chances are that he will simply read the word correctly without comment. In that case, draw the double-letter ending to his attention once he has done so, otherwise, simply explain how they are pronounced.

For the first few times, when you are dictating words for him to print, help him out by strongly emphasising the double-letter sound. For instance, 'Nan fell off a van' would be read out by you as: 'Nan fel-l-l-l-l of-f-f-f-f a van.'

Lesson 37: Double-'l', double-'s' and double-'f' endings

Exercises 69–71 contain many commonly used words. Therefore, the phonic drills should be done so thoroughly that the child reaches the point at which he can recognise the word immediately. This can generally be accomplished in one session. These words also allow for some good cursive writing practice (obviously, this can be combined with dictation).

Exercise 69: Words with the double-l ending

will	well	Bill	bell
Hell	hill	pill	mill

gill	tell	sill	rill
Nell	Jill	cull	Kill
till	dell	yell	sell

Exercise 70: Words with the double-s ending

mess	doss	fuss	muss
cuss	Jess	miss	hiss
kiss	less	Ross	pass
ass	lass	Bess	Russ
mass	moss	toss	loss

Exercise 71: Words with the double-f ending

muff	huff	Jeff	toff
guff	gaff	Goff	jiff
buff	biff	doff	cuff
puff	ruff	tiff	duff
diff	Taff	off	naff

Multiple-consonant Beginnings

A great many words start off with two or more consonants before a vowel sound comes into the picture. It is important to handle this problem very carefully because the child has to be trained to *listen carefully* so that he can pick out all of the constituent sounds. Much of the sloppy reading and bad spelling that we see about us stems from the lack of attention being paid to *discriminating listening* in the teaching of reading.

For instance, when seeing the word 'strap', children will often say 'sap' or 'trap'. Equally, when they are asked to spell it after hearing it spoken, they often write 'sap', 'trap' or 'srap'. More than anything else, it is a question of teaching the child to *concentrate*, to *listen carefully*. This requires that, increasingly, you must make him responsible for retaining what you have said. I have often seen situations in which a child is given a word to spell and then forgets what the word is while getting his pencil ready! While the learning sessions should be pleasant, they should not be so relaxed that no disciplined effort at all is required.

We must move slowly here. The hearing of some very young children will not yet be fully developed and thus they will struggle to hear the middle consonant. Writing these sounds from dictation requires a much higher level of concentration than anything the child has done previously. Be patient, slow and supportive. Practise saying these sounds slowly so that the child can hear each sound. Mistakes will occur in both writing and oral reading. Such mistakes must be rectified immediately, but gently. The liaisons should be practised until the child can read them off the page quite fluently. Some children require two or three days to do this.

Lessons 38–39: Two-consonant word beginnings

The sound combinations which we shall be dealing with next are:

bl   (as in <u>bl</u>ed: Have the child say '<u>bl</u>uh' – minimising the aspirated 'uh')

br   (as in <u>br</u>ed: Have the child say '<u>br</u>uh')

cl   (as in <u>cl</u>oth: Have the child say '<u>kl</u>uh')

cr   (as in <u>cr</u>am: Have the child say '<u>cr</u>uh')

dr   (as in <u>dr</u>op: Have the child say '<u>dr</u>uh')

fl   (as in <u>fl</u>ap: Have the child say '<u>fl</u>uh')

fr   (as in <u>fr</u>og: Have the child say '<u>fr</u>uh')

gl   (as in <u>gl</u>ad: Have the child say '<u>gl</u>uh')

gr   (as in <u>gr</u>ab: Have the child say '<u>gr</u>uh')

pl   (as in <u>pl</u>an: Have the child say '<u>pl</u>uh')

pr   (as in <u>pr</u>am: Have the child say '<u>pr</u>uh')

sl   (as in <u>sl</u>am: Have the child say '<u>sl</u>uh')

sm   (as in <u>sm</u>ut: Have the child say 'smuh')
sn   (as in <u>sn</u>ug: Have the child say 'snuh')
st   (as in <u>st</u>ep: Have the child say 'stuh')
sw   (as in <u>sw</u>im: Have the child say 'swuh')
tr   (as in <u>tr</u>am: Have the child say 'truh')

Exercise 72: Some two-consonant word beginnings

bl-	bla	ble	bli	blo	blu
br-	bra	bre	bri	bro	bru
cl-	cla	cle	cli	clo	clu
cr-	cra	cre	cri	cro	cru
dr-	dra	dre	dri	dro	dru
fl-	fla	fle	fli	flo	flu
fr-	fra	fre	fri	fro	fru
gl-	gla	gle	gli	glo	glu
gr-	gra	gre	gri	gro	gru

Exercise 73: More two-consonant word beginnings

pl-	pla	ple	pli	plo	plu
pr-	pra	pre	pri	pro	pru
sl-	sla	sle	sli	slo	slu
sm-	sma	sme	smi	smo	smu
sn-	sna	sne	sni	sno	snu
st-	sta	ste	sti	sto	stu
sw-	swa	swe	swi	swo	swu
tr-	tra	tre	tri	tro	tru

Lesson 40: Three-consonant word beginnings

Follow the same procedure as with the two-consonant beginnings. All of these combinations should be sounded out until fluency is achieved. In addition, do not forget to give the child daily practice in writing a few of these combinations as you call them out – writing is not only necessary when whole words are involved. If Exercises 72 and 73 have really been mastered, these will present few problems.

Exercise 74: Some three-consonant word beginnings

scr-	scra	scre	scri	scro	scru
spr-	spra	spre	spri	spro	spru
str-	stra	stre	stri	stro	stru

Lessons 41–42: Review of two- and three-consonant beginnings

When the child is fluent at the word beginnings in the previous exercises, let him attack the words in Exercises 75–77. Do not neglect having him write down a few words as you dictate them. This should, of course, be done *after* he has read through all of them.

Exercise 75: Review of words with two-consonant beginnings

bluff	bled	bliss	blot
Brad	bred	Brit	bran
brim	clam	Clem	cliff
clod	clad	crop	cram
crib	crud	crass	drip
drop	dreg	drum	dram
drab	drag	drill	dress

dross	flip	flap	floss
fled	flag	frog	Fran
Fred	frill	from	glad
glass	gloss	glen	grab
grim	grill	grass	gruff

Exercise 76: Review of more words with two-consonant beginnings

plan	plod	plum	plug
pleb	prod	pram	press
prim	prom	slam	slim
sled	slog	slug	smell
sniff	snag	smug	snap
stiff	staff	stop	step
stuff	swan	swig	swag
swum	swop	trim	trill
trod	trot	trad	tram
trip	tress	truss	trap

Exercise 77: Review of words with three-consonant beginnings

scram	scrap	scruff	scrum
sprat	sprig	sprog	strap
strip	strum	strop	stress

Multiple-consonant Endings

Words that end in more than one consonant sound can be

sounded out simply by reading up to, and including, the first consonant in the endings. Then the remaining consonant sounds can be blended on in order. As the child is doing this, he should be using his index finger under the word, shifting his finger along as he decodes. In fact, this is a useful habit to acquire in learning to read for a number of reasons. It keeps track of the child's place on the page, it discourages regression (i.e. letting the eye wander back over material already read) and it gradually increases reading speed (see discussion at the end of this chapter). Consider a word like 'soft'. The child should be taught to approach it as follows: s – so – sof – sof, sof, sof – sof-t.

Lessons 43–45: Two-consonant word endings and review

Start with the first row of words in Exercise 78. Make sure that the child keeps his index finger under the word, moving along as he sounds out the word. When he can do this exercise fluently and can correctly write a few of the words, let him do Exercise 79. Exercise 80 consists of words combining the features of words in Exercises 75–79.

Exercise 78: Some words with two-consonant endings

soft	kept	sift	sand
sump	bump	lift	mask
act	fact	vamp	hump
camp	lamp	jump	task
last	list	mast	must
mist	fist	fast	test
musk	desk	husk	dusk
hums	lips	lisp	dams
cusp	cups	melt	pets

Exercise 79: More words with two-consonant endings

dent	dint	sent	bunt
bent	cant	rant	rent
pant	hasp	lent	risk
rusk	gust	gasp	help
next	rift	tuft	hilt
bask	rapt	cast	felt
damp	tent	silt	cost
bulb	kilt	duct	gift
tact	hemp	tempt	pelt

Exercise 80: Words with multiple-consonant beginnings and endings

bland	plant	blimp	blunt
plump	flask	frond	flint
flops	glint	grunt	drops
clasp	claps	print	slump
slips	next	nest	trump
tract	stamp	stunt	stint
swift	swept	script	drift

Lesson 46: The 'ck' ending

Print the word 'rock' on a piece of paper and have the child read it. He may work it out correctly the first time or he may try to pronounce two 'k' sounds at the end. In either case, make a point of showing him the 'ck'. Underline it and say that there are many words that have the ending. In fact, *almost all single syllable words ending in the sound 'k' are spelled with a 'ck' at the end*. You do not have to tell the child this. He will gradually discover it through reading. However, make sure that he can correctly spell the words in Exercise 81 after he has read them.

Exercise 81: Words with 'ck' ending

rock	sock	lock	mock
dock	lick	sick	tick
Rick	Dick	neck	peck
fleck	heck	speck	beck
lack	slack	track	crack
duck	suck	luck	pluck
truck	tack	deck	black
stick	frock	stock	flock
smack	flick	clack	quack
quick	trick	crock	kick

Lesson 47: Reading passage

The child is now equipped with a considerably enlarged arsenal of spelling conventions and can bring this to bear on reading. Exercise 82 represents an easy reading passage. It should be practised until the child can read it fluently and with expression. By now you may find that your child is writing you notes or little stories. Encourage that and, at this stage, *make no comment about incorrect spellings* unless what is put down is incomprehensible.

Exercise 82: Reading passage

Quick, quick! A fox has run in.

Tim can run after it but it sat on a black
kitten. Nan is sad. Fox sat on a cat.

Dad got Fred a drum. Fred got a drum from
Dad. Did Fred grin? Fred and Fran did a lot.

Fred can scrub and Fran can mop. Fred did
not fret and Fran did not brag.

Reading and Speed Reading

In many primary schools the use of the finger or hand as a
'tracker' is actively discouraged in the mistaken belief that it is
'childish'. Omitting for the moment that children might be
permitted childish behaviour(!), the concept is incorrect. The
fastest and most efficient readers generally use their hands. In
fact, in the now world famous Evelyn Wood Reading Dynamics
courses, people are *taught* to get back to using their fingers as
trackers as a means of increasing their reading speed – and they
are also taught to *continue* using their fingers like that to *maintain* a high reading speed.

It might be useful at this point to make some comment about
the whole issue of reading speed. When phonics (as a major
method of teaching reading) first fell into disfavour with
educators in the United States, one of the arguments used
against it was that sounding out words slows the child down.
He reads much faster, of course, if he can simply say the words
right off. However, there is a serious flaw in that argument.
While we know that accomplished readers see words as wholes
and not as individual letters, there are really only two ways in
which a person can develop that skill.

1 He might learn each word 'whole' – as a shape – in the
   same way that Chinese people have to do it. As the
   Chinese themselves know, this takes a long time, and

imposes (even for the highly educated) a limit on the words they can 'know' in print. That is, there are Chinese characters that stand for words which the most brilliant Chinese scholar has not learned. That, of course, is not true of English. Even a moderately educated British person can read out *any* English word, even if he has never seen it before and does not know its meaning.

2 He might learn the 'system' – the phonic rules – which govern our writing of words. That means that in the initial stages he will move slowly, then he will pick up speed. Some people, after they learn to read silently, still keep *subvocalising* (sounding out the word in their minds) as they read. Although they become very fast at it, even at its fastest this holds them to about 400–450 words a minute. That is, they read at the rate of rapid conversation. Although that is adequate – many university academics read at that speed – it can be improved on. A person can be taught to stop subvocalising, so that his eyes take in a whole line at a time and he reads quickly down the page. However, to do that, *one has to know how to read first*. That means that the initial phonic drill stage is *vital*. Speed develops with practice and high-level speed reading can be taught *after* that.

In fact, speed reading can be compared to Kim's game. Kim's game, for those who are unfamiliar with it, involves showing someone a tray full of various objects for a short span of time, say, fifteen seconds. The person then has to try to recall all of the objects. It is an exercise in observation – he has to see *and* recognise all of the objects quickly. However, it wouldn't work very well if he didn't recognise some of the objects and had no way of describing them! In the same way, one can only 'speed read' words that one has some way of knowing. If one is restricted to a limited 'sight vocabulary', as a Chinese person has to be, speed reading would be impossible. The passage might contain words outside of the 'sight vocabulary'. A person who has been well trained in phonics becomes so adept at applying the rules quickly to unknown words that they register almost immediately.

Therefore, be patient. You will no doubt meet people who tell you that by teaching your child to sound out words you are slowing him down. Research studies have shown the opposite. A confident reader is one who gets plenty of practice and who enjoys reading. The best way to ensure that facility, and hence that pleasure in it, is to make sure that the learners can use the code.

8

Words of more than one syllable

Sight Words

At this point we shall introduce to the child a 'sight' word. A sight word is one which he cannot decode with the phonics that he already commands and which he simply has to remember whole. Great care must be exercised not to provide more than the occasional sight word, otherwise the child will develop the lazy habit of just guessing at words without using his phonic skill. This, of course, is the trouble if one *starts off* by teaching the children a few whole words and then tries to insist on phonics after!

The first sight word we will introduce is 'the'. With 'the' in his reading vocabulary and with the command of phonics that he already has, the child will be able to read much more interesting material. It will not be long now before he can read quite widely and confidently!

Write the word 'the' on a piece of paper in all lower-case letters and also with an initial capital: 'The'. Point it out to the child and have him *spell* it – first while looking at it, then while looking away. Have him write it down. Explain that eventually he will see why 'the' sounds like it does, but that in the meantime he must just remember it. Show him a page of print in a children's book and ask him to point out all the 'the's that he can find. Then print 'the' on a filing card. As each sight word is presented, it should be printed on a separate card so that every day or so you can use these flash cards to drill the child quickly on his accumulating sight-word vocabulary. There will not be very many cards because within two or three months his command of phonics will have reached the point of sophistication which allows him to sound out even words embodying irregularities.

The Building Blocks of Words

We now turn our attention to explaining to the child the constituent parts from which words are built.

Lesson 48: Explaining syllables

At this point you should teach your child about *syllables*. One way of describing the idea to a child is in terms of 'beats'. Tell him that some words have one beat, some two beats and so forth, and demonstrate it by saying a list of words, accompanying each syllabic beat with arm movements as if conducting a choir:

station	(two arm movements, so two *beats*)
dog	(one *beat*)
principal	(three *beats*)
ridiculous	(four *beats*)

After having demonstrated with a few words, speaking slowly and emphasising each syllable, read out the following list to the child. After each word, have the child repeat it to you. If he trips over a syllable or has trouble pronouncing the word, repeat it and then have him say it again. As he says it, let him try to find the beats, possibly tapping them with a pencil on a table top. Then, let him tell you how many there are. Go through the whole list in that way, one by one.

men/tor
puff
ad/ver/tise
ad/ver/tise/ment
por/ridge
big
my
soft
soft/ly
boun/ti/ful
glo/ry
suc/cess/ful/ly
op/ti/mist/ic
pes/si/mist/ic

ren/di/tion
ad/mis/sion
fel/low/ship
pan/ic
be/head/ing
choke
pen/du/lum
mo/tion
ad/min/i/strat/ive
un/em/ploy/ment

When he can do it without too much trouble – he has to learn to listen carefully, of course – you can explain that the *beats* are called *syllables*.

Now, go over the list again, this time letting him watch you read the words, with your finger moving along under each syllable. Obviously, he is not going to have to read the words, but it gradually acquaints him with the process.

Syllables and syllable identification are so basic to fluent reading that the word will be mentioned many times in the rest of this book. Make sure that your child can *say* the word 'syllable' and *knows what it means*.

Lesson 49: Explaining vowels

We now start to introduce a bit more technical vocabulary to the child. Do not do this on the same day as you teach him about syllables. Have him write out the alphabet in both capital and lower-case letters. He may not know it off by heart yet, in which case you can dictate it to him one letter at a time.

Now, explain to him the idea of a *pure sound* by having him utter the *sound value* of each letter. As he articulates each consonant, point out to him the slight aspiration at the end: a consonant cannot be sounded without another sound after it. When he comes to each vowel, point out that with those no other sound is necessary. Now, have him go through it again, picking out the letters that have a *pure* sound. With some guidance from you, he should arrive at the five sounds: 'a', 'e', 'i', 'o', 'u'. Explain that these are called vowels. Have him *count* the vowels, *sound* the vowels and *name* the vowels. When you have finished, he should be able to say, 'There are five vowels: "a", "e", "i", "o" and "u".'

Lesson 50: Explaining consonants

Let vowels sink in for a few days – of course, you must keep up the phonic work, the drill exercises and the writing on a daily basis – and test him daily to make sure that he knows what syllables are, what the vowels are and what they sound like. Then, in a subsequent lesson, tell him that all the letters that are *not* vowels are *consonants*. 'Consonants' is a hard word for a child to say – repeat it slowly, emphasising each of its three syllables. Have him print out the alphabet again, underlining each consonant in red and each vowel in blue.

Lesson 51: Two-syllable words

We now turn to Exercise 83. Here the child is introduced to two-syllable words. This is a critical stage in his reading development. By learning to articulate each syllable, the child learns to dissect the word into its constituent parts. This is extremely important for the development of both his reading and writing skills. One only has to listen to much of the reading that is done aloud – in church, at meetings or wherever – to realise how poor the general standard of oral reading is, and this is a useful clue to the standard of reading overall. Much of the sloppiness that is evident in pronunciation is due to insufficient attention to syllables.

You will find that when most children come across a long word, especially one with which they are not familiar, they tend to run through it. So, it is important to train your child to read the *whole* word – not just the beginning and the end, with a bit of a mutter in between! Insist on accurate sounding out from the beginning.

A terribly important skill for the child to develop is the capacity, when reading, to articulate each syllable so that, when encoding (writing), the child learns to dissect the word he wants to write into constituent syllables. Only when the child can correctly read aloud each of the words in Exercise 83 should you attempt to have him write them from dictation.

Go slowly at first. When difficulty is encountered – which it will be with just about every word the first time through – print the word on a separate piece of paper and lightly mark the separation between the syllables. Thus, 'attack' becomes 'at/tack'. Also, while each word is being read, ensure that the child keeps track of each syllable with his finger (not with a pencil – it marks up the book!) while he is sounding it out.

Certain clues might begin to become evident to the child. For instance, each syllable has its own vowel. That helps a great deal in separating the syllables. Likewise, two consonants together often mark the end of one syllable and the beginning of the next.

Once he has gone through all of the words in Exercise 83, have him do it again, aiming for increasing fluency. Do not leave this exercise in a hurry. It wouldn't hurt to go over it several times until a quite high degree of fluency is achieved.

The sessions will now begin to include more work and to demand an increasing level of concentration. You should no longer insist on dictating *every* word in the lists or *every* sentence in the reading passage. The correct approach is to include enough that the child spends about fifteen minutes of the session writing. Before that, though, it is important to make sure that the child can fluently do the relevant reading aloud.

Exercise 83: Words with two syllables

insect	cannot	himself	itself
flatlet	crumpet	trumpet	kitten
panic	attic	sicken	impact
Donald	fatten	bluntness	infest
antic	infect	dentist	flatten
basket	until	plastic	tepid
dampen	attack	aspect	despot
amid	happen	travel	gravel
invent	upon	invest	insist

unlock	unbend	undid	unplug
indent	inspect	instant	infant

Lesson 52: The 'nk' ending

Print the word 'rank' on a piece of paper. Have the child try to sound it out. He might, after several tries, come up with the right terminal sound. If he does not, then say it for him, emphasising the ending. Make sure that he notes the way it is spelled and the way it sounds. Tell him to close his eyes and spell 'rank'. Did he get the 'nk' correct? Test him with reading the following words: 'dunk', 'link', 'bank'. Of course, you should print them out for him in larger letters. After about Chapter Eleven, he will be able to read directly from print of this size.

Now, cover those words over and have him spell them orally as you call them out. Go now to Exercise 84. When he can handle that exercise fluently, have him try the reading passage in Exercise 85. He should read it several times, until he can do it smoothly and with expression.

Exercise 84: Words with the 'nk' ending

sink	rink	flunk	brink
clank	bank	sank	hunk
bunk	honk	kink	sink
skunk	crank	tank	lank
link	blink	blank	trunk
dank	plonk	prank	spunk
spank	pink	trinket	drunk
drunken	drink	flank	wink
blanket	sunken	plankton	plank
clink	fink	Frank	swank

Exercise 85: Reading passage

A man had a rat under the bed in his hut. The man got a cat. Will the cat kill the rat? The cat just sits in the sun. It will not kill the rat. The cat just sits and sits and licks himself. It winks at the rat but it will not kill the rotten rat.

The man went and got a rat trap and hid it in a basket on the blanket. The man set the rat trap. The rat stuck his leg on the trap. Clank! Snap! The trap got the rat.

9

Some useful beginnings and endings

Three Common Two-consonant Beginnings: 'sh', 'ch', 'th'

It is important that these three phonemes be presented on different days, as a more thorough command is secured if they are taught separately. Of course, you should include in each day's lesson a quick review of a word or so from each sound family that has been introduced already. Make a flash card for each.

Lesson 53: The 'sh' sound

Start off with 'sh'. Say to the child: 'Make the sound that comes at the beginning of "shop" and keep making just that sound.' He should make the sound 'sh-sh-ssshhh-'.

Then, explain that to write the 'sh' sound, we use the letters 's' and 'h'. Now, show him the 'sh' flash card and be sure that he says 'sh' correctly.

Next, try the child out with a few words. Do a few that you have printed first, before going on to Exercise 86: 'shop', 'ship', 'posh', 'dish', 'shell', 'crash', 'flush', 'mash', 'sham', 'shots'. Have the child read the words first, then spell a few of them out loud to you. From now on, a little oral spelling will make a welcome change from writing and is excellent practice. Once he can do this, he is ready for Exercise 86.

Exercise 86: Words with the 'sh' sound

dash	rush	hash	gush
flesh	rash	shed	blush

crush	shaft	trash	fresh
swish	gosh	plush	shall
shelf	shod	shunt	cash
potash	monkish	dishrag	fishpond
shovel	splash	splashes	crashes
dishes	shock	shucks	smash
shellfish	finish	vanish	banish
mishmash	stash	slash	flashes

Lesson 54: The 'ch' sound

The 'ch' sound is taught in exactly the same way. After teaching 'ch', have the child do Exercise 87.

Exercise 87: Words with the 'ch' and 'sh' sounds

shop	catch	hitch	chum
chaff	crutch	botch	hutch
chuck	check	such	much
chomp	champ	chimp	chess
chips	lunch	flesh	chisel
munch	crunch	bench	wench
ditch	finch	henchman	Frenchman
enchant	enchanted	flinch	chug
shreds	chunk	shank	lash
Chad	flushes	fish-and-chip shop	

Lesson 55: The 'th' sound

When you come to teach the 'th' sound, you will quickly realise that, in fact, 'th' has two sounds. The one is a *soft* sound, as in 'the', 'that'. The other is a *hard* sound as in 'Thatcher', 'thrush', 'thumb'. I have never found it worthwhile to discuss this with the child. The child already *speaks* his language and if he learns one sound for 'th', he will tend to vary it according to his needs while reading. His ear, and his growing knowledge of his own language, tell him when to use the soft and when to use the hard sound. He can now do Exercise 88.

Exercise 88: Words with the 'th', 'sh' and 'ch' sounds

that	this	then	thus
thrush	bath	cloth	filth
thug	broth	thank	think
hath	moth	mathematics	froth
throb	thrills	thrash	thresh
pith	with	path	within
chug	chin	chop	much

Two Common Endings: 'ng' and 'ing'

Some children have trouble with the 'ng' sound, especially in areas of the country where it is not sounded. If a child habitually says 'comin'' or 'fussin'', he may have problems unless you systematically correct his speech. On the other hand, there are some parts of England (Birmingham, for instance) where many people go to the opposite extreme and actually pronounce the 'g' as a separate entry, e.g. 'I'm goin-g to a dancin-g class.' Whatever political correctness may demand, strictly speaking, both ignoring the 'g' and pronouncing it separately are not regarded as good English. We aim somewhere in between!

Lesson 56: The 'ng' ending

Have the child practise repeating after you words like 'song', 'hang', 'Ming', 'lung', 'length'. Emphasise the 'ng' sound each time and then tell him that it is made with the letters 'n' and 'g'. In each, point to the 'ng' with your finger and then go to the beginning of the word and move your finger along as you say each word – slowly. Now, have him read each word. This time, as a variation, have him spell one or two of the words orally, before going on to Exercise 89.

Exercise 89: Words with the 'ng' ending

song	sang	sing	sung
Ming	thing	bang	clang
lung	thong	throng	bong
hung	fang	flung	bung
cling	rung	ring	along
spring	string	strong	long
fling	sting	stung	wing

Do not neglect to give him some words to write, as you dictate them, from Exercise 89. It should be noted, though, that while *some* written work should be given in each session, care should be taken to avoid giving more than a few minutes of it. While you may be impressed at the speed of the child's progress, remember writing is still a new skill which is tiring for little hands. If the written work is made too much of a chore, it can turn the child off reading altogether.

Lesson 57: The 'ing' ending

The next exercise serves as a review of the 'ng' sound while at the same time equipping the child with a very important verb ending. *Long* after he can read all of the words in Exercise 90 (and write them easily) it can be pointed out to him that the 'ing' ending involves a rather interesting rule of spelling governing words – but *only* after he has learned about long and short vowels. This should *not* be discussed with the child at this stage, because it is far beyond him; however, when he has learned about long and short vowels it should be pointed out. (I'll remind you in Chapter Thirteen.) Certainly, in writing any words from this exercise (e.g. 'grab' and 'grabbing') the double consonant should be pointed out to the child, but you needn't go into the reasoning behind it.

The reading passages in Exercises 91 and 92 are valuable and must be read at least twice until fluency has been achieved. Although these reading passages may seem trivial to an adult, they are of vital importance. They contain subtle phonic blends and will help the child develop a variety of related reading skills – cadence, expression, a sense of punctuation – not to mention confidence! They should be followed by dictation from the passages (no more than fifteen minutes).

Exercise 90: Words with the 'ing' ending

hopping	cropping	jumping	yelling
chopping	telling	singing	flinging
bathing	running	stamping	camping
grilling	killing	sitting	flunking
helping	slipping	getting	drinking
banding	banking	telling	vanishing
fleshing	flushing	sending	finishing
bending	grabbing	stabbing	banishing
fibbing	clapping	tipping	admitting

Exercise 91: Reading passage

Frank went on a trip on a big ship – a big red and black ship with pink planks on the

decks. On the ship Frank had six shrimps shredded on a dish. His pal on the ship hid Frank's shrimps on a shelf. A man left seven pups on the deck. The pups got shut up in a box and got sick. Frank kept the pups as pets. The pups got on the shelf and had Frank's shrimps off his dish.

Exercise 92: Reading passage

Fran got lunch. Fran got us a ham sandwich and milk. Such a lunch!

Sal had lunch with a bunch of kids – Beth, Chet, Nan and Jim. Tom and Bob had lunch with them. Tom and Bob had strong hands. Bob lifted the big chest and set it up on the bench. But Tom and Bob cannot pick up Frank's trunk. Tom has an axe. With a trap Tom catches rabbits and chops them up for lunch. Tom drank six cans of pop and is sick. Bob has left.

You may be wondering, somewhat anxiously, when your child will be able to read complete books of his own choosing. If the groundwork is being laid conscientiously through the exercises of this book, it will not take too long. In fact, after the child has been taught the rule for terminal 'e', which causes vowels to change from short to long (see Chapter Twelve), he will be well able to forage widely in his reading. In the meantime, continue reading aloud to him every day. He will no doubt look on with increasingly analytical interest as you do so and may even point out words that he wants to decipher. As I mentioned earlier, reading to your child is a most important means of ensuring that he himself later derives pleasure from reading – and it is a great deal of fun!

10

More beginnings and endings

Two More Sounds of 'y'

'Y' has already been introduced as a consonant, as in 'yes' and 'yam'. It also has three distinct vowel sounds, each of them governed by certain rules of spelling. We shall introduce two of them here.

1 If 'y' comes at the end of a one-syllable word, it is pronounced to rhyme with 'eye': 'by', 'cry', 'my', 'sty', 'fly'.
2 If 'y' comes at the end of a word with two or more syllables, it usually sounds like 'ee': 'mummy', 'daddy', 'candy', 'rusty', 'puppy'.

Lesson 58: 'Y' endings

Having explained the two rules above, print out the ten words listed. Help him sound out the first one, reminding him of the rule: 'It is pronounced "mum-*mee*" not "mum-*meye*".' Go through these words a few times until he appears quite certain of the rule. Let him print two or three of them at random, as dictated by yourself. Now he is ready for Exercises 93–95.

Generally, Exercises 93, 94, and 95 can be done in one session. The spelling rules, while easy, are important and require some practice, but not a *great* deal. The reading passage is longer. Thus, the dictation should only involve selected sentences from it. Do not forget, though, that the dictation *must* include some words from Exercise 93 and 94 to make sure that the rule is understood.

Exercise 93: The letter 'y' at the end of a short word

shy	sty	cry	fly
fry	my	try	sly
ply	pry	dry	thy
by	my	spy	fly

Exercise 94: The letter 'y' at the end of a longer word

Mummy	tummy	rummy	bunny
funny	Daddy	madly	gladly
tarry	carry	Harry	marry
Barry	Larry	parry	worry
sorry	slinky	shimmy	muddy
belly	Kelly	Milly	silly
dally	folly	lolly	smelly
doggy	puppy	holly	hilly
chilly	Shelly	richly	kitty
jumpy	candy	handy	hanky

Exercise 95: Reading passage

The man will fry a fish. The fish swam in the pond, but the man got it. The fish cannot fly! It can swim and it swam by the man's net. He did try to catch it in the net and at last he did. The fish went in the net. The man is glad. He is very hungry. His tummy tells him that he is hungry.

Yummy-yummy! A fish on a dish!

Mummy and Daddy can fry a fish by and by. It is silly if Nan will not try to fry a fish. Kitty has fish as well. Kitty cannot fry the fish, but the man will fry the fish in the big pan. Ronny had his fish on my dish.

The 'wh' Sound

One of the major difficulties that British children have is in recognising whether a word is spelled with 'wh' at the beginning or just 'w'. The reason is that, unlike some Americans, the British differentiate only slightly (if at all) between the saying of words like: 'Wales' and 'whales'.

I was invited once to talk to a fourth-grade nature-study class in Newcastle about sea animals. When I first walked in, I momentarily thought that I had accidentally walked in on a geography lesson, as one little boy was working very hard on a hand-printed sign saying 'Save the Wales'.

Most of this confusion can be avoided if, at the initial stages of reading, the child can be made aware of the difference between 'wh' and 'w'. This is done by artificially emphasising the 'wh' sound. Print the following words, then say them aloud (with appropriate emphasis on the 'wh') while he follows with his finger:

which	witch
Wales	whales
wether (the sheep, not the climate!)	whether

If this is done for a few days, or until he has become used to reading these words, he will develop an awareness of the difference that will stay with him. Therefore, in demonstrating the 'wh' sound, really hit the 'h' in it!

Lesson 59: The 'w' and 'wh' sounds

Say 'when' and print it. Point to the 'wh' at the beginning. Now, print 'wen' and say that one. Make sure that the child can *hear* the difference. Now, try him on Exercise 96. After he has a bit of dictation from that, let him do the reading passage in Exercise 97.

Exercise 96: Words with the 'w' and 'wh' sounds

which	witch	whisk	wish
wig	whist	whiff	whip
Whig	wag	wit	whit
whilst	whelp	whim	whet
when	why	whether	wind

Exercise 97: Reading passage

Can Jeff whip Tom? If Jeff hits Tom, my dad will spank Jeff. Which pond did Jeff swim in?

When Fred is swimming, Dan sits on the bench. But when Dan is on the bench, Fred smells a skunk. Dan got a whiff of it.

There will probably be time in today's lesson to include some more extraneous reading; allow the child to select it from one of his favourite stories.

A Few More Sight Words

You already have one sight-word flash card – 'the' – which the child has learned to recognise as a whole. You should now make up 11 more flash cards, one each for: 'I', 'to', 'he', 'who', 'you', 'go', 'she', 'we', 'me', 'no', 'be'.

The child should *never* learn more than one sight word a day. Indeed, one every two or three days is sufficient. Begin with 'I'. It is an important word and one he is not likely to forget. One by one, introduce the others, one every two or three days. They will begin to occur in the reading passages after the next few lessons.

Each of the Vowels and 'r'

In the next few sessions the child will learn about the three phonemes – 'er', 'ir' and 'ur' – which all sound alike, and two – 'or' (as in 'fort') and 'ar' (as in 'car') – which don't! Herein lies the first real ambiguity your child will have come across, so go slowly and make sure the child thoroughly understands each concept before moving on.

Lesson 60: The 'er' sound

We shall deal with 'er' first. Print the word 'gather' and have the child try to sound it out. In all probability he will give a rendering rather like 'gath-air'.

Now, explain what 'er' at the end of a word sounds like. Say the last syllable of 'gather'. When he seems to have understood that, print another word, like 'mender'. He should note that two syllables are involved and say the word as 'mend-er'.

When he can spell a couple of words like 'mender' and 'tanner', he is ready to tackle Exercise 98.

Exercise 98: Words with the 'er' sound

faster	setter	letter	fetter
better	netter	mother	father
rather	brother	sister	master
helper	upper	batter	mister
quicker	shelter	checker	catcher
mocker	monster	spender	lender

banter	banner	docker	clerk
jerk	perk	masher	crusher
chopper	helicopter	copper	matter
silver	crammer	jammer	setter
wetter	herself	berth	fender
her	spender	welter	cracker
ticker	blotter	fodder	welter

Let him get quite used to the idea of 'er' first before going on to 'ir' and 'ur'. Certainly, words like 'father', 'mother', 'brother' and 'rather' may take some explaining, because you will notice that the vowel sound in each is modified. Make sure that he can spell such words. The reading passage in Exercise 99 will provide some useful practice.

Exercise 99: Reading passage

My mother and father went fishing with my brother. I did not. I had a chill and a bad chest. When Mother rubs my chest it will get better.

Father will get eggs and Mother can fry up a batter. If my brother cannot get the eggs from the hen, the hen will sit under the ladder and hatch them. A chicken is better than a batter! After a bit, the chicken will get big – as big as a fat hen. Will I cry when Dad kills the hen? It is sad to kill a hen, but I am hungry.

Lesson 61: The 'ir' and 'ur' sounds

The two phonemes 'ir' and 'ur' sound *identical*, therefore, one cannot be *absolutely* sure which to use. 'Gurl' and 'girl' sound the same – why should one be right and the other wrong? Despite this difficulty, the sounds 'ir' and 'ur' can probably be taught in one session, as long as you are careful to review the 'er' words at the same time. Eventually, the child will learn which words use 'er', 'ir' or 'ur' in their spelling, but there is no point in making too big a fuss of that now. Simply dictate a few words from the exercises. If he uses the wrong spelling, just correct him and have him change it. The first task is to develop his competence as a reader.

Let him read the words in Exercise 100, and then write a few, before going on to Exercise 101. In that exercise occurs the word 'murderer', which gives excellent practice in syllable separation.

Exercise 100: Words with the 'ir' sound

bird	twirl	girl	stir
fir	first	chirp	twirp
gird	girder	shirk	shirker
shirt	dirt	dirty	flirt
flirting	Firth	birth	girded
twirler	stirrer	mirth	smirk

Exercise 101: Words with the 'ur' sound

burn	burst	burning	burner
fur	curl	murder	murderer
furl	slurp	murky	further
purr	burr	curse	curt
hurt	spurt	churn	turn

lurch   church   burp   curl

sturdy   hurdy-gurdy   spurn   lurking

If the child is both competent and confident, you can move on to encouraging him to remember which words use 'ir' and which 'ur'. This can be done by playing a game with Exercises 100 and 101, seeing if you can 'trick' him; but *remember*: make it pleasurable, as if you anticipate there will be mistakes. Do *not* aim for perfection – the number of mistakes will decrease each time you play the game. Over the next few years, sheer experience will complete the job.

The reading passage in Exercise 102 must now be read a few times, until fluency and expression with it are achieved. It also provides opportunity for practising dictation.

Exercise 102: Reading passage

My family is camping by the river. With us is Mother, Father, my brother Ernest and my sister Betty. I went on a trip with them.

First we must pitch the tents. We will set them up by a rock. It is wet in the other spot, but this is dry.

Then we cut dry ferns and had a rest on them. The birds sang and were chirping. My father and I got plenty of dry fern under a crack in the rock. At the first turn in the track, my father and mother had dinner set on a box.

Lesson 62: The 'ar' sound

Print the word 'park' on a piece of paper and have the child sound it out. Because of the 'p' sound at the beginning and the 'k' sound at the end, he will probably figure it out – even if he makes the short 'a' sound in the middle. In any case, after he has tried, say the word slowly. Point to the 'ar' in the middle and articulate that sound in isolation. Spell the 'ar' sound for him, write it down separately and have him write it as well.

Then, have him write a few words such as: 'hard', 'dart', 'tar', 'car' and 'part'. When he can do those easily, have him go through Exercises 103 and 104.

Exercise 103: Words with the 'ar' sound

park	lark	hark	bark
dark	shark	farther	mark
card	hard	lard	garden
gardener	harder	tarmac	carpark
car	cart	carp	far
barns	farm	farmer	harm
harmless	charm	party	smart
harness	mar	market	dart

Exercise 104: Reading passage

Mister Darby has a big red car. He went to the market in it from the farm. The market is far from the farm. He is clever and went along the left part of the path. He met a lot of cars. A lot of men go to market to sell the harvest. At last he parks the car.

When he went to try it after his lunch, the car did not go. It did not start. It had run dry. Its tank had no gas in it.

Lesson 63: The 'or' sound

We approach the sound 'or' in much the same way that we handled 'ar'. Print the word 'porch'. Have the child try to sound it out. He might, through giving the 'o' a broadened short sound, come out with 'parch'. However, he is not likely to have that word in his vocabulary, so he will probably discard that and keep trying. Do not let him get too frustrated. He should not be compelled to take more than four or five stabs at it before you come to his help.

Say the word slowly, pointing at the 'or' in the middle. Then, print the word 'or' and use it in a few sentences. Have the child print 'or'. Now, let him try to crack the following words, after you have printed them for him: 'afford', 'for', 'fort', 'snorkel', 'horn'. When he can do those, go on to Exercise 105 and the reading passage in Exercise 106.

Exercise 105: Words with the 'or' sound

sport	fork	cork	born
abort	Lord	shorn	corn
cord	Ford	torn	storm
torment	short	shorter	York
pork	Rory	story	Tory
port	form	former	dormitory
laboratory	lavatory	gory	glory
portly	support	snort	forth

Exercise 106: Reading passage

Norm and Henry will lift the timber on to the Ford for Father. He has held back the flap of the truck and Norm and Henry are trying to lift the lumber up into the truck. It is a very hard job, but Norm and Henry are strong. Henry stands on the porch and yanks at the planks. His shirt gets torn when he stretches the cloth. Father will mend it after he finishes the job. Norm and Henry had a lot for dinner.

Flash cards should now be made up of each of the following sounds and words: 'ar', 'are', 'or', 'er', 'ur' and 'ir'.

Lesson 64: The terminal 'le' sound

This is such a common sound that adding it to your child's phonic decoding kit will open a wide variety of words to him.

Print the word 'little'. Now, say it aloud, sliding your finger under it as you do: 'little'. Point to the 'le' and say: 'When we put "le" at the end like that, it makes the sound "ul".'

Demonstrate this using the word 'middle'. Print it and let the child attempt it first. If he is still befuddled after three or four attempts, explain it again. Now, let him sound it out with his finger. Let him write it.

Keep on doing it with other 'le' words – 'meddle', 'fiddle', 'puddle', 'muddle' – until he understands the concept. Now, let him try his teeth on Exercise 107. The reading passage in Exercise 108 will give him greater fluency with 'le' words in a more natural context.

Exercise 107: Words with the 'le' ending

paddle	saddle	straddle	handle
candle	cattle	hurdle	puddle
huddle	middle	spittle	little
terrible	horrible	cuddle	snuggle
straggle	haggle	twiddle	fondle
guzzle	puzzle	prattle	kettle
settle	shuttle	chortle	hurtle
humble	fumble	rumble	mumble

Exercise 108: Reading passage

Little Red Hen lived in a little hut by the river. Little Red Hen had a little bed in the middle of her little hut. The little hut had a little door with a handle. The little door led into the garden. In the garden is a puddle where ducks can paddle. In the middle of the puddle sat a big fat frog.

Little Red Hen waddled into her garden and gabbled to the frog. The frog grumbled to her. Then Red Hen went to get sticks. The silly hen forgot to shut the door.

The cunning sly fox went into the hut and did a terrible horrible thing. He gobbled up Little Red Hen for dinner.

Lesson 65: The 'all' sound

Print the word 'all'. When the child attempts to read it, he will almost invariably pronounce it as in 'Allen'. Tell him how it is really said, as in the sentence (which can be pointed out to him in this book):

'Bill had *all* of it.'

(Increasingly, you can begin showing him words in this text instead of printing them out for him. You will also find that he is probably beginning to notice words and phrases in the story books that you are reading aloud to him.)

Now that he knows the *word* 'all', you can show him a few words that have the *sound* 'all' in them, *before* he goes on to Exercise 109.

ball
call
hall
tall
pall

Also, show the child the sounds 'ald' and 'alt'. Print these two sounds and also print the words 'bald' and 'salt'. He will at first read these as with a short 'a', but once you give him the correct pronunciation, he will have no real trouble with words from that family.

Exercise 109: Words with the 'all', 'al', 'ald' and 'alt' sounds

fall	gall	mall	stall
small	wall	pall	tall
salt	halt	falter	halter
paltry	malt	halting	call
calling	enthral	Yalta	squall
ball	Walter	basketball	tall

After he has read the words in Exercise 109 and printed some of them from dictation, it might be pointed out to him that words that have 'al' at the beginning or in the middle (unless the 'al' is followed by 'd' or 't') usually take the ordinary sound of 'a', e.g. 'fallow', 'alley', 'callow', 'Allen', 'valium', 'stallion'.

If the child is a beginning reader, this point does not need to be emphasised. As his reading skill develops over the years, the refinements can be added. For now, though, he should be made aware of words such as 'shall' and 'Allen' as exceptions ('shall' can be introduced as a sight word).

After he has done Exercise 109, and written a selection of the words from it, he is ready to move on to Exercise 110.

Exercise 110: Reading passage

Mister Hall had a stall by the wall. He sells things to his customers every morning. A man got a tall clock from him for a hundred and fifty pounds, which is not bad for a tall clock. He will stand the clock on the deck of his small ship.

Mister Hall will try to get extra clocks to sell, for that clock went quickly. As well, Mister Hall will get a supply of balls and bats, halters for horses, salt and all sorts of other stuff. He will sell it all.

Why cannot his stall be in the mall? He can get more customers there. But he cannot go there. It costs much more to rent a stall in the mall than a stall by the wall.

You will notice that the reading passages are now becoming more demanding. For instance, certain words like 'customer' will slow him down because of their length. If he gets stuck, remind him to go at it syllable by syllable, thus: 'cus – cus-tom – custom-er'. Other words, such as 'more' and 'there' are *almost* phonic and, with the rules that he knows already, he can probably work them out – although he might need a bit of help.

When he can read the passage fluently, print the words, 'there', 'where' and 'were' on separate flash cards. Teach him those words as sight words. Have him write them several times until you are sure that he can recognise them and spell them.

11

Four important blends with 'i' and 'y'

Lesson 66: The 'ay' and 'ai' sounds

In this section we want the child to learn to read words involving 'ai' and 'ay'. Although we will not explicitly tell the child at this point, it is also of interest to note a spelling rule associated with these sounds. You may wonder how on earth we can know which 'ay' sound to use in spelling. The rule is this: if the word *begins* with the 'ay' sound, or if it has it in the middle, it is spelled 'ai'; if the sound comes at the *end* of the word, it is spelled 'ay'. There are, of course, some exceptions.

When teaching the child, start off with the sound 'ay' and leave 'ai' until later. Explain that when 'a' and 'y' go together to make 'ay', it wounds like it does in:

day

play

hay

Write 'ay' on a piece of paper and point to it while you are talking. Then, go to the list above and do each of 'day', 'play' and 'hay' in turn.

You may have to help a bit with the blending, e.g. 'p-l – pl-ay – play'. However, the child should pick it up quite readily. If he has difficulty, print the sound 'ay' on top of another sheet of paper and list a string of words embodying that form underneath. To do this, use some words from Exercise 111. When he can handle these fluently, and can also write out words from Exercise 111 as you call them out to him, have him quickly read through the words of that exercise.

Exercise 111: Words with the 'ay' sound

play	tray	flay	fray
crayfish	Fay	gay	lay
slay	may	say	stay
Mayday	nay	Thursday	pray
pay	payday	Monday	ray
spay	way	away	always
today	clay	bay	Raymond

Exception: **says**

In the same lesson, you can also present 'ai'. Say nothing yet about the spelling rule discussed above. Simply explain that 'ai' sounds the same as 'ay' and try him out on the following words:

rain

train

sail

pail

mail

As soon as he can handle these, go directly to Exercise 112.

Exercise 112: Words with the 'ai' sound

mail	aim	ail	ailment
tail	fail	hail	sail
rail	Gail	grail	trail
bail	jail	nail	pail
quail	avail	wail	maim

raid	paid	laid	Kincaid
maid	jailer	staid	Haig
Craig	wait	bait	daily
gaily	Maitland	snail	twain

Exception: said

When he has done these and can print those that you call out to him, you can introduce him gently to the spelling rule. It really is quite a simple rule to explain when you have Exercises 111 and 112 open in front of you.

Then, try him out with a bit of oral spelling of, say, five words – two from Exercise 111 and three from Exercise 112. At first you might have to keep reminding him of the rule. Keep at it until he at least has *some* idea of it.

A few words now need to be said about exceptions. The English language being what it is, almost all spelling rules have exceptions. Even the simple spelling rule that I have mentioned here has exceptions (which will not be discussed, but which have been noted in the exercises). This is not something about which you should be overly worried, but you *must* get the child to recognise 'says' and 'said' in their own right. Most children have no trouble reading 'says', and understanding it in context, even if they pronounce it to rhyme with 'raise'. But 'said' can prove difficult for some time. Make out flash cards for 'says' and 'said' and use them until he can read and spell both words.

Do not neglect to keep going through those flash cards every couple of days with your child.

Note that there is no reading passage from the book in this session. This gives you the opportunity to re-do one of the previous reading exercises, if you feel it necessary, or to allow the child to select one from his storybooks.

Lesson 67: More sight words and reading

Before going on to the reading passage in Exercise 113, print out the following words: 'minister', 'funny', 'before', 'again'. Each of these words can be worked out by phonics, so let the child practise doing so until he has become fluent. With 'before', for instance, you will have to remind him of the sight word 'be' and then of the sound 'or'. Print 'before' on a flash card and include it in the deck of sight words.

Now, go on to Exercise 113. This is the longest and most sophisticated reading passage that the child has encountered – *very* impressive after only a couple of months or so!

Exercise 113: Reading passage

Today we will all play in the den. Gail has her clay in a tray and Ray has a crayfish in a pail. The crayfish has a tail to swim with and carry her eggs under her tail. We must not hurt the crayfish. After lunch Ray will let her go again in the pond where she can stay. The pond by the haystack is where you may trap crayfish.

On Sunday, when we were at church, Fay hid a crayfish in the font. The minister did not think it at all funny! We will let the crayfish stay with us until we go for lunch. Ray laid it on a tray, but it fell off. Before lunch we will let it go. That is better than waiting until after lunch.

Gail said, 'We must let it go.'

Ray said, 'But Fay says that you are bringing it to church again next Sunday.'

'No,' said Gail. 'I must not let it go in the font again.'

The girls let the crayfish go into the pond. It can swim and play and get wet in the rain. It will be glad to be back in the pond.

Lesson 68: The 'oy' and 'oi' sounds

The similar rule of spelling applies to the sounds 'oy' and 'oi' as applies to 'ay' and 'ai', but there are more exceptions to this rule than to the one with 'ay' and 'ai'. Again, do not discuss this with the child yet.

Begin with the word:

toy

Point to it on this page. Say it aloud and have the child say it. Explain that the letters 'o' and 'y' together make the sound 'oy'. Try him out on:

Roy

soy

boy

hoy

coy

When he understands and can print and spell such words, show him the sound 'oi'. Explain that it sounds exactly like 'oy'. Let him try it out on a few words first:

boil

soil

coil

broil

point

After he has achieved fluency with these, go to Exercise 114.

Exercise 114: Words with the 'oy' and 'oi' sounds

boy	joy	enjoy	tomboy
oyster	annoy	toy	destroy
Troy	ploy	toyshop	pointer
Roy	boil	toil	toilet
soil	royal	ointment	point
appoint	disappoint	joint	hoist
loin	join	doily	foiling
poison	foist	ploy	Fitzroy

He should now do the reading passage in Exercise 115. Again, prepare him for it by printing the following words and having him work them out until he can read them readily:

present

uncle

person

store

pellets

These words are all easily phonhic and none of them need to be put on the sight-word list.

Exercise 115: Reading passage

'Can we go to the toyshop?' said May to her mother.

'Can I also go?' said Roy.

'Yes,' said Mother, 'but I think you must get back before long. Uncle Mick is going to visit me. He has at last got a job and is very happy. He did not have a job before and unemployment can be very hard on a person.'

'Let us get a present for Uncle Mick,' said May.

'Where can we get him a present?' said Roy. 'You cannot get him a thing in a toyshop. He will not enjoy that. Maybe we can get him a kettle to boil his milk in.'

'No,' said May, 'that will annoy him. You can't boil milk in a kettle. But we can go to the store next door and get him a tin of poison to kill the snails in his garden.'

'Will you be disappointed if you cannot go to the toyshop, Roy? I think that May's plan is best.'

'That's okay with me,' said Roy. 'We will go to the store next to the toyshop and get him a present. When he paints his shed, he can scatter the poison for the snails.'

'Is the poison in pellets or is it a liquid or an ointment?' said May.

12

Short and long vowels

Growing Independence in Reading

Material covered in the next five to ten sessions, especially that in Exercise 116, tends to be pivotal in a child's development of confidence and competence in reading. Comprehension of the most well-known rule for changing a *short* vowel sound, e.g. the 'a' in 'cap', to a *long* vowel sound, by adding an 'e' to make 'cape', represents a great increase in power over the code. In fact, it has been my experience that large numbers of children stop taking regular reading lessons once they have mastered this rule. They can read so much by then that when they run across the few words which make use of more involved phonic rules they are able to guess. Doubtless, if they persisted with the lessons, they would become much more proficent, especially at writing, but once a child feels that he can read, the incentive to keep learning about it drops away.

For this reason, you must be especially careful to move increasingly away from this text in the search for reading matter. The reading selections in the text are only intended to provide practice in applying spelling rules learned in the corresponding exercise. Thus, those reading exercises should certainly all be done – and dictation should be given from them – but it is only reasonable that as the child's reading fluency develops, he will begin to enjoy reading for its own sake. When this happens, he must be encouraged to acquire a taste for books by being allowed to select his own. In this context, it also would be most useful to read the section entitled 'Extraneous Reading Experience' from Chapter Thirteen.

Introducing Short and Long Vowels

Lesson 69: Short and long 'a'

Print the word 'mat' in fairly large lettering and have the child read it aloud. Now put an 'e' at the end and explain as follows: 'This is a magic "e". When I put it here –' point to the end of the word with your finger '– the word no longer sounds like "mat", but like "mate".'

Now, print both words side by side. Say them as you point to them. Have the child point to and say them. Now, point to 'mate' and ask him, 'What makes this word sound this way?'

Let him answer to the effect that it has an 'e' at the end. Now, put your finger over the 'e' and ask him what it sounds like. Do this sort of thing with a few more words, such as:

pan	pane
hat	hate
rat	rate
cap	cape

Now, have him write a few. At first do it by reading the short vowel word first (e.g. 'pan') and then the associated long vowel word ('pane'). When you are sure that he has the idea, turn to Exercise 116.

Exercise 116: The rule of 'e' to make the long vowel sound of 'a'

fad	fade	rave	daze
Gav	gave	safe	fame
cane	can	save	haze
cave	dam	dame	pave
wade	made	tap	tape
lame	name	wave	flame
Sam	same	came	cam
tam	tame	blaze	crave

brave   game   mat   graze

make   craze   shad   shade

Exception: have

Once he is sure of those and can read them fluently, explain to him the difference between short and long sounds of 'a'. Explain that each vowel has two sounds: the *short* sound which he has already learned ('a' as in apple, 'e' as in egg, 'i' as in Indian, 'o' as in octopus, 'u' as in umbrella) and the *long* sound. *The long sound is the same as the name of the vowel.* Thus, in 'cap', the 'a' is short, but in 'cape', the 'a' is long.

Now, do the reading passage in Exercise 117.

Exercise 117: Reading passage

Bill had a snake and gave it to Dave. Dave named his snake Slip-Slop and kept it in a crate. The snake was black and red.

Dave is fond of snakes, but his sister Kate hates snakes. Kate said to Dave, 'Is that darn snake going to stay with us?'

When David said, 'Yes, it is,' Kate got mad. She always tells tales and Dave's mother said that Dave had to get rid of the snake. Dave got upset and let the snake go in the kitchen.

Kate's father said, 'That snake is poison. Quick! Kill it fast. Chase it and kill it!' But the snake got under the door and hid away in the garden.

Lesson 70: Short and long 'i'

Do not introduce this topic on the same day as you deal with 'a'. Again, start out by printing a simple short 'i' word: 'pin'. Ask the child to read it.

Now, add an 'e' to the end and explain that placing the 'e' there makes the 'i' *long* instead of *short*. To make the point, say the word 'pin' with the 'e' covered and 'pine' with the 'e' uncovered.

Print these words on a largish piece of paper, having some space between them: 'Tim', 'Sid', 'rim', 'hid', 'dim', 'pip'. On a small piece of card (a flash card will do), write the letter 'e' in the same size as the letters of the words on the page. Place the 'e' at the end of 'Tim' so that the word becomes 'Time'. Make sure that the child understands the difference in pronunciation. Do it in succession with each of the other words.

Be sure that he understands the idea and can spell the words correctly. Now, have him do Exercise 118. After he is able to handle that without undue difficulty and can master the reading passage in Exercise 119, you are ready to move on to the next vowel.

Exercise 118: The rule of 'e' to make the long vowel sounds of 'a' and 'i'

fit	five	size	live
rid	ride	line	tide
pin	pine	dive	bit
vine	bite	bide	Mal
bid	wide	wade	dig
hide	pal	tin	pale
hid	side	win	mat
wine	drive	male	mine
hive	prize	grave	fan

Exercise 119: Reading passage

Blake is a boy who kept a lot of fish in a tank. Every time Blake takes a hike by the river, he takes a bottle with him. With a bottle you can make a fine trap for silly little fish who have no sense at all.

Blake's pal, Hank, can go with him if his mother will let him. Blake got mad at Hank the last time he went with him for fish. Hank had said that the bottle belonged to him and Blake had tried to grab it from him.

'It's mine, you silly fink!' yelled Blake. 'Give it back.'

'That's a pile of tripe!' cried Hank. 'My brother gave it to me last Saturday for helping him to wipe his bike dry. It got all wet in the rain.'

The boys made a horrible noise in the scuffle and the jar got bust.

'I can't get a single fish in there,' sobbed Blake. 'You are nothing but a piker. I bet you swipe things all the time!'

Lesson 69: Short and long 'o'

In the same way as we did with 'a' and 'i' (we shall come back to 'e' at the end), write down a word containing 'o' as a short sound, thus: 'not'.

Have the child read the word. Remind him, after he has done so, that the sound of 'o' in 'not' is the *short* sound. If we put an 'e' on the end of that word, the 'o' takes on its *long* sound. Say the word 'note' and print it. Emphasise the 'o' in 'note'.

To be sure that he understands, ask him to read the following words.

Tom	pop
rob	rot
lop	cop

Now, ask him to add an 'e' to each and, as he does so, to say what the word becomes. When he can do all that correctly, let him go on to Exercise 120. Having completed that, he is now ready for the reading passage in Exercise 121.

Exercise 120: The rule of 'e' to make the long vowel sounds of 'a', 'i' and 'o'

mod	mode	cove	rod
rode	pole	hope	hop
stole	wove	dome	stove
rope	bone	vote	tone
rob	drove	robe	mop
mope	pond	not	sole
note	stone	home	gave
tax	grove	Tim	shine
print	those	six	nine
pane	cave	lax	mix
hive	vine	rove	his
hide	pale	shave	shrove

wise	crave	fix	yam
brave	clove	vim	lime

Exercise 121: Reading passage

'Did you spot that pole-cat over by the rope?' Denison asked Martha.

Martha replied, 'What the devil is a pole-cat?'

Martha is from Australia where there are no pole-cats. She is visiting relatives in Canada. In Canada skunks are commonly called pole-cats and are often seen after dark.

Denison explained to her, 'Pole-cats are skunks. A pole-cat is as big as a cat and is black all over with a white stripe starting at the tip of its nose and passing back over its back and along to the tip of its tail.'

'Can you make a pet of a pole-cat?' asked Martha.

'You can if you cut off its stink glands first, when it is still a kitten,' said Denison. 'Adult skunks can let off a terrible pong!'

Lesson 70: Short and long 'u'

As before, print on a piece of paper a word containing the short 'u' sound: 'cut'.

Have the child read it. Explain, after he has done so, that is the *short* sound of 'u'. The *long* sound of 'u' is given by the name of the letter itself and is brought out by adding 'e' to the word:

cut   cute

Does he understand the long and short sound of 'u'? The best way to find out is to go on to Exercise 122.

Exercise 122: The rule of 'e' to make the long vowel sounds of 'a', 'i', 'o' and 'u'

tub	tube	but	Bute
stud	blue	Sue	nut
mute	tune	muse	assume
rude	cub	cube	cue
up	puke	dues	true
lake	pile	pill	rule
ride	rip	ripe	vote
pod	hole	fan	grab
mill	mile	file	use
abuse	misuse	fuse	muse

There are a few tricky variations in that lot: for instance, words like 'Sue', 'true' and 'blue'. They do not carry the same sound of 'u' as does 'nude'. Some children try to give it that pronunciation, cannot do so and – in struggling – come up with the real word. In the United States, people have less trouble with it because, to them, the long 'u' almost always sounds like 'oo', as in: When I was a student (stoodent), I was so stupid (stoopid) that I ate my stew (stoo) with a screw (skroo) driver. However, British children just have to learn from experience (and practice) that the long 'u' can take either pronunciation, depending on the word being used. Exercise 122 should make this clear.

At this point, you should teach the child three more sight words: 'have', 'some' and 'come'. 'Have' has already been listed as an exception at the bottom of Exercise 116, but take this opportunity to teach it thoroughly. As for 'some', if he knows his stuff, he will say 'soam'. However, he might have picked it up already as a sight word without you teaching him. This sometimes happens. Often such a word is picked up from an older sibling or from trying to read something off a cereal packet or whatever. The important thing is that he learns to recognise it, to write it and to be able to spell it orally. Above all, he must pronounce it correctly as 'sum'. Print it on a flash card and add it to his collection of sight words. Do exactly the same with the word 'come'. Put all three words on flash cards and add them to the deck. Then, have your child tackle the reading passage in Exercise 123.

Exercise 123: Reading passage

Whenever Jill comes over to Jennifer's flat to play, Jennifer's mother thinks up an excuse to stop them from playing together.

'Why has your mother got it in for me?' Jill asked Jennifer last time.

'I can't understand it,' said Jennifer. 'Maybe she is upset about your exam results. She did not like it when you scored better than me. You did better than me in arithmetic and also in music. That made my mother angry.'

'But that's silly,' said Jill sadly. 'I just like studying.'

'Yes,' replied Jennifer, 'I think it's silly to go

on like my mother. You study and I play, but
we are still pals. Tests in class just amuse me.
When I get home I just like to play some tunes
on my flute and on my trumpet. Who cares if I
get bad scores and fail exams?'

Lesson 73: Short and long 'e'

There are fewer words exemplifying the same rules with 'e'
itself, but there are some. Look at the following words:

here	he
mere	she
sere	be
see	me

Read each word to him, emphasising the long 'e'. Have him
read them back to you. Note that 'he', 'she', 'be' and 'me' have
been learned as sight words.

From 'see' ('e' after 'e') he can then work out that two 'e's
together make the *long* vowel sound 'e', as follows:

Ben	been
bet	beet
red	reed
met	meet

Thus armed, he can now do Exercises 124 and 125.

Exercise 124: Introducing two forms of the long vowel sound of 'e'

here	red	send	mere
flee	see	seen	been
seed	deed	greed	feed
she	heed	steed	steep
he	glee	me	green
sheep	be	tree	sleep
peel	creep	feed	feet
feel	deep	free	greet
leed	fleet	sweet	three
complete	these	Swede	grebe

Exercise 125: Reading passage

'Come here and see this,' called Ted from the back of the shop. 'I've trapped a big spider under this jar on the toy bench.'

'What sort of spider is it?' said Derek. He panicked every time a spider came inside.

'I'm afraid,' shivered Derek. 'If that spider gets at me it will be my punishment. I stole a pile of cupcakes from my grandmother yesterday. Maybe fate sent that spider to bite me for my crimes.'

'But these spiders haven't even got poison in

them. If it bites you, you bleed a bit, but it can't kill you. You can complete your life in safety with no worry at all,' said Ted. 'In fact, we will keep the spider trapped in the jar until my father gets home. We will see what he says. He can recognise all sorts of spiders.'

Remember in Chapter Nine I mentioned there was an interesting rule of spelling which would be introduced after you had instructed the child in long and short vowels? The rule is this. If we want to change, say, 'shed' to 'shedding', we *double* the *consonant* before the 'ing'. (This is not necessary if the word already ends in two consonants, e.g. changing 'shell' to 'shelling' or 'jump' to 'jumping'.) We will do more work with this rule in the next chapter.

13

More work on syllables

Breaking a Word into Syllables

From this point on, it is generally a poor idea to do two word-list exercises in one day. Each such word-list exercise represents an increased level of spelling sophistication, and best results are obtained if you allow at least a day for the child to become thouroughly familar with each.

In dictations you can now begin to be more fussy about punctuation marks, quotation marks, etc. You can even start to dictate from sources other than the reading passages in this book.

Lesson 74: Compound words

Your child already knows that separate syllables each have their own vowel sound, e.g.:

sep/a/rate
dis/til/late
un/bend/ing
hel/i/cop/ter

Write these words without the stroke marks and, as each one is written, have the child sound it out. If he gets stuck, write the word again *one syllable at a time*, as indicated by the strokes.

This is an important skill to develop, *so go slowly*. Your child must learn to divide or break words up into syllables so that words can be more readily attacked and recognised.

To continue teaching syllabication, then, we can introduce *compound* words. A compound word is one that is made up of two or more separate whole words. Teach the child the formal expression 'compound words', although he cannot be expected to read the phrase yet.

Before doing Exercise 126, review 'some' and 'come' as sight words. Once he has mastered these, move on to Exercise 126.

Exercise 126: Some compound words

become	into	mailman
gladsome	hatrack	upon
backstand	handsome	carpark
wherefore	rainfall	somewhere
cannot	therefore	something
income	fishhook	railway
sometimes	welcome	beforehand
underhand	nevertheless	unwelcome

Lesson 75: Open and closed syllables

If a syllable begins with a vowel, it is said to be *open* at the beginning. Likewise, if it has a vowel at the end, it is said to be *open* at the end. On the other hand, if a syllable begins with a consonant, it is said to be *closed* at the beginning. Likewise, if it has a consonant at the end, it is said to be closed at the end.

Teach the child to divide the word into syllables, using pencil strokes on words you have written on paper. Usually, if two consonants come together in the middle of a word, we split syllables between the two consonants, e.g. 'at/tain/ment'. However, that should not be done if it involves breaking an already existing word, e.g. 'bender' must be broken as 'bend/er'. It would make no sense to divide it as 'ben/der'. (Once the child has done work on prefixes and suffixes, he will develop greater facility at deciding where to divide between syllables.)

Before attempting Exercise 127, try him out on these words:

malevolent   afterward   banishment

For instance, 'malevolent' should be broken up as follows:

'mal/ev/o/lent' – 'mal' is closed at both ends, 'ev' is open at the beginning, 'o' is open at both ends, and 'lent' is closed at both ends.

In Exercise 127, tell him to write each word (by copying – he doesn't have to try to spell them yet) and then to try his hand at breaking each one into syllables. For each syllable thus produced, he must say precisely whether it is open at either end or closed at either end.

Exercise 127: More polysyllabic words

extraordinary	battleship	optimistic
glorify	Landrover	pessimistic
magnify	wartime	retrenchment
exemplify	fundamental	bandana
establishment	fundamentalist	cannibal
mandible	cannibalism	cannibalistic
atavistic	mentality	mandible

At this point, you should be allowing at least fifteen minutes for writing/dictation work and fifteen minutes for reading aloud from a book chosen by the child.

Extraneous Reading Experience

We are about to embark on teaching a difficult rule – but one which will become easy once the child is used to it. However, it is an extremely important rule, so time should be taken in its teaching and you must persist until the child has a thorough command of it. This may take several sessions. While he is working on this topic, especially if it lasts for several days, he should continue to read to you each day.

At this point, it is worth mentioning the importance of expanding the child's reading matter to broaden his lesson material – and to maintain his interest (and yours)!

Go to your local library or bookstore and get an attractive storybook, the subject matter of which might appeal to your child in particular. You will find that there are a number of words in any such book that he cannot read yet – although there will be surprisingly few. Be sure to read the book carefully yourself first. Lightly (so that the marks can be erased later), underline with pencil all the words which the child's phonic preparation up until now has not prepared him to handle. The vast majority of these, words such as 'though', 'house', 'station', 'what' and 'was', will within the next few weeks be covered as his phonic skills increase. Therefore, do *not* attempt to teach these as sight words. Simply *say* the word to him as he comes to it, though it would obviously be useful – in some cases – to let him *attempt* a phonic analysis. Doing so would give him an incorrect rendering of the word, but possibly one that is so close to what it should be that he might get it by context.

For instance, take the sentence: 'Timothy knew that he should not do it.' The child will work out: 'Timothy … that he … not … it.' There is almost no way that he can work out 'knew' – it embodies two things he has not yet learned: he does not know the 'ew' sound and he has not yet had silent letters explained to him. So *tell* him. When he comes to it, simply say, 'That word is *knew*!'

He has never seen 'should', but when he gets to it, let him try. He will get the initial 'sh' sound and the terminal 'd': 'Sh…d, sho…d, sh-[mumble]-d.' *After* he has attacked it a few times, tell him. The advantage of this is that he will doubtless run across it again in the same story and, when he starts to work it out again, the process will take less time.

'Do' is a word that the child will usually figure it out, even though later on we shall list it as a sight word.

The important thing to bear in mind is that you should not become discouraged. It may strike you that there seems to be an awful lot that the child cannot read. Remember this: phonic training is *exponential* in its impact. That is, the command it will give the child over written English is *not* in direct proportion to the amount of time he has spent learning. If forty hours of work on phonics has given him command over about 20 per cent of the words he meets, then it will not take eighty hours of work to give him command over 40 per cent of the words he meets. It accelerates. Where forty hours gives command over 20 per cent of the words, maybe forty-five hours will give command over 80 per cent of the words.

If you become discouraged, you might be tempted to switch to a look–say system. It seems so unambiguous. But remember: look–say is *not exponential* in its impact, as far as ability to recognise words is concerned. In fact, maybe it is even *negatively* exponential, in the sense that the greater the number of words one has to learn whole, the *less* likely it is that they will all be distinguished from one another.

Even worse, though, is the effect that look–say has on the child's reading habits. He stops relying on phonics and starts to guess. As long as the material is juvenile enough, such guessing works quite well, but it imposes a drastic limit on the level of sophistication he can reach with his reading. It also carries with it psychological difficulties. For instance, since word guessing is a bit risky, with a fairly high level of error possible, it introduces tension into reading. It makes the child understandably reluctant to tackle new material or to engage in spontaneous reading. On top of that, the attempt to spurt forward by a concentrated drive on whole-word recognition makes it difficult for the child to go back to phonics later. Even when he does, while ostensibly trying to methodically apply phonic skills, subconsciously he will be trying to guess at the whole word. This has the effect of never letting him develop sufficient fluency at phonics to attack new words quickly with a high expectation of success.

Therefore, do not let yourself be upset if most of the words that the child meets in his extraneous reading defy his present kit of phonic-analysis tools. Instead, revel in the amount he has learned in a relatively short amount of time. Persist a few weeks longer, and the increase in the fluency of his command over the phonic rules he has already learned, plus the new phonic material that he learns in the coming few weeks, will increase his reading effectiveness many times over.

Now, let's turn back to the rule mentioned before this discussion.

Two Consonants Keep a Vowel Sound Short

Lesson 76: Doubling a consonant

Let's take another look at the rule for doubling a consonant. The reason for doubling the consonant is that, if there is only *one* consonant between a vowel and the 'ing', the vowel takes on the *long* sound. The doubling of the consonant, or the presence of two consonants already, insures that the vowel sound stays short. Consider, for example, the word 'slop'. Here we must double the 'p'.

The water will *slop* over the edge.
The water is *slopping* over the edge.

With only one 'p', the word would be 'sloping' as in:

The plank is *sloping* up to the kerb.

Lack of knowledge about this simple phonic rule accounts for a large percentage of spelling errors in the community!

Now, to teach the child the rule, write the word 'hop'. Have the child say it.

On another strip of paper, using letters of the same size, write the sound 'ing'.

Now, bring the 'ing' up to join on at the end of 'hop'. Ask the child, 'What is the word now?' Almost certainly the child will say 'hopping'. But, of course, that is not right.

Explain that, because there is only *one consonant* between the 'o' and the 'i', the 'o' *is given the long sound*. Thus, 'hoping' rhymes with 'soaping'.

But rabbits *do* hop. How do we describe what they are doing? We want to keep the 'o' *short* like it is in 'hop'. We do that by *putting in an extra 'p'*. Thus, it becomes 'hopping'. Explain this very carefully, then have the child read the following:

The rabbit *hops*.

The rabbit is *hopping*.

The rabbit *hopes* and it *hops*.

It *hopes* to see a carrot.

It *hops* along to get it.

The rabbit is *hoping* while it is *hopping*.

Of course, understanding this rule makes a great difference in spelling. Even in secondary school one sometimes sees students putting down things such as: 'I was writting an essay.' However, if the rule we have just discussed were taught early enough, and consistently enough, such sloppy spelling would soon diminish.

Now, before going on to Exercise 128, have the child read *and write* the following pairs of words:

pining   pinning

diner   dinner

planing   planning

Like most rules of spelling, this one is *not* watertight. For instance, it doesn't work with 'i' before 'v' – obviously 'river', is correct, not 'rivver' – and there are also other exceptions to it. But it generally works. When the child is comfortable with the words above, move on to Exercise 128.

Exercise 128: Keeping a vowel sound short by doubling the follow-ing consonant

caning	fated	ratting	rotter
canning	fatted	grating	grabbing
patting	robing	matter	grading
noting	passing	rating	noted
plummet	lading	robbing	spotting
plume	mussed	mused	music

accused	fussing	fusing	copping
coping	petting	mating	matting

Lesson 77: Two unalike consonants

The double-consonant rule holds true, not *quite* universally, but in most cases, when there are two consonants which are not a double separating the vowels, e.g. the 'u' in 'humping' as opposed to the 'u' in 'human'.

When he can see the point, have him do Exercise 129. It would also be useful for him to look over Exercise 90 again. The sounding out of those words – and their spelling – will now make a lot more sense. Follow this with the reading passage in Exercise 130.

Exercise 129: Two unlike consonants keeping the preceding vowel sound short

human	stump	making	lapping
puking	stupid	linger	baring
mucking	Cupid	liner	barring
tuning	cuspid	limping	staring
stunting	masking	lining	cater
chatter	pelter	Peter	crater

Exercise 130: Reading passage

'Come and see what I've got,' said Jane to Robert. 'I got some bits of metal from my father – shavings from his lathe – and I made a spinner with them.'

'Yes,' said Robert, 'but what can you use

something like that for?'

'Well, I suppose I will tie it on the end of a strong line and catch an absolute monster of a shark with it.' Jane spoke rather angrily. 'Besides, I never said it is to be used for something. I make things just for fun.'

'Maybe a shark will bite and swallow it,' replied Robert. 'You can't tell with sharks. Fish are not very smart and if a shark thinks that your spinner is something edible, it will come along and swallow it.'

'That's not true,' said Jane. 'Sharks hunt by smell. A shark is not likely to fall for a spinner made of metal. Steel hasn't the correct smell. I will tell you what. Let's try it. I will hang the spinner over the side of the jetty and, if a shark comes, you can jump in and try to interest it in my spinner!'

Robert did not think much of that plan.

14

The 'ou', 'ow', 'oo' and 'ol' sounds

Vowel Combinations

We have had some vowel combinations with the rule of 'e'. As we have discussed, when 'e' is added to the end of a word, it will almost always make a vowel long, whether there is a consonant between them or not. 'Flee', 'tie', 'toe', 'hue' and 'home' are all words that show this rule. In this chapter we will look at several other vowel combinations.

Lesson 78: The 'ou' sound

To teach the child the 'ou' sound, write it on a piece of paper, then tell the child that *usually* when 'o' and 'u' come together, it sounds like the first part of 'ouch'. Have him say the sound 'ou' several times and let him write it. Now, show him the word 'spout'. (You can show it to him in the book, without writing it separately).

Before letting him try to sound it out, ask him what the 'ou' in the middle sounds like. When he tells you, let him sound out the word:

spout

Now, ask him to write it from memory.

At this point, let him go on to Exercise 131. You must not forget to give him some spelling words from that exercise.

Exercise 131: One 'ou' sound

out	lout	clout	cloud
mount	amount	hound	round
around	sound	ground	dismount
cloudy	aground	without	pout
spout	rout	tout	slouch
couch	shout	stout	grout
mound	pound	bound	bounty
county	douse	found	foul
joust	louse	lousy	mouse
house	noun	wound	clouded

Once he is comfortable with those words, introduce a few more sight words. They are: 'could', 'should, 'would' and 'they'.

With 'could', let the child take a stab at it himself. He will get the initial 'c' and the terminal 'd'. He will *then* apply the rule for 'ou' and come up with 'cowelled' – or something of that order. Tell him that the word is actually pronounced 'could' and see if he can read the following sentence: 'Max could have come, but he went home.'

Once he has read 'could' several times, and has correctly printed it, he can be tried on 'should'. He may struggle a bit, but it won't be too long before he can correctly read 'could' and 'should'. Now, introduce 'would'. Write each of these on a separate flash card and add it to the deck. Shuffle the deck well and run through all the flash cards with him.

Now, show him the word 'they'. It is not a difficult word to remember on sight, because its phonic elements are so suggestive. Make a flash card for that one too and add it to the deck.

If you now let your child tackle the reading passage in Exercise 132, you will see what he does when he runs across the word 'eventually'. It may well not even be a word in his speaking vocabulary, let alone his reading vocabulary! But don't let that worry you. Once the child has a really good command of phonics – that is, after he has finished this book – he will often sound out words he has never heard before.

This is another good reason for using phonics when teaching reading: it leads to a very rapid growth of vocabulary, which does not happen with a child who has been reared on a look–say method. The phonics-trained child, who is always testing out his skill, will often run across a big, juicy word. He will sound it out and – if he doesn't know what it means – he will go and ask someone. Suppose the word was something like 'unscrupulous'. He will not bring the book with him, point to the word and ask, 'What does that say?' Instead, he will ask, 'What does "unscrupulous" *mean*?' When you answer, the word will become part of his vocabulary.

What would a look–say child do? Well, if he *were* looking at print at random and he ran across a word like that, the only way he could find out what it said would be to carry the book (or paper or whatever) to someone and say, 'See this word here,' assuming he hadn't lost it in the meantime, 'what does it say?' But *why* would he do so? It is unlikely that he would take the trouble, because *most* words he sees outside the carefully controlled vocabulary of his reading material are foreign to him – every bit as foreign as 'unscrupulous'. There is no reason for him to pick on one word more than any other. Indeed, he has quite enough to do remembering the shapes of the whole words he is learning at school without voluntarily burdening himself with more.

What will your child do, then, when he sees 'eventually'? No doubt he will get as far as 'event-' and then stop.

You can help by pointing out that the 'u' has to have its *long* sound because it is followed by another vowel. There's no need to go into any greater depth than that. He should come up with something like: 'event-eventyou-eventyoual [rhyming with 'ball] –' don't correct that mistake, let him finish the word '– eventyoually'.

Have him repeat it a few times until he can say it from memory. Now, you say 'eventually'. Repeat it a few times, then ask him: 'Do you know what it means?' If not, explain its meaning by using it in a simple sentence, e.g. 'Eventually it will stop raining'.

Then, have the child start back at the beginning of the sentence in which 'eventually' occurs.

Exercise 132: Reading passage

Peter found a ball in the junkyard at his father's shop. He called all of his mates up and they came along to see what else they could get for free. They dug around in the rubbish and eventually found an overwound clock. The glass and the stand were a bit broken, but the hands were still on. If they could fix the spring, even the alarm would go.

'Should we ask your father if we can have it?' said Bill.

'Well, I suppose we should,' said Peter, 'but he will refuse. What would you do then?'

'I think we should just nick it,' said Henry. 'There's so much junk here, he wouldn't even see it missing.'

'Come on!' said Bill. 'It's a bit of a cheek to rob Peter's dad when Peter is standing there. Turn around Peter. Then you won't see us swipe the clock!'

Just then Peter's Dad came out. 'Hello boys,' he said. 'You wouldn't be planning to take that clock, would you? Somebody inside could tell what you were saying and they said to me that some boys out the back were about to make off with a clock!'

The boys went home in a hurry. You can bet they were embarrassed.

Lesson 79: The 'ow' sound

The letters 'ow', when found together, make the same sound as 'ou'. Tell the child this and explain that 'ow' usually comes at the end of a word, while 'ou' usually comes at the beginning or middle. Write them both and have the child spell them.

Test him out on the word 'cow'. If he has no trouble with it, go right on to Exercise 133 with him (otherwise, do a bit of review). Then, do the reading passage in Exercise 134.

Exercise 133: One 'ow' sound

fowl	owl	cowl	cowling
down	flower	power	powder
tower	cow	plow	how
prowess	bow-wow	town	now
vow	vowel	towel	chow
shower	power	bower	dowry
Dow	prowler	prowl	growl
howl	wow	crown	brown
drown	gown	crowd	downy

Exercise 134: Reading passage

How foul is it to keep fowl in the kitchen! When I had a hen, I kept it in the shed. All birds such as hens, ducks, geese and turkeys are called fowl.

I went downtown last Tuesday to see if I could get a trowel to scrape dirt off my hen-house. While I was in the paint shop discussing my problem with the shopkeeper, who should come in but the bloke from next door to me. He shouted at me. 'I found your fowl sitting on the back of my car where my wife laid her towel to dry. That disgusting hen of yours left its droppings all over the towel and the car. I'll bet that you are the sort of person who lets fowl foul up your kitchen. I'll tell you now, if I see that fowl on my car again, it will end up in my kitchen – in a pot!' He got extremely angry and growly, but I hope he gets over it.

Lesson 80: More 'ou' and 'ow' sounds

Once he has mastered the work in the previous two lessons, it should be pointed out that 'ou' and 'ow' each have *another* sound. 'Ou' not only sounds like the 'ou' in 'pound', it also sounds like it does in 'soup', 'you' and 'group'. Write these three words, and with each *say* the word and then *point* to the 'ou'.

Likewise, 'ow' not only sounds like the 'ow' in 'vow', but can also sound like 'oe', as in: 'blow', 'low' and 'grow'. Write these three words and have the child say them and spell them. Now, try Exercise 135. There is no need for him to write or spell these words, but he should know of their existence, though some of them, like 'troupe', may not be in his speaking vocabulary. Once he has done that, let him do the reading passage in Exercise 136.

Exercise 135: Alternative 'ou' and 'ow' sounds

grow	group	croup	you
bowl	throw	below	snow
crow	troupe	soup	blow
slow	glow	window	show
flow	tow	row	stowaway
low	growth	grown	own
mow	mown	sow	sown

Exercise 136: Reading passage

When Dad used to be a kitchen-hand in the Army, he made the best soup in the camp. On a very cold winter's day, all the men were sick with croup. A small group of men were up, but all the rest were in bed. My father was up as he had to get dinner for all the others. They all asked him to make a yummy soup. He said, 'Okay, I will make you a soup like you have never tasted before, but you men who are up have to get some stuff for me. I need somebody to get me a crow. Then somebody else has to row out into the middle of the lake and bring back the fish that died out there a while back. Then will somebody else shift the snow and dig up frozen worms? While you are all getting those different things, I shall start to scrape that smelly green stuff off the window sill and put it in a bowl. With all of that, I will make a first-rate soup!'

All the men felt even sicker after that, so my dad said, 'It's only a joke, fellows. If somebody peels the spuds and the carrots and cuts up the onions, I'll chop up some beef and make you all the very best soup this army has ever had.'

Lesson 81: The 'oo' sound and review

This is a sound that children seem to get a great deal of satisfaction out of learning, for some reason. Explain it using the word 'boot'. He will have no trouble learning the sound. Now, do Exercise 137 with him. He will work out 'school' without much trouble, because of the 'oo', but it should also be put in with the sight words.

Exercise 137: One 'oo' sound

mood	scooter	rooster	loot
loop	troop	coop	stool
tool	fool	drool	droop
spool	Liverpool	cool	school
moon	loon	spoon	moo
croon	boon	coon	goon
hoop	goose	boost	noon
soon	swoon	food	brood

Use the rest of the lesson to review areas in which the child might be having some difficulty, to do dictation and to focus on extraneous reading material.

Lesson 82: More 'oo' sounds

When the child can read the words in Exercise 137 fluently, and print them quickly and accurately, we have to introduce him to a mildly complicating feature, namely that 'oo' has two slight variations to its sound. You immediately become aware of it if you say the words 'zoom' and 'look'.

You must mention this to the child at this point. Have him re-read the words in Exercise 137 and then read those in Exercise 138.

Exercise 138: Alternative 'oo' sounds

look	hook	cook	shook
nook	took	room	broom
wood	good	hood	stood
understood	foot	soot	hoof
rook	crook	crooked	book

At this point, introduce two number words as sight vocabulary: 'one' and 'two'. Print a flash card for each. There is no easy way of remembering them, they just have to be drilled along with the other flash cards. He can now read the reading passage in Exercise 139.

Exercise 139: Reading passage

One day three criminals planned to carry out a big robbery at a bank. Two of the crooks were men. They were Scar-Mug Harry and Chomp-Chomp Charley. They were sinister in every respect. The third criminal was a lady. She could be just as bad as the other two. Her name was Kissing-Killer Kate and she always had two guns up her sleeve.

They planned to stick up a bank in Liverpool. They had three fast scooters and they also had shooters. They also had sacks to take away the loot and some make-up to fool the men in the bank. Before they got to the bank, they were going to dress up as nuns. Who would suspect nuns of robbing a bank!

'Nobody would ever think such a thing,' said Scar-Mug to Chomp-Chomp.

'But nuns are ladies, so Kissing Killer better say whatever has to be said,' observed

Chomp-Chomp. 'If you or I say something, they will catch on that we aren't nuns.'

'Holy smoke, I didn't think of that,' replied Scar-Mug.

'What would a nun say in a bank?' asked Kissing-Killer Kate. 'I've never been a nun before.'

'Well, gang, unless we can get around that problem, we can't make the robbery,' said Scar-Mug.

They are still thinking hard about it, but so far they haven't come up with a good plan. They are not very clever crooks. In fact, if they were clever, they wouldn't be crooks.

Lesson 83: The 'ol' sound

Write the sentence: 'The old man had no teeth left.' Have the child try to read it.

At first, he will pronounce 'old' as 'ald', as in 'called'. From the context of the whole sentence, though, he is likely to discover its correct pronunciation. When you have taught it to him, have him move on to Exercise 140, being sure to have him write some words with 'ol' in them as you call them out. Then he can tackle the reading passage in Exercise 141.

Exercise 140: Words with the 'ol', 'old', 'olt' and 'oll' sounds

bold	old	told	fold
gold	mold	hold	cold
dolt	colt	sold	folder
golden	soldier	Holt	jolt
roll	volt	poll	stroll
troll	roller	holder	untold
scold	holding	roller	bolder

Exercise 141: Reading passage

A bold person is a person who is very brave. One day there came to a little town two horsemen. They were bold and strong. The children of the town told these men on horses that everybody had been afraid to go outside after dark for there were witches and goblins around. 'How can we get rid of them?' asked the children.

One of the horsemen then said, 'Well, as it happens, I can turn myself into a witch. It's a little trick my old father taught me. He used to drive along in his Landrover and suddenly turned into a witch just to scare the traffic cops for a joke. Sometimes he would even scare black cats while he was out for a stroll.'

'That is amazing,' said the other horseman. 'You see, I can turn myself into a goblin. Whenever I got bored in school, I used to turn into a goblin. It drove the masters crazy.'

'That solves our problem,' said the first horseman. 'I'll turn myself into a witch and you turn into a goblin and we'll get rid of the lot!'

And that's what they did.

15

The various 'ea' sounds

Lesson 84: The most common 'ea' sound

Explain to the child that 'ea' usually sounds like 'ee'. For instance, look at these two words and have the child read them from the page:

heel   heal

Can he use each of them in a sentence? Encourage him to do so, then let him read these two sentences:

The *heel* on my slipper needs mending.

The cut on my finger will *heal*.

Now, move on to the words in Exercise 142. You will notice that there are more of them than usual. It is important for the child to learn to recognise instantly the three or four main sounds which 'ea' can take on. To be able to do this, he must be thoroughly grounded on the most common rendering of the sound. In that way, and by using a rapid process of elimination, he will gradually learn to recognise variations on it.

The child should write out, in dictation, at least ten of the words at one time.

Exercise 142: One rendering of the combination 'ea'

steal	real	meat	peal
weak	dear	team	each

eat	flea	tea	leap
beast	beach	zeal	beam
bean	cheat	preach	cheap
reach	heap	lean	east
peach	teach	gear	clear
fear	rear	speak	neat
ear	squeak	spear	streak
leaf	bead	scream	reap
yeast	stream	steam	hear
near	wheat	beak	heat
veal	seat	seal	dream
mean	year	feast	easy
easily	cream	peas	Jean
heat	teacher	creak	treacle

From now on, before each reading selection we shall introduce some sight words. This is not because the words concerned cannot yield to phonic analysis, but because they do not *easily* come apart and because they are so common that the child will become frustrated if he keeps running across them in his reading.

The sight words, then, that should be thoroughly learned and spelled before doing the reading passage in Exercise 143, are: 'was', 'any', 'guess'.

Before actually teaching them one at a time to the child, have him try to figure out each one in the following sentences:

1 Bill *was* at home playing tapes.

2 Kerry said that she didn't have *any* tapes.

3 I bet you can't *guess* where Bill hid them!

With each sentence, if he cannot work out the 'mystery word', tell him what it is. Show him, by sounding it out, how close it comes to what it is supposed to be and then write it on a flash card.

Before incorporating those new sight words into the pack of sight words, have the child study each of them a little more. Now, ask him to *spell* them. Then, let him *write* them. After that, shuffle the new cards into the sight word pack and quickly go through the whole lot. This shouldn't take more than a few minutes and should now be done every day, because he is accumulating a fair collection of sight words.

Now, go to the reading passage in Exercise 143.

Exercise 143: Reading passage

Jonathan Jones was very proud of his name. On anything that he owned, he printed it in big letters so that everyone could see it. No one was going to steal any of his property if he could help it! I guess anyone who did take something of his would be embarrassed to have something with the name 'JONATHAN JONES' printed on it.

Not only was Jonathan always printing his name on things, he did it very neatly. He was clean and never made a mess with the ink that he used, or the paint. In fact, he used a felt-tip pen. Each time that he printed anything, he looked at his hands and his jeans to make sure that there were no streaks on his clothes. He was a real fuss-pot about it. He always appeared neat in school. He would never dream of leaving his desk untidy or his books in a heap.

Maybe it was easy for him to keep his gear in order and to clear up for the teacher. Should we all be that neat? I'm not. What about you?

Lesson 85: 'Ea' as in 'learn'

Have the child read the following sentence:

Can you *learn* how to read?

No doubt he will say, 'Can you leer-n to read?' From that, he may figure out the word 'learn'. Whether he does or not, tell him that 'ea', when it is followed by 'r' *sometimes* sounds like 'ur' – not 'eer'. Now, let him do Exercise 144.

Exercise 144: The combination 'ear' sounding like 'ur'

learn	earn	pearl	early
earth	heard	search	research

There are not many words that are affected by that sound of 'ea'. Many more make the 'ea' sound like 'a' in 'ake'. Therefore, in the same teaching session as Exercise 144, review material that you have done already. The dictation should be a fairly extended passage by now, involving at least ten sentences and attending to punctuation. Also, let the child read from a book of stories of his own choosing.

Do *not* try doing the next section on the same day, because to introduce three sounds of 'ea' on the same day might cause confusion.

Lesson 86: 'Ea' as in 'break' and 'death'

We shall teach both of these sounds for 'ea' at one time, because context generally makes them clear. Start off with 'break'. Have the child read the following sentence:

Did you *break* my window?

If he reads: 'Did you breek my window?', he will recognise that the sentence lacks sense and thus be likely to change it. In any case, make sure that he understands that 'break' rhymes with 'lake'. Then, let him read this sentence:

The meals of the day are: breakfast, lunch and tea.

There is no such meal as 'brake-fast' (although that is its linguistic origin), so he will conclude that in that case 'break' sounds like 'brek'. You can then point out that there are quite a few words in which 'ea' sounds like short 'e'. Just to get him started, let him read these three:

dead

meadow

head

In fact, the short 'e' sound is much more common than the 'ay' sound for 'ea'. Now, go on to Exercise 145. In each case he will have to experiment to ascertain which of the two sounds is appropriate. You may have to help him with some. When he has finished the exercise once, have him read it again. Then, let him read it a third time in a different order, say, down the columns instead of along the rows. Do this as often as is necessary to secure fluency. Note that such words as 'tear' and 'read' each have two legitimate pronunciations meaning different things.

Exercise 145: Alternative renderings of the combination 'ea'

instead	wear	dead	weather
swear	spread	breath	ready
feather	health	steak	breakfast
bread	steady	sweat	head
wealthy	break	pear	dreaded
meant	tread	threat	heavy
tear	leather	great	deaf
heaven	breadth	thread	bear
sweater	wealth	dread	dreaded
heavier	spreading	already	dealt

Before going on to the reading passage in Exercise 146, present the following sight words: 'people', 'believe', 'taught'.

Introduce them one at a time employing the technique described earlier in this chapter. Use the following sentences:

1 Some *people* like school, others do not.

2 Some people *believe* that you must go to school.

3 In school you are *taught* how to count.

Whether or not the child works out through context any given sight word, tell him precisely what it is after he has tried it a few times. Make sure that he can spell each word correctly and can write it. Write the words yourself on separate flash cards and shuffle them into the flash card deck. Now, quickly run through all of the flash cards. If the child misses any, just lay those to one side and then do those few again after you've been through the whole deck.

Now, let him attack the reading passage in Exercise 146.

Exercise 146: Reading passage

Father always sings while he is working.
He says that he dreads some of the jobs he
has to do and unless he sings the work
becomes deadly. Some people swear when
they have to work at something unpleasant.
They would rather play or rest instead. But it
is no good swearing. You just have to bear
it.

Sometimes the work is so heavy that it takes
your breath away. After breakfast, everything
has to be cleared away. You have to be
careful not to break any dishes. The bread is
put away and the table is wiped down ready
for lunch. Then, with a feather duster you
have to clean the furniture. When the weather
is warm, the work can make you sweat. It
would be great if you didn't need to clean
up!

But my father taught me to sing while I work.
He even taught me some good songs to use if
the job is a really horrible one. I believe that
he is correct. I've always believed that if you
believe that something will work, it will. Some

of the songs he taught me would make you laugh, but I enjoy them. It is my belief that other people would too.

16

The sounds in 'kind', 'wild', 'load' and 'few'

Lesson 87: The 'ind' and 'ild' sounds

These two phonic sounds can often be learned initially in context. For instance, let the child try to read each of the following sentences one at a time:

1 A dog is tame, but a dingo is *wild*.

2 The *blind* man can't see anything.

After he has tried the first sentence, and has either worked out or been told the pronunciation of 'wild', let him sound out the following three words:

child

mild

wild

Now, do exactly the same thing with the second sentence, letting him then sound out:

rind

find

mind

When he can handle those words, and spell them and write them, he is ready for Exercise 147. That exercise includes many other words carrying the long 'i' sound. After the child has read them, when doing spelling dictation from this exercise, be sure to include a few of each type of sound represented.

Exercise 147: Various combinations giving the long vowel sound of 'i'

mild	child	tried	flies
find	tied	die	blind
lie	bind	rind	grind
mind	skies	wild	kind
fired	pies	pied	cried
hind	behind	unkind	shies

Before going on to the reading passage in Exercise 148, some more sight words have to be introduced. These are particularly easy in that they all belong to a family of words using 'u'. They are: 'put', 'pull', 'bull', 'full', 'push'.

As usual, use the following sentences to put each in context:

1 Polly *put* the kettle on.

2 'Molly, *pull* it off again!'

3 The cow's husband is a *bull*.

4 The teapot is *full* of tea.

5 You should not *push*.

Following the established practice, allow the child to try to work each word out. Whether he succeeds or not, finally pronounce it clearly yourself. Let him spell it and then write it. Then, go on to the next sentence. Write all five words on separate flash cards and incorporate them into the growing deck of sight words. Now, shuffle them thoroughly and quickly flash through the whole deck. Go on to Exercise 148.

Exercise 148: Reading passage

Kara Mullins has a farm on which she breeds
cattle. It is great fun to look on while she
struggles with her animals. One time her prize
bull wandered off and got lost in the woods.
Poor Kara nearly went berserk trying to find
him. She had been taught to take care of her
livestock. You can be sure she didn't laugh
about it.

I guess the flies got too much for the bull.
They were biting and stinging and tormenting
him so much that he went wild. He was
practically blind and couldn't tell where he was
running. He ended up in the woods. Kara
looked there, but people wouldn't believe how
hard it is to find a bull in the woods.

However, at last Kara found him. He was
stuck in the mud. Kara went up behind him
and tied a rope around his front legs and
across his chest. She put the other end of the
rope around the winch of her jeep and started
the motor. Eventually, with a great slurping
and sucking noise, she pulled the bull free,
then she carefully pushed him on to dry

ground. She got her boots full of mud, but she
was very kind to the bull. Kara was so glad
that she laughed and laughed. But she also
learned a lesson from it. It taught her to make
better fences to keep the bull safe.

Lesson 88: Variations on the long vowel sound of 'o'

The child has already experienced 'ow' as is 'snow', 'o (consonant) e' as in 'cope' and 'ol' as in 'old'. However, there is yet
another combination which produces a long 'o' and that is 'oa'.
Before teaching him that sound, let him take a crack at this
sentence:

Put on your coat and hat.

No doubt he will guess 'coat' correctly. Now, ask him the
following question: 'What sound do "o" and "a" make
together?' He *should* say 'o' (as in 'pole'), but if he does not, then
tell him.
    Now, have him read through Exercise 149. Included in that
exercise are various other renderings of the long 'o'.

Exercise 149: Various combinations giving the long vowel sound of 'o'

soap	rope	coast	most
boast	so	low	road
coach	toll	blow	old
bolt	toad	mow	told
boat	goes	woe	goat
oar	soar	doe	throw
row	crow	sold	coal

gold	oath	bowl	coax
toast	scold	foe	show
hold	growth	coach	roach
roast	tow	glow	slow
loaf	scroll	cold	throat
toes	go	goal	loan
roar	uproar	roam	oats
bold	jolt	foam	growth
moat	groan	load	float

The next sight words to be learned are: 'young', 'course', 'laugh'. They are all awkward and so take even more care than usual to deal with them separately.

Let the child try to read the following sentence:

When my father was *young*, he was just a boy.

After he has taken a few runs at 'young', say the word clearly and have him say it after you. While he is looking at it, ask him to spell it to you. Now, ask him to close his eyes and spell it. When 'young' has thus been learned, write it on a flash card and insert it in the deck.

Now, we come to the word 'course'. Let the child read the following sentence:

'Of *course* you can have some more to eat,' said Mother.

Follow the same procedure as with 'young', again taking great care to ensure that he has learned the word completely.

When we get to 'laugh', we have problems. The spelling renders it very obscure. The best way to teach it is purely by repetition. Have your child read the following:

The clown *laughs*.

He has to *laugh* even if he is sad.

He is paid to *laugh* and the people are supposed to *laugh* at his tricks.

Even after the child gets it, he will keep forgetting it. It really has to be well drilled. Have him spell it – first looking at the word and then with the word covered up. Then, have him write it. Once he is confident, slide it into the sight-word deck. Shuffle the deck and quickly go through the sight-word drill.

At this point, the child is ready to go on to Exercise 150.

Exercise 150: Reading passage

'Good gosh!' shouted Ann. 'There is a fire among the fir trees over on the other side of that growth of bushes.' Everyone stopped what they were doing, of course, and took a look. All along the coast and most of the way up the road you could see a thick coat of smoke rolling forth. Other people could see it too.

'I hope the wind isn't blowing this way,' said Jeff. 'We'll roast if those flames ever get here.' Jeff was only a youngster himself.

'I believe it is coming!' said Ann.

You could now see sparks soaring into the air. Ann, who had good ears, claimed that she could hear the fire roaring. She told Jeff to get the horse tied up before it bolted. He did not understand horses and only laughed when she told him to coax it into the stable.

As Jeff led the horse along, it pulled back against him. He swore at the poor horse. Just then, a doe ran out of the forest and headed for the lake. Jeff groaned as he said, 'What on earth can we try if it gets anywhere near our house?'

'I guess we would have to get in the boat and row like mad,' said Ann. 'Of course, I can't find the oars, but we would be safe in the middle of the lake.'

But they did not have to. The fire veered away. That evening, a great rainstorm put it out and they were saved. Those young people were so happy about that. They never forgot the event. They always had been taught about the perils of fire in the bush, but they hadn't really believed just how bad it could be.

Lesson 89: Long vowel sound of 'u' in disguise

We have already encountered the long 'u' in connection with the rule of 'e' and in words like 'blue'. However, there is another combination that has the same effect, namely 'ew'. Let the child read the following sentence:

The bird *flew* away from its nest.

So sometimes 'ew' sounds like 'you' and sometimes like 'oo'.

Can the child spell and write both 'new' and 'flew'? If so, he is now ready for Exercise 151. Be sure to teach the exception: 'sew'.

Exercise 151: The combinations 'ew' and 'ue' sounding like 'oo' or 'you'

glue	flew	hue	strew
drew	blew	cue	blue
new	chew	dew	screw
Sue	news	true	slew
Jew	brew	flue	drew
threw	crew	newspaper	newest

Exception: sew

Now, introduce some more sight words; the child will already know most of them from day-to-day usage which makes things a lot easier. The words are: 'go', 'so', 'to', 'do'. Let him read them over. Virtually the only one which might be new to him is 'do'. Have him read the following sentence:

What will we *do* if it rains?

He should get it from context. Say 'do', then have him spell and write it. Make a flash card of it and shuffle it into the deck. Do a quick run through the flash cards. Include a flash card for 'sew' as well.

He is now ready to try the reading passage in Exercise 152.

Exercise 152: Reading passage

It is a rainy afternoon and there is nothing for Tom and Mary to do. They believe that there is something going on down at the docks. On the news it was said that a submarine was in port and that people were welcome to come down and view it. The crew would show people over.

The children went and they saw that the sub had a blue flag with a white star on it.

'The Jews own this sub,' said Mary, 'because that is the Jewish flag.'

'Do they come from Israel?' asked Tom. 'Let's go on board.'

As they were clambering down the narrow gangplank, Mary's skirt caught on a hook and tore. 'I'll have to sew that,' she observed, 'but first I am going to see this sub.'

The crew were very kind and helpful. They showed the children all over the boat and even let them look in the galley. The cook was in there brewing some stew. He said that the youngsters could have some, but only if they joined the Jewish fleet! Then he laughed.

17

Plurals with 'y' and further work on short and long vowels

These rules are not very complicated, but often they are not thoroughly learned in school, if the essays I've seen are anything to go by! Go very slowly. Be patient. Make sure the child *understands* the concepts and *can explain them* to you. Don't forget to do oral reading and dictation.

Lesson 90: Plurals of words ending in 'y'

Words ending in a consonant plus 'y' can *only* have an 's' added at the end if the 'y' is dropped and is replaced by 'ies'. This takes place either when making a noun plural or when conjugating a verb. Thus, 'candy' becomes 'candies' and 'fry' becomes 'fries'.

All of this complexity need not be explained to the child. Just let him see the pattern applied a few times and it will sink in. Show him the following words:

one candy

Ask him to read them. Now, show him these words:

three candies

Ask him to read them. Explain that we cannot write 'three candys'. We must drop the 'y' to make '*cand*' and then add on the 'ies' to make '*candies*'.

If the child is old enough, of course, you can employ the terms 'singular' and 'plural', but that would not be appropriate with younger children.

In the same way, let the child read the following two sentences:

1 Mother will *fry* the fish.

2 Mother *fries* the fish.

Now, go on to Exercise 153.

Exercise 153: Changes to the terminal 'y': 'ies', 'ier', 'iest' and 'ied'

nutty	twenty	jury	ladies
gladly	bunnies	sadly	buggies
foggy	likely	daddies	daddy
chillier	Bobby	sleepy	hurries
puppies	Peggy	daily	uglier
ugliest	handily	carried	silliest
thirty	thirsty	Betty	scurries
hardy	dirty	dirtier	dirtiest
dirties	candy	candies	parties
snappier	kitty	penny	bodies
likeliest	worry	worried	hurried
pennies	dizzy	dizziest	lazy
sunniest	stories	happily	scurried
berry	berries	parties	hardier
tabby	chirpy	buggy	baggy

There are two definite stages to this development. At the first stage, the child *appreciates the rules* and *can read* words such as 'relies' correctly. At the second stage, he *remembers the rule* and *can apply* it to his spelling. We want to ensure his mastery of both stages. Therefore, after he has read aloud the words in Exercise 153, give him enough practice writing dictated words from that list to ensure that he has a thorough command of the rule.

Of course, words like the noun 'valley' or the verb 'play' end in 'y', but *not* a consonant plus 'y'. Thus, the plural of 'valley' is 'valleys' (not 'valleies') and it is 'plays' is not 'plaies'. This need not be gone into at this stage, though, as it is far too complex.

Lesson 91: Short or long vowels with words ending in 'y'

The child has already learned this rule in a somewhat different context. We shall re-inforce his insight into it in this section. Take the words:

holy   holly

Ask the child to look at both and say whether or not they are both pronounced the same way. He will not realise that, although 'y' is regarded as a *consonant*, when it comes at the end of a word it behaves like a *vowel*. You can simply explain to him that in 'holy', because there is only *one consonant* between the 'o' and the 'y', the 'o' is given its *long* sound, whereas in 'holly', because there are *two consonants*, the 'o' is given its *short* sound.

Once the child understands this, you can review Exercise 90 and Exercise 128 with him, then go on to Exercise 154. After he has read Exercise 154, dictate a few words from it for him to write.

Exercise 154: Short and long vowel sounds with words ending in 'y'

Molly	dolly	roly	roly-poly
sorry	gory	story	stories
golly	Tory	glory	ivy
ladies	Amy	Jody	worry

navy	gravy	cabbies	cozier
crazy	Mary	marry	pony
tidier	Tony	fury	nutty

Lesson 92: Words ending in 'ed'

At this point it would be a good idea to give the child some practice with the past tense 'ed' at the end of words. As you know, sometimes the 'ed' is articulated (as in 'matted') and sometimes not (as in 'looked'). Without complicating the issue by teaching the child elaborate rules, simply let his ear tell him. Have him read through the words in Exercise 155. When he comes to write out a selection of those words as a dictation exercise, then he will have to listen carefully for the ending. Such a dictation exercise, if it is not persisted with for too long, helps to improve his concentration span.

Exercise 155: Short and long vowel sounds with words ending in 'ed'

matted	added	wiped	parked
needed	dropped	trapped	rugged
hissed	puffed	canned	trailed
growled	stuffed	hemmed	pointed
aimed	wished	hatched	leaped
cooked	sniffed	planned	nagged
ragged	pinned	whipped	wicked
crashed	boxed	mixed	called
spotted	cracked	jumped	tipped
buzzed	boiled	stopped	fished
snapped	hushed	counted	skipped
scuffed	wished	wheeled	fussed

marched   rested   snacked   stacked

helped   spotted   matched   snaked

Before we go on to the reading passage in Exercise 156, we need some more sight words. They are: 'sign', 'piece', 'friend'. We handle these in the usual way. Have the child attempt to read the first sentence of the three given below. If he works out what 'sign' must be, all well and good. If he does not, tell him. In either case, have him spell it aloud – first, while looking at the word; then, without looking. Finally, have him print it. When that is done, write 'sign' on a flash card and shuffle it into the deck. Do each of the other two in the same way.

1 Will you please *sign* this form on the bottom?

2 I will give you a big *piece* of cake.

3 I play with my *friends* after school.

Now, run through the deck of flash cards as quickly as possible. Then, go on to Exercise 156.

Exercise 156: Reading passage

Have you ever had a pet parrot?

People think that all birds are stupid, but that is a great mistake. I had a cockatoo lent to me by a friend who had nowhere to leave it when he went overseas. He had taught it tricks. I carried the bird over to my flat in a box with wire mesh across the front. My landlady did not like the cockatoo at all. She said it gave her the willies!

Willy, for that was the wily bird's name, had heard me say to the landlady, 'It's silly to be afraid of a bird like Willy. He couldn't put anything over on us!'

Willy did not like that comment one little bit. One day he saw how I latched the mesh across his box. As soon as I was out of the room, he undid the hasp and out he flew. Before I could turn around, he was out of the window. There was no sign of him anywhere.

What in Heaven's name could I say to my friend when he found out that his cockatoo was lost? It was a good thing that I told my landlady, because she told the story to her husband. When he went outside to throw away some dirt, he looked down the street and saw Willy sitting on a pole about 30 metres away. He could hardly believe it. He cried out to me to come and I was able to rescue Willy. I was most thankful to get him back. That taught me to keep his box locked without letting him see how I did it. When my friend returned, he signed a contract to work in another town and took the cockatoo with him.

You have now had about three months' worth of sessions and should be both impressed by and proud of what you and your child have accomplished. There are only a few more spelling/phonics rules to master!

18

Hard and soft 'c' and 'g' can deceive unless you believe!

Lesson 93: Hard and soft 'c'

Explain to the child that 'c' can have either a *hard* sound or a *soft* sound.

It has the *hard* sound in words such as: 'cat', 'cod', 'crib'. It has the *soft* sound in words such as: 'cell', 'cinder', 'cesspool'.

Now, explain the rule to him: 'c' takes on its *soft* sound if it is immediately followed by 'e', 'i' or 'y'; otherwise it is *hard*.

The best way of illustrating the rule in all its glory is to consider a word such as 'successful', which gets spelled incorrectly with monotonous regularity!

Let's look at it and have the child try to read it:

successful

The correct pronunciation immediately becomes obvious if we divide it up into syllables: suc/cess/ful.

The 'c' in 'suc' is *hard* because it is not followed by 'e', 'i' or 'y', but the next 'c', the one in 'cess', is *soft* because it is followed by 'e'. When you think about it, it would be difficult to spell 'success' sensibly in any other way. If students were taught these rules more systematically, there would be little reason for them to be unsuccessful at spelling!

Just to make sure that the rule has stuck, try your child out on:

lacy   (Remember, the 'a' has to be long and the 'c' soft.)

commend   (hard 'c')

fancies   (soft 'c' before 'i')

truncate   (hard 'c because it is not followed by 'e', 'i' or 'y')

Now, try him on the words in Exercise 157.

Exercise 157: Hard and soft sounds for 'c'

doc	practical	pace	truce
truck	peace	piece	electric
slice	slick	slicing	pacing
piercing	lacy	laced	rice
hectic	Bruce	custard	spicy
content	princess	prince	mince
France	voice	parcel	Nancy
service	mice	space	city
tracer	circus	grace	dancing
cinders	Alice	cell	pounced
fancy	twice	centre	braced
icing	circle	officer	cinch
cuddle	fences	cider	groceries
face	concert	mercy	merciful
cent	race	advice	citizen
spruce	glancing	nice	concern

Before he goes on to the reading passage in Exercise 158, there are some more sight words to be learned. They are: 'want', 'eight', 'because'. 'Want' is easily worked out in context, while 'eight' and 'because' are consistent with phonic rules which will be introduced later. However, for now, all three should be treated as sight words.

Introduce them in the usual way, initially using context as a clue, then having the child spell each of them orally and write them. Some useful sentences are:

1 The children *want* some food.

2 One, two, three, four, five, six, seven, *eight*, nine.

3 I let the bird go *because* it was unhappy.

Once each of these three sight words has been learned, write them on separate flash cards and shuffle them into the sight-word deck. Then, do a drill through the whole pack.

You can now release the child onto Exercise 158.

Exercise 158: Reading passage

Joyce believes in being nice to people and that is a good thing. Her father and mother taught her that. Too many people think that it is impractical to be nice. But if we treated everybody else the way we wanted to be treated, we would have peace at last. We wouldn't need police officers – except to help people and give advice. Being polite is really a sign that you like people.

One day Joyce decided that she wanted to have her friends up to her flat to hear pop music. But she remembered that the people in the flat next door liked classical music and found pop records irritating. So she went next door and said, 'I'm afraid I have a piece of bad news for you. Eight of my friends want to come by at about eight this evening to hear my new Pop-Chart records. It seemed to me that I should tell you ahead of time because that would give you a chance to go out or something.'

'Thank you very much for warning us,' said the man, 'because I believe there is a concert on and my wife and I can go to that while you play your pop.'

So Joyce called up her friend Janice and together they purchased a few groceries – salami, crackers and some cheese dips. They were going to have a really nice party with pop music setting the pace. They put a sign on the door so that all the friends would find the flat.

Lesson 92: Hard and soft 'g'

Tell the child that 'g' also has a *hard* sound and a *soft* sound. It has the *hard* sound in words such as: 'dog', 'gas' and 'get'. It has the *soft* sound in words such as: 'bridge', 'gem', 'gist' and 'gypsy'.

The rule for 'g' is exactly the same as it is for 'c'; before 'e', 'i' or 'y', it is usually *soft*; otherwise it is *hard*. Have the child read the following sentence several times until he has the idea.

Gypsies from Egypt got going in a rage at the engineer who grabbed the goat.

Then, move on to Exercise 159. After the child has read all the words successfully, don't neglect to give some of them in dictation.

Exercise 159: Hard and soft sounds for 'g'

passage	page	energy	germs
gentleman	tinge	badge	gently
ridge	magic	bridge	stingy
dodge	strange	forge	wedge
German	fudge	wage	gem
hedge	garbage	midget	hinged
nudging	engine	pledging	ginger
maggot	change	urge	gurgle
bulge	sledge	lodge	rage
George	gene	urgent	stranger
cabbage	damage	rage	staging
huge	cringe	fringe	stag

At this point, instead of introducing any more sight words before moving on to the reading passage, it would be an excellent idea to thoroughly review the sight words the child has already accumulated. Select the few that he has most hesitancy in responding to and concentrate on learning how to spell those. Then, go on to Exercise 160.

Exercise 160: Reading passage

'I believe it is raining,' said Mother. 'What will you do about the cement path? You wanted it started today.'

'That is going to be an urgent problem,' replied Father, 'because I've already engaged an engineer to design a cement ridge up to the hedge. He has an assistant to lay the cement. The assistant, who is a Polish gentleman, has already been given his wages. So I owe a huge amount.' Then he added, 'Maybe I could urge them to just leave the heavy equipment in the passage where it wouldn't get damaged and start the job tomorrow.'

'Tomorrow! Tomorrow! Tomorrow!' screeched the budgie from its cage.

So Father went out to chat to the engineer and his assistant, and they agreed to Father's plan.

'If we tried to run the engine in the mud in a rainstorm,' said the Polish gentleman, 'it would be using up energy for nothing.'

They put all their sledges, hammers and

tools in the passage, along with all the heavy
equipment, and wedged a piece of wood
under the door to keep it shut. Not all people
have been taught not to steal!

Lesson 95: Words with 'ie' and 'ei'

In the word 'believe', which the child has already had as a sight
word, 'ie' sounds like 'ee'. That same long 'e' sound is also
sometimes given to the combination 'ei'. Worse than that, some
words have 'ei' pronounced as 'ay' and 'ie' pronounced as a
short 'e', as in 'friend'. Altogether, these variations represent
some of the most confusing parts of English spelling, which
interestingly (but frustratingly!) reflect its rich linguistic
origins.

In this section we shall simply acquaint the child with some
of the more common rules which deal with these spellings.
First of all, if the 'ie' or 'ei' is to sound like 'ee', the rule is: '"I"
before "e" except after "c".' As you may yourself have found,
this little rhyme is a useful device for remembering the rule.
Have the child learn and recite the rhyme.

First, show him a word with 'ie' after a letter other than 'c':
'believe', and say: 'In "believe" the "i" comes *before* "e" because
it is *not* after "c".' Now, show him a word with the 'ei' after 'c':
'receive', and explain: 'In "receive" the "i" comes *after* "e"
because it *is* after "c".' Repeat the rhyme.

You must also remind him that the 'c' is *soft* because it is
followed by 'e'.

Now, have him compare:

receive   believe

Have him account for the use of 'ei' and 'ie' in each of these
words in terms of the rhyme he has learned. After that, have
him spell those two words and then let him write them.

There is only one thing left to clear up before he can attack
Exercise 161, and that is that 'eigh' often sounds like 'ay'. The
Americans have a clever little rhyme which follows on from the
rhyme just taught and which helps to explain this exception to

the 'i'-before-'e' rule. It goes like this: 'Or as sounded as "ay" as in "neighbour" and "weigh".'

You can remind the child that he has already learned 'eight' as a sight word, so he knows this configuration. Present him with the following 'family' of words:

eight

freight

neigh   (a horse's noise)

neighbour

weigh

Make sure that he can read them all and write them as dictation before going on. When he can, have him read the words in Exercise 161.

Exercise 161: The combinations 'ie' and 'ei' to render the long vowel sound of 'e'

field	believe	deceive	receive
conceive	sieve	siege	sieze
fierce	belief	relief	niece
chief	thieves	sheik	priest
handkerchief	relieves	shriek	grief
yield	piece	pier	Charlie
grieving	shrieked	beliefs	shielded
neighbour	weigh	weighty	freight
sleigh	weighing	eighteen	neighed

Exception: friend

Before going on to the reading passage in Exercise 162, three more sight words have to be introduced: 'four' (which the child has seen already in context), 'hour', (phonic except for the silent 'h') and 'done' (a linguistic hangover!). They should be handled in the usual way, using the following sentences to establish the context:

1 In a deck of cards there are *four* aces.

2 There are 24 *hours* in a day.

3 I've *done* all my homework.

Once the child can read, spell and write these three words without trouble, write each on a separate flash card. After shuffling them into the deck, do a fast-paced drill on the complete deck. Now, let him work on the reading passage in Exercise 162.

Exercise 162: Reading passage

When Brenden was only four, he could sing quite loudly. The neighbours used to ask him to keep quiet, but he had great difficulty doing that. To him, if he wasn't allowed to make noise, the hours just seemed to drag.

One day he was out in the turnip field when he saw a fierce boar coming at him. He shrieked, of course, but the boar kept coming. Much to Brenden's relief, the boar believed that Brenden had a gun so he concealed himself behind a bush. Brenden started to cry.

He had no handkerchief to wipe away the tears, so he tore off a piece of his shirt which he had received as a birthday present.

Then he remembered that one day at church the priest had said that, if you sing, your problems sometimes go away. Brenden tried it out. He sang out for about an hour and when he had done that the poor boar couldn't take any more. He ran off and Brenden's problem disappeared!

Now, when anyone asks him to be quiet, he says, 'Look! A horse can neigh and a freight-train can roar and I can sing. It takes away all my problems!'

Lesson 96: Review

This lesson constitutes a review day and gives you and the child a chance to practise fluent reading using rules already learned. Go over any concepts which have been giving the child difficulty, then work on the reading passage in Exercise 163.

Exercise 163: Additional reading passage

'Have you been taught the eight times table yet?' said the teacher to all the people in the class.

'No,' responded the children. 'All that we

can tell you about eight is that it comes before nine!'

'You mean, you haven't done any of the tables yet, not even the fours?' She couldn't believe that.

'Well,' said Gregory, 'our next-door neighbour reckons that his horse can count. All it can do is neigh and neigh, but the silly fellow thinks it is counting.'

'When you weigh it all up,' said Betty, 'I guess it would be impossible for a horse to count. I can't believe that animals can do such things. It is really quite inconceivable.'

'That's not true,' replied Jerry. 'When my father was doing relief work for the hospital, he said there was a woman in there whose dog could add and multiply.'

'I wish I had that dog's brains,' remarked Albert. 'I have to work for hours to do my number work!'

'Did you do yesterday's homework?' the teacher asked Albert.

'Yes, I've done it all. It took me three hours. If I had been that dog I could have done it in one hour. But I guess it would not be very nice to be a dog. Imagine having to scratch your fleas in class!'

Then the teacher said, 'I want to see the homework. I want all of you to put your homework on the desk!'

'Holy cow!' exclaimed Robert. 'I've left out four sums.'

19

More common sounds

Lesson 97: The 'tion' ending

Words that end in 'tion' have the final sound 'shun'. In addition, while 'i' always keeps its short sound, sometimes 'a', 'e', 'o' and 'u' are given the *long* sound. However, at first, just teach the child that 'tion' sounds like 'shun'. When he understands, try him out on the following words (he needn't read through the accompanying explanations):

1 traction   The 'a' is *short* because a consonant comes between the 'a' and 'tion'.   ·

2 invitation   The 'a' is *long* because it comes right before 'tion'.

3 mention   The 'e' is *short* because it doesn't come immediately before 'tion'. There is another consonant in between.

4 completion   The 'e' is *long* because it comes right before 'tion'.

5 rendition   The 'i' is *short*. It always is when followed by 'tion'.

6 option   The 'o' is *short* because a consonant comes between the 'o' and 'tion'.

7 notion   The 'o' is *long* because it comes right before 'tion'.

8 disruption   The 'u' is *short* because a consonant comes between the 'u' and 'tion'.

9 solution   The 'u' is *long* because it comes right before 'tion'.

It is sufficient that the child be able to *read* the words. With each one, tell him whether the vowel is long or short. When the vowel is short, simply say, 'Look, there's a consonant in there'

– point to it – 'so the "tion" doesn't make the vowel long.' Gradually he will work this out for himself. Only when he is a bit more sophisticated is it worthwhile explaining the rule in all of its detail.

Carefully go through all the words two or three times, until he can get them all right. Then, let him write them from dictation. For some days he will keep making mistakes, but eventually he will get it right. As much as anything, it is an exercise in concentration. Now, let him go on to Exercise 164.

Exercise 164: The 'tion' sound

invitation	rendition	contradiction
diction	fiction	ambition
friction	contrition	function
sanction	nation	ration
faction	station	question
education	action	fraction
ruction	obstruction	vacation
mention	notion	addition
dereliction	attention	distribution
notion	solution	interruption
elation	enunciation	relationship
infraction	restriction	faction

You will probably notice by now that your child is attempting to do a lot of extraneous reading. He may be especially interested in tackling the stories that you read aloud to him. That's fine! If he is doing that, he is still running across a fair number of words that he doesn't know. Some of these he *can* work out, but he needs to be reminded of the rule or sound involved. In those cases, don't make him feel guilty about it or you will turn him off reading! Just remind him gently. On the other hand, there will be some words that defy his present command of phonic skills. In those cases, just tell him what the word is. Don't jump the gun and try to teach him extra phonic rules.

We shall only provide a few more reading passages in this book. After that the child will be able to cope with a wide range of material of his own choosing. He will not be confined to a particular set of school readers, but will roam as his interests take him. Even then, from time to time he will run across words that he cannot work out. Tell him what they are when he asks and encourage him in this newfound independence.

For the next reading passage, he will need three more sight words: 'suit', 'thought' and 'though'. Approach the matter in the usual way, using the three sentences that follow:

1 The man wore his good *suit* to church.

2 The boy *thought* that he would like to swim.

3 Emily can fix cars, even *though* she is a child.

The word 'suit' belongs to a family of words exemplifying a phonic rule which will be dealt with later. For now, the child should learn it as a sight word. 'Thought', 'though', 'through' and 'thorough' traditionally cause trouble. They needn't if the approach is careful. For now, we will deal only with 'though' and 'thought'. They are presented together because they are frequently confused. The child should be shown both of them written out close together so that he can compare them. The terminal 't' should be brought to his attention and the word 'thought' said with heavy emphasis on that final 't'. Point out, when you say 'though', that it has no 't' sound at the end. Drill the child in the *spelling* of those two words. Let him write them out several times. Now, you are ready to go on to Exercise 165.

Exercise 165: Reading passage

Charles Templeton ran a clothing store in town. He wanted people to believe that it was the best store in the city for men's clothes. However, even though his prices were low, a lot of people thought that they could get better clothes somewhere else.

During the summer vacation he thought of a plan to attract customers. He would have a huge sale of men's suits, because that is what people wanted. Also, he would advertise boys' school uniforms because people are always interested in education. He went down to the printing shop by the train station and said to the printer, 'Do you suppose you can run up some advertising posters for me? I want them next week, though, so you would need to work fast. I thought maybe you could get it done in time.'

'Of course,' said the printer. 'If I have no wedding invitations to turn out in a hurry, I can do it. The print machine only takes about four hours to set up. Have you got a design there showing what kind of sign you want?'

'Here it is,' said Mr Templeton. 'I need one hundred copies.'

The printer looked it over and thought about it. 'You see where you have the word SUITS in capital letters,' said the printer, 'should that be in red?'

'Yes,' said Mr Templeton.

'It will cost quite a lot – at least fifty pounds.'

'That's okay with me,' replied Mr Templeton.

'Fine,' replied the printer. 'Sign the contract here. You have to look after the distribution yourself, of course, and remember that it is an infraction to post any advertisements in the station. The police had a big function on the other day and even they couldn't advertise in the station.'

Lesson 98: The 'ous' sound at the end of words

Have the child look at the word 'enormous'. When he tries to work it out, he will at first probably say 'enormouse' because of the 'ou' sound. Tell him the correct pronunciation. Let him now try it out on the following list:

nervous

marvellous

generous   (Don't forget the soft 'g')

dangerous

famous

Once he can get those, acquaint him with the sound 'cious', as in 'delicious'. Now, move on to Exercise 166.

Exercise 166: Words with the 'ous' ending

curious	nervous	dangerous
obvious	wondrous	generous
tedious	melodious	enormous
porous	horrendous	famous
adventurous	ravenous	jealous
serious	gorgeous	marvellous
dubious	vexatious	delicious
vicious	luscious	anxious
suspicious	precious	gracious
unctuous	ferocious	odious
marvellous	noxious	atrocious
venomous	tremendous	rambunctious

At this stage, if he can now learn to *read* the words in Exercise 166, that will be sufficient. Spelling some of them could easily be a taxing exercise – unnecessarily so. Once the child can *fluently* read the words in Exercise 166 (it will take several sessions of practice), the spelling will gradually become evident. This will be especially so when he is old enough to use some of these words in his daily life.

For reading practice, let the child read to you from any book he chooses. Correct his mistakes without being too critical. From now on, this should be done for at least a few minutes every day.

Lesson 99: Other 'sh' and 'ch' sounds

We now want to acquaint the child with all of the 'sh' and 'ch' sounds in their more general aspect. He has already seen 'tion' and 'cious', but they are special cases. The general rule is this: before a vowel, 'ti', 'ci' and 'si' all sound like 'sh'. Examples are:

station

special

vision

Go over these words with the child and explain the rule.

We also find the 'sh' sound in the ending 'sure', albeit somewhat softer:

assure

treasure

erasure

Finally, 'ture' at the end of a word gives the 'ch' sound, as in:

picture

puncture

rapture

To explain all of this you will need to write down the sound and the words on pieces of paper and also to say them aloud. Give the child plenty of practice on the words listed above. He should be able to spell with confidence the ones that are most meaningful to him, e.g. 'station', 'picture', 'treasure', 'delicious', 'television'. Devote as many sessions to this as it requires before going on to Exercise 167.

Exercise 167: Various combinations giving the 'sh' and 'ch' sounds

exception	addition	mission	passion
nature	picture	future	compassion
creature	creation	mixture	permission
occasion	vacation	patient	suspicious
treasure	measure	pleasure	leisure
nurture	feature	mansion	expression
action	suture	usual	unusual
unusually	usually	special	notion
motion	television	derision	mature

You must not forget to have the child read to you *every day*. He can read from a book that he chooses (in which case it may well contain a lot of material he cannot handle) or, preferably, a book that you have gone over and selected for him. He should read to you for *at least* five or ten minutes a day, though he may well want to do more than that. If so, that is okay, but don't allow him to exhaust himself.

After he can read Exercise 167 fluently, introduce the following new sight words: 'does' (he now will know 'does' and 'done'), 'neighbour' (already learned in phonic context) and 'eye' (difficult to sound out!). Present them in the usual fashion, using the following sentences to give them the necessary context:

1 Who *does* this book belong to?

2 Love your *neighbour* as yourself.

3 He wore glasses because he had bad *eye*-sight.

Again, after each of these words have been learned, spelled and written, make a flash card for each of them. Shuffle them into the deck and do a drill on the entire pack. Then, have him read Exercise 168 as often as required to ensure fluency.

Exercise 168: Reading passage

You shouldn't mention black cats to superstitious people. Of course, we know that all of that hocus-pocus is a lot of garbage, but there are some people who still believe in it. They get some sort of pleasure out of it. Some even think that they can predict a person's future just by looking them in the eye. If nervous people believe in magic like that, it can be very dangerous. Usually magic and fortune telling is simply treated as a joke, to be used for fun at social gatherings. Does it worry you when a black cat wanders across your path? If you break a mirror, does that make you anxious? If it does, stop worrying. There is no truth in these things. You should be suspicious of people who speak about such things as the 'evil-eye' or who come up with atrocious predictions about your future just from staring wide-eyed into a silver ball.

Lesson 100: Three awkward combinations

In this section, we are going to introduce the child to three phonic combinations all in one go! They are: 'au' as in fault, 'aw' as in jaw and 'alk' as in talk. 'Aw' and 'au' should be written out first, each on a separate flash card. Although they are not words, even after the child knows their sound they should be included in the sight words. They both sound like the *short* sound for 'o'. Make sure that he can *use* 'au' and 'aw' in context. Have him read the following words:

hawk

awkward

taunt

haunt

Although it need *not* be pointed out to a young reader, notice that 'aw' can begin or end a word, but rarely occurs in the middle.

As for the 'alk' sound, it can best be learned by contextual clues. Have the child read the sentence:

You must not talk during church.

Once he has worked out 'talk', point out that it belongs to a family of words. Have him read the following list:

talk

chalk

walk

stalk

Now, have the child read Exercise 169. Again, you should not worry him about spelling more than a few of the words – and then only those he uses most commonly. His insight into their phonic structure will *gradually* make an impact on his spelling development. Make sure, though, that he can *read* each of the words, even the ones for which he does not know the meaning.

Exercise 169: Various combinations giving the short sound of 'o'

awning	lawn	law	flaw
claw	dawn	talk	stalk
chalk	caulking	caulk	haul
bawl	yawn	thaw	balk
draw	drawn	paw	raw
walk	sprawl	fraud	shawl
taunt	gaunt	haunt	saw
fault	crawl	lawsuit	straw
launch	brawl	Paul	hawk
jaw	tawny	maul	hauler

Let him do the reading passage in Exercise 170 *after* he has learned the following sight words: 'woman', 'women' and 'their'. They can be introduced in context, in the usual way, using the following sentences:

1 My mother is a *woman*.

2 We see a lot of *women* at Mothers' Visiting Day in school.

3 Good children put *their* toys away.

Again, be sure that the child can recognise each of these three words, that he can spell them and that he can write them. Then, go on to the reading passage.

Exercise 170: Reading passage

Two men decided to bring a lawsuit against someone who sold them a parrot that couldn't

talk. They purchased the parrot from a pet shop because the shop owner said it talked a blue streak. They thought about it for a long time. Even though it cost a lot of money, they agreed to go for it because they wanted to give it to the old woman up the road. She was a pensioner and could hardly walk. She wanted a pet to keep her company. A dog would be no good to her because she would have to do too much for it. It would have to be taken out for a walk, would mess up the lawn and would wipe its muddy paws all over the carpet.

The two men put their money together and got the parrot. They took it to their office to hear it talk, but all it did was to screech from dawn to dusk.

'That pet shop man is a fraud,' they said and they got in their automobile and went back to the shop. They tried to get their money back, but the owner would do nothing for them. Two women were in the shop and they also thought that the men should have their money back.

'Not at all,' said the pet shop owner. 'You

see, I said that the parrot talks a lot – and, by George, it does. I did not say that it talks English, though. It talks parrot language, I guess!'

One of the two men looked at the shopkeeper in the eye and said, 'You have cheated us. We will see what the law says about it. We shall go to the police station now.'

20

The 'ph' and 'gh' sounds and the fourth 'y' sound

Lesson 101: The 'ph' sound

A large number of English words, generally those of Greek origin, use the combination 'ph' to sound like 'f'. As usual, the best way to make the point clear is to let the child discover it in a carefully controlled context. Let him read the sentence:

One day the phone rang and it was for me.

Explain that the letters 'p' and 'h' together sound like 'f'. Now, have him work out the following words:

telephone

phonics

elephant

phantom

Once he can do that easily, and can spell them and write them, he is ready for Exercise 170. He should have fun with 'electro-cardiograph' and 'encephalograph', especially if he is older and is interested in word roots. Even if he is not, he will still feel extremely proud for having mastered such long words!

Exercise 171: The combination 'ph' sounding like 'f'

alphabet	orphan	phonograph
triumph	photograph	hyphen
pamphlet	nephew	phrase
Philip	Phil	Ralph
autograph	pharmacy	trophy
telegraph	electroencephalograph	
kymograph	electrocardiograph	

Lesson 102: The 'gh' sound

The 'gh' combination wandered into the English language through its Saxon roots. It masquerades in various ways, sometimes silent (as in 'though'), sometimes as 'f' (as in 'tough'), sometimes as 'g' (as in ghost), etc. In this section, we shall only present it in its 'f' sound. Teach the child the word 'laugh', which he already knows as a sight word. We can point out that in that word, the 'gh', or actually the 'ugh', sounds like 'f'. Exercise 172 contains some of these words. Go slowly here and practise thoroughly. These words should be learned fully and spelled out several times a week.

Exercise 172: The combination 'ugh' sounding like 'f'

laugh	laughing	laughter	rougher
cough	tough	tougher	toughest
roughest	rough	roughly	enough
coughs	trough	coughing	laughable

Lesson 103: The fourth 'y' sound and review

The letter 'y' takes on one of four sounds, depending on context. We have learned three already. The four sounds are:

1 As in 'yak', when a beginning consonant.
2 As in 'fly', when the terminal vowel of a short word.
3 As in 'puppy', when the terminal vowel of a longer word.
4 As in 'system', when a middle vowel.

When explained in context, the new 'y' sound should not present any difficulty. Exercise 173 presents 'y' in all of these forms.

Exercise 173: The four possible 'y' sounds

system	Lynda	Egypt	gypsy
Flynn	yet	yes	yak
young	yellow	cry	yell
try	spy	my	by
ply	fry	sty	mummy
daddy	puppy	cryptic	cuddly
cubby	Barry	yard	yesterday
yummy	yawn	dizzy	cynical
cylinder	rhythm	folly	mystery

After he has mastered that exercise, he can go on to the reading passage in Exercise 174, for which he will need three more sight words. They are: 'know', 'knew' and 'colour'. 'Know and 'knew' exemplify the silent 'k', other than that are perfectly phonic. At a later stage in this book silent letters will be dealt with systematically, so now simply present 'know' and 'knew' as sight words in context.

1 They *know* where Timothy lives.

2 Timothy *knew* his spelling words.

When those two have been mastered, spelled and written as well, then make a flash card for each of them.

'Colour' belongs to a large family of words which, in American spelling, are phonic but which in British spelling end in 'our' instead of 'or'. For 'colour', give the child this sentence:

3 I know what *colour* my shirt is.

Once he has mastered it, including its peculiar spelling, show him the following family of words:

rigour

vigour

valour

labour

splendour

Have him read them.

Shuffle the cards 'know', 'knew' and 'colour' into the sight-word deck and run through the lot.

The reading passage in Exercise 174 contains some ideas which are more difficult than those previously encountered. For that reason, it is followed by an additional reading passage in Exercise 175 for the very young reader, who may find the first passage a little complex.

Exercise 174: Reading passage

Do men and boys see colours when they dream? This seems like a strange question, but some people used to believe that only women and girls saw colours in their dreams.

That is one of those things that we know now to be incorrect. There are men who dream in colour and there are women who only dream in black and white.

If you could take photographs of what you saw in your dreams during your sleeping hours, you could really be sure. However, that may never happen. Of course, you never know. A hundred years ago no one knew that one day we would have the telegraph or even phonograph records. The triumphs of technology are truly amazing. Last century, if you had told someone that a system would be invented by which computers could be taught to read out loud, using an electromagnetic alphabet, they would have laughed. Likewise, suppose you said that one day people would be able to see each other over huge distances, they would have said that nobody has eyes that good!

Just as no one knew then what would happen now, we cannot assume that we can predict the future today. It is hard enough to keep your mind open without setting limits on future knowledge.

Exercise 175: Additional reading passage

The other day, I phoned my friend and asked him if he knew of a good game to play because I was bored. His name was Phil Randolph. Phil said, 'Yes. I know of a good place to play games. They know me there and they will let me bring a friend.'

'What kind of games do they have?' I asked. 'And where would I have to go?'

'You know that old church hall down near the photography shop? It's beside the bakery and across the street from the orphanage. Every Saturday they have games there,' said Phil. 'It only costs twenty cents to get in. Once you get in, they give you a coloured badge. The colours go according to your age and with each colour you are allowed in the games of your age-group. They do that because some of the older kids can get a bit rough.'

'Oh well,' I said, 'that should be good for a laugh. I'll ask Aunty if I can go. She's got a nasty cough and she may want me to stay behind to help. Also, I need to know whether she can give me enough money to get in.'

'When you know,' said Phil, 'phone me up.'

21

Some word families

Understanding Word Families

Word families, in the sense that the term is used in this book, are groups of words which display strikingly similar spellings, however the similarities do not usually apply to a sufficient number of words to make a phonic rule. In addition, their meanings and/or roots may be entirely unrelated, as say, 'face' and 'lace'. Therefore, word families should be regarded simply as convenient tools to help the child tackle similar-looking words, especially when he is encountering new and unusual words for the first time.

Over the next ten lessons, the child will be taught a number of spelling conventions. These should not be rushed – only do one exercise a day. This will give the child ample time to learn the convention, to read aloud from a book he has selected and to do fifteen minutes of dictation. By the time your child has completed this section, he will be able to read almost anything he chooses with a minimum of difficulty.

Lesson 104: The 'thought' family

Present the child with the word 'thought', as printed in Exercise 176. He has already learned it as a sight word. Using 'thought' as a model, he should be able to work out the rest of the words. Go over them several times until he can read them almost instantly in random order and can spell them and write them on command.

Exercise 176: The 'thought' family

thought

ought	**sought**	**thoughtless**	**brought**
bought	**fought**	**wrought**	**thoughtful**

Lesson 105: The 'taught' family

The word 'taught' has also already been learned as a sight word. Use Exercise 177 in exactly the same way as the preceding one. Always makes sure that the words can be read fluently and in random order, and that the child can spell them and write them on command, before going on to the next exercise. Also, dictate a few words from the previous exercise to keep in mind the conventions already learned.

Exercise 177: The 'taught' family

taught

aught	**naught**	**fraught**	**naughty**
distraught	**daughter**	**slaughter**	**caught**
haughty	**retaught**	**fraughtful**	**naughtiness**

Lesson 106: The 'work' family

The child has already learned the words 'world' and 'work' in context. Again, be sure he is completely fluent in spelling, writing and reading the words from Exercise 178 before moving on, and remember to review words from previous families.

Exercise 178: The 'work' family

work

worm	world	worst	workers
worth	word	worthy	working
worsening	worthless	unworthy	worldly

Lesson 107: The 'high' family

We now introduce a family with which the child is not familiar. Following our established routine, we shall do it in context. Let the child read the following sentence:

The hang-glider was flying sixty metres *high*.

Tell the child that the letters 'igh' *usually* sound like the long sound of 'i'. Make sure that he can spell the sound quickly and write it on demand. Now, let him tackle Exercise 179 until he can read, spell and write all the words with facility.

Exercise 179: The 'high' family

high

sigh	sight	might	nigh
fight	almighty	right	flight
blight	night	fright	highly
frighten	frightful	higher	light
delight	thigh	lightning	delightful
bright	tight	slight	tighten
knight	brightness	tonight	mighty

Lesson 108: The 'air' family

Again we introduce a new family. Consider, with the child, the following sentence:

We need *air* to breathe.

Once he has thoroughly learned what the word 'air' sounds like and refers to, move him on to Exercise 180.

Exercise 180: The 'air' family

air

fair	pair	Gairy	pair
Blair	flair	hairpin	haircut
airy	stair	fairy	lair
chair	hair	airsick	clairvoyant

Lesson 109: The 'father' family

We made the observation near the beginning of this book that anomalous spelling and distortions of nice, neat phonic rules occur in any language, and occur much more frequently with those older and more intimate words connected with the person, his state of being, relationships, etc. Consistent with this idea, we find that 'father', 'mother', 'son', 'brother', 'cousin', etc. all, to some extent, violate the rules. The word 'father' is particularly useful in this regard, because a large number of common words in English use the 'a' pronounced as 'aw'. The child should be told this and then should go through all of the words in Exercise 181. This exercise should *not* be left until he can read, spell and write each of the words in it with fluency and confidence. Remember to keep reviewing words from previous families.

Exercise 181: The 'father' family

father

watch	want	squash	wash
swan	water	wand	swamp
wasp	washtub	swat	wander
squat	quarrel	Washington	what
quality	quantity	swatter	quantify

Lesson 110: The 'busy' family

We must introduce another new word which at first may defy the child's reading skill. Have him read the following sentence:

The workers are very *busy* fixing the road.

Be certain that the child can read the word, spell it and write it. Now, go on to the words in Exercise 182. Notice that most of them use 'ui', not just 'u'. Therefore, be very particular that the child cannot only correctly *read* them, but that he can correctly *spell* and *write* them as well. They are very common words, even for a young child, and should be an assured part of his working vocabulary.

Exercise 182: The 'busy' family

busy

business	busied	busier	busily
build	built	building	guilt
guilty	guild	builder	guiltiness

Lesson 111: The 'Australia' family

Call it personal bias, but one word that any child should learn early in his reading career is 'Australia' – it also is a nice example of the 'ia' sound. Once he can spell 'Australia' without trouble, let him read the words in Exercise 183. Also, remember to review.

Exercise 183: The 'Australia' family

Australia

media	Austria	dahlia	azalia
Ophelia	dementia	Lydia	radian
hernia	mania	phobia	trivia

Lesson 112: The 'suit' family

The child has already learned the word 'suit' as a sight word. He is also aware that the long 'u' is sometimes pronounced 'oo'. He therefore should have little trouble with the words in Exercise 184. And remember: review, review, review!

Exercise 184: The 'suit' family

suit

bruise	nuisance	cruise	cruiser
fruit	juice	suitor	fruitful
juicy	suited	bruising	cruising

Lesson 113: The 'active' family

The child will need to learn the word 'active'. It is so obvious, especially in context, that it will present no problem. Have him read the sentence:

The child was very *active*.

The 'ive' at the end of such words is the critical thing – even adults often omit the silent 'e' at the end. Let him read through all of the words in Exercise 185, spell them and write them.

Exercise 185: The 'active' family

active

restive	negative	abusive	native
positive	explosive	elusive	attentive
passive	divisive	detective	expensive
abrasive	captive	olive	tentative

He can now go on to the reading passage in Exercise 186.

Exercise 186: Reading passage

Ken Blair and his friend Kate Gairy used to like to play together. Sometimes they pretended to be pilots. They were fascinated by anything to do with aircraft and they were active children.

One day they thought they would try to launch a kite carrying a china doll that Kate's mother had had since she was a little girl. It was very valuable to her. Kate used a hairpin to hold the doll in place firmly.

A high wind was blowing. To their delight, the kite took off without any trouble. They kept it up for about an hour and then they began to get bored. They had eaten all their sandwiches and fruitcake, and had nothing much to do. Like silly children, they began to quarrel about who should hold the kite string and they even fought about whether or not to bring it down.

In fact, they were so busy fighting and bruising each other that they did not watch the kite. It swooped towards a new building. They both knew that they must not break Kate's mother's precious doll. They should have thought of that sooner. Before they could do a thing, the kite cruised into the building. They both felt guilty as they looked at the shattered doll.

What was even worse was that Kate's mother was walking down the road when it happened. She had just been to the shops to get some bait to go fishing because she didn't want to bother going to the swamp to dig up worms. She saw the doll smash. Naturally, she was very upset with her naughty daughter.

'You ought to be ashamed of yourself,' she said. 'I hope that this has taught you a lesson.'

Further Reading

Exercise 186 is the last reading passage in the book, but not the last reading your child should do aloud for you to hear. Even after learning the material in this book, he will still need consistent and wise guidance on your part.

It is said that good readers develop what is referred to as 'reading independence' in about the fifth or sixth year of primary school. This is only a rough average, of course, sometimes it occurs earlier, sometimes considerably later. Motivation is a major factor.

But what do we mean by 'reading independence'?

A child who enjoys reading and does it well has not necessarily achieved reading independence, although taking pleasure in reading is pretty well a necessary precondition to attaining this independence. Reading independence has been achieved when the child *voluntarily* reads on his own for the sheer joy of it. He even stops showing you what he is reading and stops keeping track of how much he has read. He just does it whenever he has time on his hands.

Until that time has come, you must provide every encouragement, which may need to go on for some years even after he has acquired the mechanical skills of reading. Set a specific time of the day for him to read to you, and keep on reading to him at bedtime. If he shows no inclination to pick out his own books, select them for him – taking his skill level and interests into account. However, in reading to him, cover a wide range of literary genres. If you only read to him about topics which seem to interest him (say, horse books or sport stories), his tastes will never broaden. Read poetry, novels, adventure stories, graphic political material and news accounts. Encourage him to talk about what he has read and to apply it to his day-to-day experiences. You should also cultivate his writing habit: thank you letters, poems and stories, and keep a folder of his literary efforts. Above all, he *must* see that reading is an important part of your life.

The balance of the formal reading instruction in this book consists of two sections which you *must* go through with him: 'silent letters' and 'prefixes and suffixes'. No reading passage is specifically tied in with either of these, but make sure that he reads to you during each of these lessons. You can use any children's book that he seems to enjoy, as long as it is not *so* elementary as not to involve him in the consistent use of his reading skills.

22

Silent letters

Lessons 114–122: Exercises on the silent letters

The child has already experienced a few silent letters at random in his reading: the silent 'k' in 'know', silent 'gh' in 'high', etc. In this part of his instruction, we shall systematically consider all of the silent letters in the language in their most common contexts. Eventually we want the child to be able to spell all of these words. Therefore, *never do more than one exercise per day*. Some exercises might take two or three sessions. Stay with each set of words until he can read them rapidly in any order of presentation, can spell them orally and can print them on command.

Carefully, then, work your way through Exercises 187–195. You must not neglect to keep drilling the sight words. They needn't be done every day any more, but should be practised at least once a week until the child is reading fluently and widely. You will, of course, run across awkward words other than those specified in this book which can be added to the sight-word list. These would be words that strike you as common or which the child frequently runs across in his own reading, but which do not easily yield to phonic analysis. Of course, as I have mentioned before, if you are careful and think through most awkward-looking words, you will find that they *do* yield to phonic analysis. In that event, it is *much* better to explain the phonic rationale for the word to the child – even if you have to repeat the explanation on several occasions – than for him to have to remember it as a sight word.

Exercise 187: Silent 'k' words

knee	knew	knelt	knot
kneel	know	knell	knowledge
knit	known	knives	unknowable
knitted	knock	knack	doorknob
knuckles	knave	knob	kneeler

Exercise 188: Silent 'g' words

gnash	sign	consign	gnashed
design	resign	gnaw	malign
gnat	gnome	gnarled	gnu

Exercise 189: Silent 'w' words

wren	wringer	wrench	typewriter
wreck	wrap	wreath	wristwatch
wreckers	wrist	wrung	handwritten
wrong	wrapper	write	wholemeal
wring	answer	written	wholesome
writer	sword	wrote	handwriting
whole	wretch	wretched	wrapping

Exercise 190: Silent 'b' words

lamb	limb	comb	dumb
numb	climber	debt	climb
crumb	doubt	doubtful	debtor
doubtless	plumber	thumb	bomb

Exercise 191: Silent 'l' words

talk	calm	walk	chalk
balm	stalk	balk	caulk
half	folk	yolk	alms
almond	calves	halves	talker

Exercise 192: Silent 'h' words

honour	ghost	stomach	honest
hurrah	schematic	John	hour
school	Thomas	ah!	scheme
headache	oh!	ache	honestly

Exercise 193: Silent 't' words

listen	Christmas	bustle	gristle
castle	christening	hustle	soften
fasten	often	hasten	whistle
jostle	apostle	epistle	rustle
nestle	whistling	whistler	bristle

Exercise 194: Silent 'gh' words

straight	although	bough	night
straighten	thought	plough	righteous
bought	thorough	sought	lighter
daughter	slaughter	naughty	fighting
silent	might	flight	blighted
height	through	naught	though

Exercise 195: Words with various silent letters

knight	scissors	autumn	psalm
science	column	muscles	condemn
wrestle	scene	damn	hymn

23

Prefixes, suffixes and polysyllabic words

With the lessons in this chapter, generally only do one exercise a day in the same way as you have done with the lessons in the previous chapter, though Exercise 196 and Exercise 197 may require several days. Exercise 205 is the icing on the cake! These are 'super-duper' words, as one youngster called them. Don't worry that the child does not know what they mean (though you may want to have a dictionary close at hand in case he asks) – they are fun to decode and encode, and getting them to slip nicely off the tongue can be the occasion for much mirth, but look *carefully* at each syllable so that *you* get them right.

Lessons 123–125: Prefixes

A 'prefix' is generally a letter or combination of letters placed before a word which adds meaning. In primary school, we commonly run across eleven prefixes. Have the child learn them, as it will expedite his reading and writing immensely.

Teach him each prefix *with* a word, as well as separately from it. He should be able to say what each means and to explain how it affects the word to the beginning of which it is attached.

Prefix	Meaning	Example
1. com-	together with	commotion
2. con-	together with	confess
3. de-	down, from, out of	depend
4. dis-	apart from, reversing	disrepair
5. en-	in, within	enlarge
6. in-	into *or* not (two different meanings)	inflate, inconclusive
7. pre-	before	prefix
8. pro-	put forward, go forward	proclaim

9.	re-	back again	refine
10.	ex-	out of, thoroughly, former	except
11.	un-	not	uneasy

The beauty of these prefixes is that, once they are recognised, they are pronounced separately from the rest of the word. This greatly facilitates the reading of long words. Exercise 196 should now be done. Have the child read each word, then learn to write each one. It will take several sessions!

Exercise 196: Some common prefixes and words using them

com-	con-	de-	dis-
comfort	concede	depend	disarm
combine	conflict	decrease	discover
complain	confide	deflate	dismiss
commotion	condone	demote	dispatch
commend	confess	describe	disrepair

en-	in-	pre-	pro-
enjoy	inflate	prefix	progress
enlarge	infest	predate	produce
engage	inject	prearrange	prolific
endorse	intrude	preexist	procession
encourage	inflict	predict	proclaim

re-	ex-	un-
reduce	explain	uneasy
refine	expect	unbend

remit	expense	unkind
recline	except	unpainted
rebuff	exhibit	unpaid

Lessons 126–129: Suffixes

A suffix is a letter or combination of letters placed at the end of a word or part of a word to confer added meaning. In school, we commonly run across thirteen of these suffixes. They are:

	Prefix	Meaning	Example
1.	-able	capable of, worthy	comfortable
2.	-al	pertaining to	political
3.	-ance	state, quality, condition	appearance
4.	-ful	full of, abounding in	graceful
5.	-ing	used in, does, results from	revealing
6.	-ive	tending toward	active
7.	-less	without, beyond the limit	boundless
8.	-ly	adverb, similar in manner	quickly
9.	-ment	state, act of, quality	statement
10.	-ness	condition	tiredness
11.	-ous	state or quality	famous
12.	-tion	action, state, result	contention
13.	-y	full of, result of	filthy

As with the prefixes, have the child learn each one both separately and with a word. The meaning of each suffix should also be learned and an older child should memorise them. He should also be able to explain how a given suffix affects a given word. In doing Exercise 197, he will find that knowledge of the suffixes enables him to recognise many long words much more easily than would otherwise be the case.

Exercise 197: Some common suffixes and words using them

-able	**-al**	**-ance**	**-ful**
comfortable	postal	appearance	successful
bendable	mental	contrivance	beautiful

culpable	regal	distance	graceful
inflammable	political	countenance	deceitful
teachable	presidential	circumstance	wonderful

-ing	*-ive*	*-less*	*-ly*
exciting	active	baseless	finally
revealing	elusive	useless	stupidly
lending	massive	boundless	quickly
exalting	inventive	faceless	formally
demeaning	defensive	restless	formerly

-ment	*-ness*	*-ous*	*-tion*
statement	tiredness	famous	contention
casement	joyousness	dangerous	mention
banishment	fondness	devious	portion
excitement	kindness	enormous	portion
punishment	bluntness	glorious	affliction

-y
filthy
needy
soapy
giddy
sunny

Lessons 130–136: A parting shot at syllables

By now the child should be developing an eye for syllables and be gaining proficiency in breaking long words into syllables. Of course, compound words are the easiest in this respect and should give no problem. Have him break the words of Exercise 198 down to their constituent words.

Exercise 198: More compound words

overseas	understatement	makeshift
overcoat	overdue	within
wherewithal	extraordinary	therefore
schoolteacher	underwear	beforehand
underworld	undertaker	overseer
photocopier	dishmop	typewriter
fishpond	meathook	overpayment

Beyond compound words, there are certain rules which will help immensely in breaking down polysyllabic words. Teach him those rules, as presented below, and give him plenty of practice on the exercises indicated.

1 Every syllable has at least one vowel sound; moreover, a word *cannot* have more syllables than vowel sounds. Caution: *One* vowel *sound* may have *two* vowels in it, e.g. 'ea', 'ou', 'ie' each have two vowels but are a single vowel sound. See Exercise 199.
2 If two separate consonants (or consonant sounds) occur right after a vowel, the division of syllables usually comes between the consonants. See Exercise 200.
3 If only one consonant follows a vowel, this consonant either terminates the preceding syllable or starts the following one. See Exercise 201.
4 If a word ends in 'le', the letter before the 'l' should be added to the last syllable, e.g. ex/pen/da/ble. See Exercise 202.

5 If a prefix is used, the division is between the prefix and the rest of the word. See Exercise 203.

6 Generally, if a suffix is used, the division of syllables comes between the suffix and the rest of the word. Exceptions will include some words in which the suffixes begin with vowels, e.g. wond/rous, not wondr/ous. See Exercise 204.

Exercise 199: At least one vowel sound per syllable

one vowel sound	two vowel sounds	three vowel sounds
beast	gro/cer	pen/e/trate
poise	fea/ture	pro/mo/tion
roll	poi/son	sup/por/tive
foam	fen/der	con/fis/cate
a	fi/at	com/for/ter

Exercise 200: Two separate consonant sounds following a vowel

frank/ness	laugh/ter	or/deal	park/ing
grind/er	farm/er	pans/y	fal/ter
sup/port	roost/er	melt/er	af/ford
mor/tar	brash/ly	con/nive	

Exercise 201: Only one consonant following a vowel

mo/tor	ga/ther	driv/el	phan/tom
me/tal	pro/mise	pan/ic	gar/ish
be/gin	so/ber	at/om	dup/ing

fe/line   ne/ver   lim/it   for/est

smo/king   a/gain   fat/al   vis/it

Exercise 202: Consonant before the 'le' included in the last syllable

Bi/ble   sad/dle   sta/ble   bun/dle

fa/ble   pes/tle   fee/ble   tic/kle

terri/ble   lit/tle   bea/dle   this/tle

tric/kle   fum/ble   tram/ple   muf/fle

bat/tle   gar/gle   trun/dle   trem/ble

Exercise 203: Using a prefix to divide a word

con/found   pre/tend   in/spire   de/fend

pre/empt   re/tain   pro/tect   com/plex

dis/miss   re/peat   re/flex   en/noble

un/nerve   in/jure   ex/cuse   ex/pire

Exercise 204: Using a suffix to divide a word

ex/pend/able   fra/grance   mo/dest/ly

frac/tion   per/miss/a/ble dole/ful

glad/ness   e/lec/tion   un/us/u/al

con/test/ing   re/strict/ive   haz/y

clean/li/ness   pend/u/lous   a/tro/cious

de/le/tion   fin/al/it/y   per/ni/cious

re/sent/ment   re/jec/tion   ren/di/tion

Lesson 137: Polysyllabic words

Once the child has had thorough instruction up to this point, he will be ready to attack the last exercise in this chapter: Exercise 205. This is simply a reading exercise. Its purpose is to cultivate and reinforce skill at articulating sounds in sequence, which is fundamental to good speaking and to effective oral reading. Encouraging a consciousness of cadence, of correct pronunciation and of clear enunciation not only makes the child a better oral reader, but it makes him a more discriminating and alert silent reader as well. As he completes each section, have him re-read it until he can do so fluently. It is excellent practice. Unless he is an older child, he need not concern himself at this point with spelling the words or with their meaning.

Exercise 205: Syllabication practice

certainly	penitential	unprepossessive
December	reverence	unresponsive
necessary	astigmatism	uniformed
frequency	evaluative	uninformed
frequently	undermined	undetermined
recondite	dreadfully	advertisement
solipsism	absolution	contradictory
murderous	performance	malediction
mutuality	bedazzling	maliciousness
maladroit	particularly	phenomenological
theological	apologetics	epistemological
theoretician	practicality	practicalities
abysmal	punctuation	unpretentious
ontological	ephemeral	phylogenetic

recapitulates   apostolic   recapitulatory
expostulatory   succession   condemnatory
statistical   fanciful   microscopists
redemption   attribution   eschatological
gladiatorial   illegal   heterogenesis

24

The writing side of literacy

Writing Independence

The only writing with which we have involved the child so far is the writing, from dictation, of lists of words and possibly the odd sentence or two. It is, however, critically important to take him beyond this stage. As with reading independence, if literacy is the goal, we must also aim for writing independence.

The achievement of writing independence involves several well-defined stages, some of which the self-motivated child will attain by himself. If, on the other hand, you are dealing with a child who has already experienced difficulty with reading in school, you will almost certainly be contending with a reluctant writer. It is therefore a good idea to be aware of the stages in the development of writing independence so that you can structure the situation to best suit your child.

Even with very willing children, as mentioned at the beginning of this book, writing poses problems at the purely mechanical level. Until the child's fine motor control has reached a certain stage, the physical act of writing is laborious and sometimes painful. One of the first aims in learning how to write, then, is to establish as relaxed a method of doing it as possible. Ultimately this involves learning how to write some kind of cursive script (what children call 'running' or 'joined-up' writing). If your child is slightly older, you may already have begun teaching him cursive script; if not, see Chapter Twenty-six for instruction on how best to do this.

In the meantime, we must continue to train and cultivate the child so that when he does learn an easy, quick-flowing cursive script, it is not too long before he has something to say that is worth writing about!

The Stages

The stages by which writing independence are reached are:

1 Knowing what sentences are and being able to write four or five consecutive simple sentences dealing with one theme. At first, this is done almost exclusively by you dictating to the child. The theme must be entirely non-abstract.

2 Writing six or seven consecutive sentences dealing with the same theme, but using the child's own words. The theme must be entirely non-abstract.

3 Adding several sentences to an already existing, non-abstract, descriptive passage that has been presented to the child. Initially this is done by you asking the child questions one at a time, each of which he answers by adding one more simple sentence to the description. The thematic material must still be relatively mundane!

4 Adding several sentences to an already existing passage, but in response to questions which he articulates (aloud) by himself.

5 Formal instruction on sentence structure.

6 Developing an understanding of what a paragraph is.

7 Writing two or three paragraph descriptions of action sequences given to him in picture form. Well-drawn comic strips – with the words obliterated – are good for this.

8 Describing a series of events connected with one of his own experiences in two or three paragraphs.

9 Cursive writing skills – as discussed above, these can be taught when appropriate, according to the child's needs.

10 The structure of a simple theme: introduction, development, conclusion.

Let us now deal with each one of these in turn.

Lesson 138: Sequences of simple sentences

You must be certain that the child understands what a sentence is, but, having said that, let us be clear as to what we mean by understanding! At this early stage in his development, the child's 'understanding' of a sentence need entail little more than being able to recognise the difference between groups of words which are sentences and those which are not. You tell him, of course, that a sentence makes a definite statement about something. Whether what it says is true or false is not the point, but it *must* be meaningful to say of a group of words: 'That is true' or 'That is false', otherwise the group of words is not a sentence.

The best approach is to explain it several times, using graphic and startling examples that easily make an impression.

The dog bit his leg off.

That is a sentence. Of any dog we could say whether or not it is true!

The dog bit.

That is also a sentence.

That dog bit his.

That could be a sentence if something else was said first.

The dog bit his leg.

That is definitely a sentence.

The dog bit his off.

Again, it could be a sentence if another statement came before it. However, have the child consider each of:

The dog his leg off

The dog his leg

The dog his

The dog off

The bit his leg off

The bit his leg

The bit his

Not one of these is a sentence. To make the point, ask the child if it makes any sense to say: 'It is true that the dog his leg off.'

Of course, as an adult, you will be itching to tell the child about a sentence having to have a subject and a verb. To *us*, as adults, the idea is that a sentence:

1 Introduces something (a subject).
2 Indicates what it did or what was done to it (a verb).

But that is far too abstract for a young child.

When the child can unambiguously recognise simple sentences and can put a collection of words into sentence order – e.g. transform 'three', 'the', 'pigs', 'ran', 'little', 'away', into 'The three little pigs ran away' – we can really give him some Stage One practice. Let him do Exercise 206 before proceeding further.

Exercise 206: Simple sentences

Indicate which of the following are not sentences and why those which are not sentences are not.

1   Jacob and Moses are Bible characters.

2   Breathing heavily, the dog with his coat covered in paint.

3   Cats, rats and mice are mammals.

4   Cats, rats and mice are mammals but not.

5   I saw where four green men and a great high space-ship.

6   The water all grey and soapy.

7   Mother said not to.

8   But the cow with the crumpled horn
knocked over the bucket.

9   The two snakes slithered and slid.

10 If you bend the cardboard along the dotted
line it.

Now, read the following paragraph, first aloud on your own,
then together with the child:

Washing the Dog

Toby is a white poodle and he was dirty. We filled
the laundry sink with warm soapy water. We
stood Toby in it and washed him. Then, we rinsed
him off. After that, we dried him and let him
play.

Now, do it as dictation. The child should have become sufficiently familiar with the sentences you are intending to use
before the actual dictation so that, during the dictation, he can
almost tell you word for word what is to come next. Exercise
207 can provide useful practice.

Exercise 207: Dictation of six simple themes

1   *My Cat*

My cat is a tabby tom. His name is Mick. I like
him because he is gentle and purrs a lot. We
are all kind to Mick.

2   *Singing Lessons*

I like going to singing lessons because I like it
when we all sing the songs together. First, the

teacher plays the tune on the piano. Then, she plays while we hum. After that, she shows us how to fit the words in. At the end of the lesson, we can all sing the song.

3 *Camping in a Caravan*

Last summer we went for a summer holiday to Land's End. We stayed in a rented caravan near the beach. Every morning, my Dad and I went fishing. It is a good thing that we brought food with us because we caught no fish! Even so, we all enjoyed our holiday.

4 *Reading and Writing*

I like reading, but writing is much harder. You have to be careful to shape each letter properly. Also, you must not make any spelling mistakes. When I am grown up, I shall write books for other people to read.

5 *Grandma*

My grandmother is a very old lady. She is my mother's mother and tells funny stories about when Mummy was small. I like Grandma a lot. When she baby-sits so that Daddy and Mummy can go out, she plays games with me. Once she even let me stay up past my bedtime.

6   *Putting Toys Away*

The problem with having a lot of toys is that you have to put them away! It is great fun playing with them all at once, but it makes a terrible mess. If I don't put them away, someone might step on one of them and break it. Also, it would not be fair for Mummy and Daddy to put them away because they didn't play with them. Next time I think I will only play with a few things.

Practise several short paragraphs like that with him, before going on to Stage Two.

Lesson 139: Writing using his own words

In Stage Two, use almost the same procedure, except have the child suggest the sentences to you. This encourages the child to acquire the very good habit of framing entire sentences in his mind and revising them before committing them to writing.

Whatever the topic, his first proposed sentence is almost certainly going to be too long, too complex (if not compound!) and contain too much extraneous detail. After he has formed it, explain that it is best to use two or three shorter sentences – each one saying only *one thing* – than to try to make one sentence do all of the work.

He can then reframe his sentence, rendering it as a couple of shorter ones. Let him then 'polish' each sentence. This is very much a matter of taste and aesthetic development and should not be leaned on too heavily at this point. But he should become accustomed to the idea of getting the 'feel' of a sentence right by saying it and thus testing its oral impact. Eventually, if this is done carefully, he will develop an awareness of style. At this stage it is sufficient if he renders a sentence in, say, two slightly different ways and then is guided to select the 'better' one.

Eventually, he will be able to articulate the theme in a logical progression of no more than six or seven short sentences. When he can do that, with a little help from you, let him dictate the paragraph, phrase by phrase, to himself as he writes it down.

Lesson 140: Writing in response to your questions

You have no doubt heard of the journalist's six friends. They are: *who? what? where? when? why? how?* As we shall see, the most important of these, for helping a person to extend a piece of writing to include more detail and comment, is 'why?'. An older child, say, over eight years of age, can be introduced to these six friends directly. With a younger child, perhaps we should not be so specific.

Present the child with an incomplete passage and have him read it aloud. It might be something like this:

The Missing Ring

One day my mother was hanging out the washing. Her wedding ring fell off. She tried to find it and was very upset because she couldn't. First she looked among the wet clothes in the basket.

Now, ask the child to add to the passage, one sentence at a time. You can make some ground rules. For instance, the ring is somewhere around the clothes line and is not in the laundry. Each sentence suggested should be refined *first* (as described in Stage Two) and *then* put down in writing. Note that this differs from the previous practice of framing a whole paragraph before putting any of it down. The effect is that it increasingly restricts the choices open to the child as the theme unfolds.

Once one such sentence has been added, ask the child if he can think of another one. *Each sentence must advance the theme a step further*. He may think of two or three before he dries up. If he does dry up, ask him to read the whole theme up to and including his last complete sentence and then ask a question, such as: How?, Why? or Where? That will elicit a response or an explanation that can be rendered as yet another sentence.

Avoid keeping the process up for too long. Seven or eight additional sentences are ample. It is possible to keep going for much longer, of course, by the questioning technique, but you will find in practice that it quickly leads either to banality and tedium, or alternatively to such highly contrived rationalisations as to move off the original thrust of the theme, which can be quite wearing for both child and adult.

The child should have the experience of augmenting several partial passages in this way, but ideally he shouldn't attempt more than one on a given day. Either make up about half a dozen beginnings yourself, drawing on themes that you know are of particular interest to your child, or use Exercise 208. In doing this, strive for variety. For instance, while it is true that the thematic material should not be abstract, it shouldn't always consist of a story line. It might be a description ('My Guinea Pig') or an essay ('Why I Like Maths').

Exercise 208: Unfinished passages

1   The Search

I was walking by myself along the beach, when I saw two soldiers ahead of me. They were shouting at each other and seemed worried. One of them had a buzzing thing like a metal detector and they kept jabbing it into the sand.

2   Sunday School

Some of my friends think that Sunday school is boring, but I don't think so.

3   The Angry Wasps

One day my brother and I saw a grey thing like a Rugby League football hanging from the edge of the garage roof. My brother said it was the best wasp's nest he had ever seen and that he wanted it in his room. The trouble was that it was full of nasty yellow and black wasps. You could see them going in and out of the hole in the bottom and a loud buzzing was coming from inside.

4   *Owning a Dog*
If you want to own a dog, you have to take care of it. It would be cruel to lock it up all day because you are too lazy to take it for walks. Also, it needs feeding.

5   *My Favourite Season*
Of all the seasons of the year, I like Spring the best. In Spring, the weather is not too hot and school is nearly over.

6   *The Car Crash*
One night when we were having our tea, we heard a loud screech of brakes and then a huge crash. You could hear glass breaking and people crying. Daddy ran out to see if he could help and he told us to stay there. But ...

Lesson 141: Asking the questions himself

In this stage the child will advance from the previous stage even though the techniques employed will be similar. As previously, let the child put down sentences until he runs dry.

In fact, he may put down a string of half a dozen or so coherent sentences, in which case, that is enough. In that event, let him have another theme the next day. You may even find that he can expand freely on each of several themes you give him. That simply means that he has already achieved this stage of development himself and that you can go on to the next one.

If such is not the case, though, the child will run out of ideas and have to make use of some of his 'six friends'. When this happens, it is important for him to develop flexibility, both in asking the questions and in answering them. There will be several choices of questions he can ask at any given time. Have him articulate all the choices that he can think of and then decide which one will make the most interesting or productive springboard for the subsequent development of the theme.

Such strategies are elementary, but at this stage they do not represent a serious obstacle to the child's progress, it is the *attitude* one cultivates that is important. Later, when he is writing at a more sophisticated level, the early inculcation of a strategic 'look ahead' attitude to essay writing will stand him in very good stead indeed.

Paragraphs from Exercise 208 which were not used previously might be used with good effect at this point, unless you can think out half a dozen thematic beginnings of your own which are more closely linked to the child's experience.

Lesson 142: Writing as personal expression

A psychological observation is in order here. Presumably, we want the child to feel completely at home in expressing himself through writing, so that it is virtually as natural to him as speaking is. The schools are full of students to whom writing is an alien and alienating business – difficult, artificial and hence poorly done. Not a few such people even filter into the universities. Obviously, if such an attitude toward writing can be avoided, it would be of great benefit to the child. Much of his school work would become a pleasure rather than an obstacle and in all sorts of other ways his sense of well-being and effectiveness would be enhanced. The problem is to arrive at a strategy for making the writing process natural.

Until the child learns to write in cursive script, the sheer mechanics of it are a stumbling block. However, another stumbling block is apt to be the thematic material about which he is asked to write. The usual approach is that children in primary school are asked to write about simple descriptive subject matter, while as students move through secondary school, the themes becoming increasingly idea centred and abstract. Of course, this is a logical progression, but along with it something else must be kept in mind: for several years at least of a child's writing development, the thematic material *must be largely personal*.

This is something which is easily lost sight of in schools, for instance, where the tendency is for children to be called upon to write about things external to their experience. It is important that they are able to cope with such 'externalised' writing, of course, but they will not be able to do so effectively unless they get plenty of practice with more intimate material, both *before* they reach the stage of formal thematic writing in school and *while* they are engaged at that level in school.

There are several ways of encouraging this, but the two most effective are writing letters and keeping a diary. The child who grows up in a situation in which he is expected to write thank you letters for birthday gifts and the like, and to correspond on a regular basis with some distant relative, is fortunate in this regard. Also, writing needs to be given its due place in the home as an 'art form'. For instance, one will often see a child encouraged to play a piece on the piano for a favoured guest or even as a gift for his parents or for a sibling. That is good and is based on the well-accepted idea that music is an art form and hence a suitable vehicle for the expression of feelings. Might we not also stimulate the rendering of essays and poetry in the same light?

This was standard practice in my home. On looking back, I can appreciate that there were sound economic reasons for it, but we were entirely unabashed about giving one another pieces of creative writing for presents or in producing them for such special occasions as 'Harvest Day', etc. It is not difficult for the child to realise that a gift that he has had to work at for several days is much more likely to be treasured than something he has bought in five minutes at the local supermarket!

Lesson 143: Formal instruction in sentence construction

By now the child is accustomed to producing sentences and it is no longer a hurdle for him. We can therefore afford to insist on refining the process! Have the child read the following passage to you.

The Clowns

The circus came yesterday and we went. The clowns were the best part. The first clown was dressed in a red cloak with green boots and a yellow hat. The others wore all sorts of bright colours. The clowns had a pretend fight and the lion trainer broke it up. The circus ended so we went home.

Obviously, one can find all sorts of things wrong with it. It is, by the way, a genuine article, submitted as English homework in a Year 7 class in Melbourne. However, for the present, let us avoid the finer details of literary criticism and ask the child what he notices about it. It should not take him too long to observe that every sentence is constructed almost identically. They all begin with 'The' and each one introduces a primary subject, then disposes of it and finally gives a consequence. The effect, of course, is monotonous.

At this stage, we want the child to become highly conscious of sentence *beginnings*. How many sentences can he say in a row, each beginning with a different word? Have him try it. Point out to him that in writing we generally try to avoid, as far as possible, repeating the same sentence beginning and we do this in order to keep the passage more interesting. There are several strategies that we can point out, even to a young child, for varying sentences. Three of the more elementary ones will now be considered.

Changing word and idea order

How many *different* sentences, meaning the same thing and using most of the same words, can you make out the following one?

The cat ate the ice cream.

An obvious variation is:

The ice cream was eaten by the cat.

However, both of these begin with 'The'. It is not always possible, especially with a short, simple sentence, to avoid that if we confine ourselves only to the words in the original sentence. But there are other strategies!

Introducing the sentence with an adverb

The child, if he is young, will not know what a *verb* is, let alone an *adverb*, but we can give him plenty of examples of words which end in 'ly'!

Greedily the cat ate the ice cream.
Slowly the cat ate the ice cream.
Quickly the cat ate the ice cream.

Let the child experiment with that sentence using other 'ly' words: 'furtively', 'joyfully', 'thoughtfully', etc. Have him think of several. Each one lends a slightly different meaning to the sentence. It might not be enough to say, 'The cat ate the ice cream'. Maybe *how* she did it matters!

After he has played with that sentence for a while, present him with the following:

The train moved quickly as it left the station.

Explain first that we can begin the sentence *either* with the train *or* the station. To an older child, of course, we say that we can begin either with the subject or the object.

The train moved quickly as it left the station.
Out of the station quickly moved the train.

That immediately makes for interesting variations in sentence beginning; but we can go further and begin with part of the verb:

Moving quickly, the train left the station.
Quickly moving, the train left the station.

A younger child will only appreciate this by analogy, but an older child can grasp it in the more technical sense if he has been taught a little grammar. In the next chapter of this book a little rudimentary grammar is introduced. It might be helpful to use it in this context.

Substituting key words

Fluency in writing depends, as does fluency in speaking, on vocabulary. Always encourage the child to use synonyms as a means of avoiding repetition. For instance, have the child read the following sentence and some of the variations on it which can be rendered using different words.

The boy was late for school.

The lad arrived late for school.

The lad reached school late.

The youngster was late getting to school.

By the time he got to school, the boy was late.

Notice that in these variations we have not substituted anything for the word 'late'. If we had used such expressions as 'tardy' or 'after the bell', many more variations could have been made while still communicating the basic idea.

When dealing with a young child, you are fairly restricted in what you can show him about sentence variation, but even at that elementary level, it is important to make him *aware* of the issue. Then, as he studies grammatical structures and the like more thoroughly in school (if he is fortunate!) and as he reads more widely, he can use this basic awareness to good advantage. For such a young child, Exercise 209 might be stimulating, while an older child might appreciate Exercise 210.

Exercise 209: Sentence variation

Start the sentence below in six different ways, as indicated.

The train pulled out of the station.

1   From the station ...

2   Making its way slowly ...

3   Without delay ...

4   Noisily ...

5   With a ... (hint: With a sudden jolt ...)

6   Quickly ... (hint: Quickly gathering
    speed ...)

Exercise 210: Sentence variation

Change the following sentence to begin in four different ways,
as indicated.

A dog wandered into the milking shed.

1   The object first

2   The verb first

3   A preposition first

4   An adverb first

Lesson 144: The paragraph

An important stage in the development of reading independence is the ability to construct paragraphs. The best way of
helping a child toward this goal is to draw his attention to
examples of paragraphs in whatever book he is reading.

First of all, point out the physical features of a paragraph.
Each paragraph usually begins with the first word indented.
That is how we recognise when one paragraph ends and
another begins. Point out more examples to him.

Once he understands that, we come to the more difficult task
of explaining the *uses* of paragraphs. At the very elementary
level, we point out that quotations are set off in paragraphs
from the surrounding writing. Also, quotations by different
people are given separate paragraphs. Children's books

abound in plenty of good examples to show him.

However, we do want even the young child to have *some* appreciation of the subtle idea that a paragraph deals with *one* issue or idea. As soon as a *different* issue or idea is introduced, a new paragraph must be commenced. Again, awareness of this develops as the child matures, but only if he is familiar with the concept to begin with. Periodically in his reading, draw attention to the reasons for a change from one paragraph to another. Avoid using newspapers, for they often make a separate paragraph out of each sentence. Look yourself at your daily newspaper and you will probably notice this. It is not something of which people are ordinarily aware. Of course, the journalistic practice stems from the need to be brief and dramatic. In theory, in popular journalism, each sentence *is* intended to convey a new idea. In fact, newspapers sometimes use the rule of paragraphing as though that were always the case – a convenience for typesetters – but rarely does each sentence in a news story legitimately qualify as a paragraph. Therefore, to avoid confusion, use examples from stories or other books that the child is reading.

Once you have been doing this for a while, start to become just a *little* more critical of the child's use of paragraphing in his own written work.

An easy way to do this is to read his material aloud to him, asking *him* to decide when a change of ideas has occurred and thus when a new paragraph should be started. The usual fault is for children not to paragraph enough.

Lesson 145: Written responses to picture sequences

This very effective technique is now widely used in schools. In days gone by, almost all children were taught to write only in response to topics set by a teacher or an examiner. But, as indicated previously, this does little to encourage writing as a means of spontaneous self-expression. Responding to pictures necessitates a much more personal involvement. No two children will respond in *exactly* the same way to a picture sequence and such sequences do not restrict the highly creative child.

For instance, I once gave a class of six- and seven-year-old children a picture sequence consisting of three panels:

Panel 1:   A cat waiting by a mouse hole.
Panel 2:   The same cat with 'z-z-z-z' written in a balloon above its head, indicating it had fallen asleep.
Panel 3:   A mouse running out of the hole with a suitcase and waving goodbye to the sleeping cat.

Each child was asked to write about the picture sequence.

The most meagre response was: 'The cat is trying to find a mouse. But it got away.' Had I simply told the children to write me a story about a cat and a mouse, I would have had no response at all from *that* child! The picture approach does encourage *some* response, even from the most lethargic student. At the more creative end of the spectrum, however, there seems to be no limit to children's imaginations. Following are three responses from that class (mistakes intact!) in increasing order of creativity:

A bit fat cat whanted a mouse for diner. It wated and wated by the mouses hole but the mouse never mooved. When it was late, the cat fell asleep. The mouse herd it snoreing and came out. He had to find a new hole but that was O.K.

Slightly more involved:

There was once a very wise and sly and cuning pussy cat who disided to catch a mouse. He was old and that's why he was so wise but he has arethritess and he coldnot run so he thohgt of a plan. He ate a pile of chees so his breathe stank of chees and then he sat by the hole and breathed down it. But he ate to much chees and fell asleep. The mouse came out for the chees but when he seen the cat the mouse said Oh my God and left.

Finally, a highly technical rendering:

This cat wanted to catch a mouse, but the mouse was nuctronal [nocturnal] and only came out at night. The cat like to sleep all night, but he staid up one night to cach the mouse. The mouse was prety smart and he could see that cat there even tho it was dark. So he went down the mouse tunel until he came to the cave where they keep the guns and he took a lead case with urenum [uranium] in it and bringed brut it to the near the hole. Then he opnd the lid and hide behind the lead and all the rays hit the cat and killed it. Then he wen running out and got away.

You can give your child plenty of this kind of practice – and it is good fun even for older children – by using well-drawn comic strips with the words blanked out. Another course of similar practice, but more appropriate for older children, is photographs from newspapers and magazines. Especially when working with a single photograph, as opposed to a sequence, the response need not be a story at all, but the development of an idea or a viewpoint.

Lesson 146: Extended writing from personal experience

As indicated previously, from the very earliest stages of writing, personal experience should be the source of as much spontaneous practice as possible. In the earlier stages, however, such spontaneous writing is likely to be superficial and largely descriptive and/or synoptic: the 'first we did this, then we did that' sort of thing. With an increase in facility at getting ideas down on paper, and this only comes about through extensive practice, the child gradually is able to become more introspective in his writing. This is an important stage – and it is a stage that is very much enhanced by keeping a diary.

The child may not be willing to show you his diary, but he can be encouraged to give public expression to his personality by being asked to write about such 'big themes' as war, racism, school or pollution *from his own perspective*. One very effective stimulus in this direction as the 'Pretend that you are ...' approach:

> Pretend that you are the explorer Sir Humphrey Gilbert. Tell what he was trying to find out on one of his sea voyages.

Or:

> Pretend that you are Fidel Castro. Why are you not friendly with the United States government?

Such an approach accomplishes two important purposes simultaneously. It encourages the child to express *himself* but also forces him to empathise *outside* of himself. It gradually extends his awareness of what *he* is while making him more aware of what *other people* are at the same time. It causes him to ask questions, for one thing, and that in itself is a tremendous source of creative growth.

Lesson 147: The structure of a simple theme

One cannot *really* feel satisfied that a child has achieved writing independence until he can, without undue exertion, produce a short composition. It need not be complicated, but it should effectively introduce a topic, logically develop it and unambiguously conclude it. This three-fold structure (sometimes referred to in school as 'Beginning, Body and End') is an important one to master early, and facility in using it will not only ensure that as the child matures he can write effectively, but also that he can appreciate the structure of any written work he is called upon to read or study.

Begin specifically to inculcate an awareness of this soon after Stage Seven. Encourage the child to *plan* his themes with structure in mind by asking himself questions, e.g. How will I introduce the topic?

The introductory paragraph, or 'Beginning', should clearly indicate what is being discussed and also elucidate what the child's relation to it is or was. It should usually answer such questions as What? Who? and Where? The succeeding two or three paragraphs should *develop* the theme. They should answer such questions as How? When? and Why?

Another way of getting the child to work on structure is to think of the introduction as 'setting the stage'. It does not contain much *action*, but principally establishes a scene and a context for action that will follow. As the child matures, he should be encouraged to become conscious of *anticipatory* writing, that is writing which piques a reader and impels him to read on through the development of the theme. This, of course, requires taste, skill and experience. It also requires that the student has read a great deal of good literature himself. However, even with the earliest themes (once paragraphing has been mastered), we can begin to make the child aware of it.

The 'Body' or development of the theme generally encompasses all of the action. If it is an event that is being described, for example, the development typically embodies rapid scene changes and variations in tense. With respect to this latter aspect, strict attention to the rules of grammar should be insisted upon in a child's writing. Established geniuses can break the rules and get away with it, but only because they know how and when to do so! The point is that, whereas the introduction to a theme has a static quality about it, the development contrasts with it by being dynamic. This is so even if it is an idea, rather than a description of an event, that is being developed. If the theme is dealing with an idea, the nub of the argument is contained in the development section. Therein is set forth the reasoning behind one's opinions, so that the development is persuasive in character.

The 'End' or conclusion should, ordinarily, draw the theme to a rapid and forceful close – for our purposes, preferably in one paragraph. A conclusion that is too long runs the risk of unintentionally introducing new thematic material.

Teach the child to plan his theme by sketching out briefly what he intends to include in each area: introduction, development and conclusion. This will allow him to detect whether he has confined the major action to the middle section and whether the conclusion briefly and unambiguously resolves the issue, or issues, raised in the body of the piece.

25

A simple account of some grammatical rudiments

Why Grammar?

For some years now, debate has raged in the educational and (more especially) in the linguistic fields as to whether formal grammar should be taught to primary school children. Some linguistic scholars go so far as to say that rules of grammar in English are 'lies' because the rules are based on the Latin origins of English when, in fact, the language did not evolve either directly or completely from Latin. Others look at the issue psychologically and suggest that a rigid concern for form discourages spontaneity.

However, neither view need concern either the parent or the teacher who feels that a little 'incidental' grammar might be of use in helping a child to read intelligently and to write with greater clarity. A knowledge of a little of the rudimentary vocabulary of grammar provides both child and teacher with basic points of reference in discussing such aspects of reading as comprehension, expression or use of punctuation, and all of the relevant research does indicate that children who have had *some* instruction in formal grammar derive greater enjoyment out of reading and writing and tend to be more creative in their use of language. They certainly become better at understanding (and inflicting!) puns. But how much grammar and when should it be taught?

About this point the research is not of much help. In my experience. I have found it useful to give children enough grammatical instruction to be able to:

1 Name the parts of speech and recognise them.

2 Understand tense.
3 Know basic rules of sentence structure.

This sounds simple, but it is not. For instance, if a child is only five or six when he has learned to read and write effectively up through Exercise 208, then you should *probably* acquaint him with only a *few* parts of speech: nouns, verbs, adjectives, adverbs and prepositions. Tenses should be confined to present, past and future and only the active voice should be mentioned. In dealing with the sentence, he *should* be acquainted with subject and object as quickly as possible. Children who grow up with a good grip of that have *much* less difficulty later in developing a more sophisticated understanding of language. It really *does* confer power. An older child, or one who is particularly interested in the subject, obviously could be taught more. Therefore, how much – if any – of this grammatical material you share with your child is very much an individual matter. On no account should it be forced if the child is reluctant.

To that end, I have indicated in this chapter those grammatical structures that I would regard as so fundamental that a knowledge of them can only aid in a child's development toward literacy. However, that does *not* mean that you should feel compelled to teach it all. Even though it is only rudimentary, much of it (especially the discussion of the verb) is intended as a reference in helping children who are highly motivated and deeply interested. Certainly, a knowledge of these rudiments can help in one's reading comprehension and writing, but only if both the parent doing the teaching *and* the child receiving the instruction derive intellectual pleasure from the exercise. Grammar badly taught can prove a real impediment to pleasure in reading or writing. Therefore, use this chapter carefully and eclectically. Read it through yourself. Teach the basic parts of speech, but don't go into detail where you feel uncertain of your own ground or where you feel that the child is finding it burdensome. It is a chapter that both you and the child can come back to from time to time to find out a little more or to refresh your memory as the need arises.

As to when to introduce these rudiments, that depends very much on the child. The grammatical 'bits and pieces' incorporated in this chapter can be taught, even to a young reader, at the stage at which he is starting to write freely and spontaneously. Certainly, they must never act as a *barrier* to his enjoyment of reading or writing, nor must the parent make the mistake of attaching some sort of overweening 'moral' force to the idea of correct grammar. It should be seen as an interesting and useful technical description of how language works.

Often children are not made aware at all of the technical aspects of language until they come to learn a foreign language in secondary school. This seems a great shame, for grammar – like any mathematical structure – has a certain aesthetic appeal to it. Presented properly, it can be fascinating in its own right and, as well, it can lay a useful groundwork for the later study of any other language. I have always found that introductory Latin and Ancient Greek are also good fun – if sensitively handled, of course – and confer tremendous power and subtlety on a child's written expression if started at age eight or nine. However, that is not a view that is widely shared in educational circles in Britain.

The Need to Name 'Parts' of Speech

The idea that our day-to-day speaking and writing has 'parts' – like the engine of a car – is often a source of considerable interest to children. They take language so much for granted that such an idea may strike them as completely novel. What do we mean by 'parts' of speech? The following motivational discussion is especially effective with older children. With a younger child, it may be best to skip this discussion, unless he is of a particularly analytical frame of mind, and move right on to the following section.

At the simplest level, we can make the point clear to a child by presenting him with the following sentences:

1　Tom ate crumbs.
2　Stones hit cars.

In the first sentence, we have three sounds: 'la – la – la'. However, each of these three sounds *does* something different. The first sound *introduces* something (or someone). Until that sound is uttered, we don't know *what* the person who is speaking (or writing) is thinking about. Once he has made that first 'la', though, we know! He is thinking about 'Tom'. However, if someone came up to you and said: 'Tom' and then made two more sounds you didn't understand, you would be in a bit of a fix! You would know that the fellow was referring to something – possibly a person, but it also could be a cat, some other pet or even something non-living – so there would be *some* communication between you. You would both be thinking about something called Tom.

Let the child think of as many three word sentences as he can that begin with 'Tom'. It will not be long before he realises that for the communication to be useful, we not only need another word after 'Tom', but another *kind* of word. 'Tom' tells us *what* we are talking *about*. We now need a word that tells us *what* Tom is *doing*.

Tom ate.

Good! We now know that the sentence introduced a creature to us called 'Tom' and we further know that Tom *ate*. The child should be made aware of the face that 'Tom' and 'ate' are not only different words, they are different *kinds* of words. For instance, could we take a photograph of 'Tom'? Could we take a photograph of 'ate'?

Finally, he can be led to appreciate that 'crumbs' is another *what* kind of word, like 'Tom', but it has a relationship *with* Tom. In the following sentences the *relationship* between Tom and the crumbs is different.

Tom ate crumbs.
Tom kicked crumbs.
Tom crushed crumbs.
Tom sees crumbs.

Thus 'crumbs' is really a different kind of word, in some sense, from each of 'Tom' and 'ate'.

The first sentence introduces Tom and tells us about something he did. He may have done it many times, he may be doing it now and he may do it tomorrow. Maybe he eats crumbs continuously, maybe twice a day. Maybe he *never* is *supposed* to eat crumbs, but *one* time he did. The sentence by itself cannot help us answer any of these questions. It just says that at one point, Tom ate crumbs. Now, consider the first variation with the child in much the same way. It is a different kind of sentence from the first, even though they are both 'la – la – la' in sound.

Next, look at the second sentence – Stones hit cars. It can immediately have two meanings. What might they be?

In one sense, it could be that a person was describing a riot or something similar, in which an angry mob was pelting police cars with rocks. Somewhere in the middle of such a description, the sentence could easily occur: 'There was a loud metallic rattling noise as the rocks hailed down. Stones hit cars. Other stones shattered windows.' On the other hand, the sentence might have been referring to something far less exciting. It could be, for instance, that one driver was warning another driver about the perils of driving fast on gravel roads. In the first instance, with the police cars, the 'hit' refers to something which has already happened. In the second instance, the 'hit' refers to something that *might* happen in the future, or which *does* happen every time one drives fast down a gravel road.

Discussions like this (especially with an older child) establish a need for some way of describing what function different words have in sentences. This can open the way to a description of what we can call the parts of speech.

The Parts of Speech

Just as even the largest of whole numbers and the smallest of fractions can be made with only ten symbols (0, 1, 2, 3, 4, 5, 6, 7, 8, 9), so it is with English speech. The most complicated speech or piece of writing consists of a huge variety of words, but there are at most only nine types of words in any sentence.* You can confidently explain to the child that, once he knows these nine parts of speech, he can classify a word in any sentence in English (and in most other languages as well). The nine parts of speech, then, are:

1 nouns
2 verbs
3 adjectives
4 articles

*Some linguistics reduce it to eight because 'articles' can be included as 'adjectives'.

5 pronouns
6 adverbs
7 prepositions
8 conjunctions
9 interjections

Before going on to explain what any of these mean, have the child read over the list several times. Make sure that he can pronounce all of the terms and can spell them correctly. None of them represents any phonic difficulties.

Nouns

At the first session, you can certainly acquaint him with 'noun' and 'verb'. The best way of going about this is to use simple sentences as examples. Do not give any formal definitions yet, simply state that a *noun* is usually something that you can see, feel, name, photograph or whatever, whereas a *verb* tells what a noun is doing. A verb is an action word.

Next, compare the role of each. For instance, you might consider the following sentences:

1 The cat runs.
2 Toby eats.
3 Roosters peck.
4 Harold sleeps.
5 Mary sings.

Explain that a cat is certainly something you can see. Even if you don't see it right now, say, because it is under the house or in a different town, you *could* see it if you were close enough. 'Cat' is a noun. 'Runs', on the other hand, is not something you can see by itself. If a man runs, you see a *man*, but you *don't* see 'runs' itself. It only makes a picture in your mind if there is also a noun around to give it meaning. Similarly, he should see that: 'Toby', 'rooster', 'Harold' and 'Mary' are all *nouns*; while 'runs', 'eats', 'peck', 'sleeps' and 'sings' are all *verbs*.

Thus, on the first day you should be able to get across a rough idea of what a noun is and what a verb is. That opens the way to a more sophisticated approach to nouns. We can begin with a formal definition: a noun is a *naming* word. It is the name of a person, a place or a thing.

Have the child read the definition several times. He should be given plenty of practice reading that definition. There is certainly no harm in memorising it, if it is applied immediately to sentences. Let him read the following sentences:

1 Henry sat on the chair.

2 China is a large country.

3 The dogs and cats dug holes in the garden.

In each sentence, consider *each word*, but only with respect to whether or not it is a *noun*. Thus, 'Henry' is a noun. Why? Because it is the name of a person, etc. To do this systematically will take time, but it is time well spent because it constantly requires the child not only to memorise the definition, but to *use* it.

We can go one step further even with very young readers, namely to differentiate between *common* nouns and *proper* nouns. It can be explained that *proper* nouns name a special or a particular person, place or thing. About the only successful way of making this understood is through the use of examples. Certainly it is worthwhile to go over the three sentences he has just done and point out *why* 'Henry' and 'China' are proper nouns, while the other nouns are common nouns. But one then needs to go further. Give him a list of nouns and ask him to show which are proper and which are common:

Rover	fridge	Tibby	winter
magician	Thomas	cat	Molly
music	Newport	fellow	girl
temper	Portugal	minister	St John
Concorde	crabs	Dr Watson	Wales
Wendy	fish	envelope	country

You should also explain that all proper nouns begin with a capital letter, but not all nouns that begin with a capital letter are proper nouns. For instance, in the sentence 'Dogs destroyed her hedge.', 'dogs' begins with a capital, but only because it is the first word of a sentence. It is still a common noun because it does not refer to a *particular* group of dogs.

With older children we can go further by pointing out that nouns can also be classified according to whether they are *concrete* or *abstract*. A concrete noun is not necessarily a cement block! It is any person, place or thing that we can *touch* or *physically locate*. An abstract noun is any noun which is not concrete. For instance, while 'God' or the 'Holy Spirit' are nouns naming 'persons', they do not name persons who can be physically located or who we can touch in the ordinary sense. Likewise, Heaven and Hell are the names of places, as is the Land of Oz (the one where the Wizard lives, not the country!), but they are not physical places, they are 'ideas'. Abstract nouns, like 'justice', 'honour', 'peace', 'temper', 'fear', 'virtue' etc., name ideas. They are not concrete.

Another way of explaining abstract nouns to older children is to point out that abstract nouns are names of *qualities*. They exist in the mind. As well, we can make many abstract nouns by adding 'ness' to certain descriptive word stems, e.g. 'happiness', 'politeness'.

To round off your discussion of nouns with an older child, you should mention *collective* nouns. When we have one word that refers to a whole collection of persons, places or things, then that word is a collective noun. Examples are: 'federation', 'union', 'flock', 'herd', 'crowd', etc.

Thus, we can classify nouns as:

Proper or Common
Concrete or Abstract
Singular or Collective

Verbs

With a young child, it would not be advisable to do much more than to indicate that a verb is the 'doing' word of a sentence. It indicates what some noun is up to! You should also make it clear that some verbs do not indicate a very lively or exciting mode of action. For instance, consider the following sentences:

1 Rover is a dog.
2 Bill became a lawyer.
3 Jane has a doll.
4 The weather was cold.

Have the child identify the verb in each case. If the child is quite young, it will take him a long time and require many more examples than these four to get the point across that 'is', 'became', 'has' and 'was' are verbs.

On the other hand, when you are dealing with a child of late primary school age or older, you can afford to become a little more technical. We can, first of all, introduce him to what we mean by the *tense* of a verb. The sophistication with which you do this depends on the child, but you can certainly mention three basic tenses: past, present and future. To make the point at the simplest level, consider the following three sentences:

1 Sara gave the dog a bone.
2 Sara gives the dog a bone.
3 Sara will give the dog a bone.

The first sentence embodies the verb in a *past* tense, the second in a *present* tense and the third in a *future* tense. Notice that in the future tense, the verb involves *two words*: 'will' and 'give'. This is a characteristic of English, German and some other languages, but not most European languages, which get around the problem by using special verb endings on the one stem to indicate tense. English is not an easy language to learn! Further evidence of this is that both the past tense and the present tense can also be indicated using two words for the verb:

1 Sara has given the dog a bone.   (past)
2 Sara is giving the dog a bone.   (present)

For the sake of completeness, later we will return to such complexities. However, before delving too deeply into the details of *tense*, the older child should also be made aware of *person*. In the grammar of verbs, we speak of three 'persons singular' and three 'persons plural'. The persons singular are:

1 I
2 you (when it refers to one person)
3 he, she or it

The persons plural are:

1 we   (the plural of 'I')
2 you ('you', when it refers to a number of people, is the plural of 'you', when it refers to one person)
3 they ('they' is the plural of 'he', 'she' and 'it').

Let the child analyse this a bit before going further: suppose *one person* says, 'I love cookies.' Now, if instead of *one* person wishing to express that thought, there was a group of twenty people who wanted (collectively) to say the same thing, how would they do so? Obviously, they would say, 'We love cookies.'

Thus, it is reasonable that the *first person singular* is 'I' and the *first person plural* is 'we'. Likewise, the *second person singular* is 'you' and the *second person plural* is 'you'. In certain parts of the community, you hear people using 'youse' as a plural of 'you', e.g. 'Are youse going out?' Of course, it is hopelessly incorrect grammatically, but it has a charming logic about it! Again, the *third person singular* is 'he' (or 'she' or 'it') and the *third person plural* is 'they'.

Now, there is yet another complicating factor when we are dealing with the grammar of the verb. We not only have to contend with *tense* and with *person*, but also with *voice*. It is very difficult indeed to explain precisely what is meant by 'voice', but the use of examples makes it clear.

1 Tom gave the present to Joan.
2 The present was given to Joan.

In the first sentence, someone – Tom – was *active*. He *gave* a present to Joan. In the second sentence, the action seems to happen without anyone being active. Joan just got a present. In the first sentence, we say that the verb was in the *active voice*, but in the second sentence the verb was in the *passive voice*.

Up until now in our discussion, we have only talked about verbs having a person, a tense and a voice. Verbs like that are called *finite* verbs. Later on we shall see what we mean by *non-finite* verbs, but before going into that, let's continue with tenses, as it might be worthwhile for a *very* keen child to come back and do a more complete job on them. The principal tenses are twenty-four in number: twelve active and twelve passive. Do *not* introduce all of these tenses unless the child is particularly interested. They are as follows:

Active Voice

1 I eat.	(simple present tense)
2 I am eating.	(continuous present tense)
3 I have eaten.	(present perfect tense)
4 I ate.	(simple past tense)
5 I was eating.	(imperfect past tense)
6 I had eaten.	(past perfect tense)
7 I shall eat.	(simple future tense)
8 I shall be eating.	(continuous future tense)
9 I shall have eaten.	(future perfect tense)
10 I should eat.	(future-in-the-past tense)
11 I should be eating.	(future-in-the-past continuous tense)
12 I should have eaten.	(future-in-the-past perfect tense)

Passive Voice (each corresponding with an active voice form)
1 I am eaten.
2 I am being eaten.
3 I have been eaten.
4 I was eaten.
5 I was being eaten.
6 I had been eaten.
7 I will be eaten.
8 I will be being eaten.
9 I will have been eaten.
10 I would be eaten.
11 I would be being eaten.
12 I would have been eaten.

As mentioned previously, only a particularly keen child might find the above interesting. My own view is that it can be extremely helpful in reading to have a rudimentary knowledge of the tense and voice of verbs, but many educationists regard it as unnecessary. It is one of those things, I suspect, that depends on the teacher. If the teacher is himself fascinated by it, the child or children he is teaching tend to pick up his enthusiasm. This had never struck me until one day, when I was teaching remedial reading classes in California, another teacher said to me, 'How come your kids are so damned interested in grammar?'

The lesson to be learned from this is, if you are interested, then the material is here so that you can show it to your child. I am convinced that it helps both reading and writing. But if you find it distasteful or distressing, forget it. If you do and you attempt to teach it to your child, your own dubious feelings about it will come across and it will do more harm than good.

Having said that, we cannot really leave finite verbs until we have mentioned *transitive* and *intransitive* verbs. With a *transitive* verb, the action or feeling *passes over* (trans) from the 'doer' to the 'done-to'. For instance, consider the sentence 'Farmers kill foxes.' The 'farmers' are the 'doers' and the 'foxes' are certainly the 'done-tos'! The verb *kill* connects them in that relationship. With *intransitive* verbs, no such action or feeling crosses over, for instance:

1 Farmers sleep.
2 John comes.
3 Father smiles.
4 Mother falls.
5 I kneel.
6 Baby lies. (*That* has two meanings!)

In each of those six sentences, the verb is *intransitive*.

Having spoken so much, then, about *finite* verbs, what do we mean by *non-finite* verbs? There are two main types of non-finite verbs, namely *infinitives* and *participles*.

The *infinitive* is the form of the verb before it has had anything done to it, before it has been given a person or a tense. In English, we use the word 'to' in front of the verb to show that we mean the 'infinitive'. For instance, one might say, 'Put the verb "to kill" in the present tense, active voice, third person singular.' The response, of course, would be: 'He kills.' However, the important thing for the purpose of our discussion is that the expression 'to kill' is an infinitive.

To make any sense in a sentence, an infinitive has to be linked to some other verb, for example: 'The mayor came to eat at my house.' In this sentence, 'to eat' is linked to 'came'.

Another thing to note is that an infinitive is often used as a noun, as in: 'To skate is dangerous.'

We shall not say much about participles in such a rudimentary account of grammar, except to indicate that there can be *present* participles or *past* participles or their passive voice equivalents. Again, these are most clearly explained through examples.

1 The singing boy was shot.
2 The decayed food stank.
3 The boy being beaten cried out.
4 The food having been eaten was gone.

'Singing' is a present participle, 'decayed' is a past participle, 'being beaten' is a present passive participle, and 'having been eaten' is a past passive participle.

If the child has come this far with you, and if both you and he have enjoyed the journey, you are both to be congratulated. The child now has a reasonable grasp of the place of the noun and of the verb in sentence-writing. The other parts of speech will be dealt with much less thoroughly.

Adjectives

Adjectives, it can be explained to the child – even to a young child – are words that 'describe' nouns. A more mature child can be introduced to the word 'modifies' in this context. An adjective *modifies* a noun. Let the child read the following three sentences:

1 The beautiful house stood back from the road.

2 Jean saw a brown and white horse.

3 That was not a good idea!

In the first sentence, there are two nouns: house and road. The road is not described at all, but the house is. We are told that it is 'beautiful'. The adjective is 'beautiful' and that adjective describes or modifies the noun 'house'.

In the second sentence, have the child pick out any nouns.

Now, ask him if any of them are described or modified. He should see that the noun 'horse' is modified by the adjective 'brown and white'. The third sentence is a trifle harder because an abstract noun is involved. The noun is 'idea' and the adjective modifying it is 'good'.

At the rudimentary level it would not be appropriate to say any more about adjectives. The adjectives discussed so far are known (reasonably enough) as descriptive adjectives. There are others, such as: demonstrative adjectives, possessive adjectives, quantitative adjectives, distributive adjectives, etc., but these should be left until the child studies grammar formally in school.

Articles

As was mentioned earlier, some grammarians say that there are only eight parts of speech, rather than nine, because the articles can be regarded as adjectives. However, because the word 'article' is so often used in connection with sentence structure and reading, it should be presented to the child as a part of speech in its own right. It is perhaps the easiest part of speech to understand, possibly because so few words belong to that category. These are two types of articles: *definite and indefinite.*

The *definite* article is 'the' and the *indefinite* articles are 'a' and 'an'. Thus, there are only three articles in the whole language. Have the child read the following three sentences:

1 The dog ate the goldfish.

2 The girl ate a sandwich.

3 The worm ate an apple.

In the first sentence, the *definite article* occurs twice: the phrase 'the dog' refers to a *definite* dog, not just any old dog, and 'the goldfish' refers to a *definite* goldfish, not just any goldfish that was swimming around.

In the second and third sentences we have one *definite* article and one *indefinite* article. We should draw the child's attention to the fact that the phrase 'a sandwich' does not refer to a particular sandwich. We don't know whether it was a cheese and lettuce sandwich or a jam sandwich or what. We don't even know whether it was the girl's sandwich. She might have taken someone else's. The 'a' is an *indefinite* article. The same is true of 'an' in the phrase 'an apple'.

Pronouns

The child can be told that a *pronoun* is a word that stands for a noun in a sentence. Illustrate this by use of the following example:

Felicity Mary Phillips put John Smith's book on the table.
She put his book on it.
She put it on it.

If we are talking about a person, we usually introduce them by name (or in some other way) in the first sentence and then in the next few sentences we refer to the person by the appropriate pronoun: 'he', 'him', 'his' for a male; 'she', 'her', 'hers' for a female. It makes for shorter sentences and avoids awkward repetition! Likewise, a common noun can be replaced by the pronoun 'it'.

In the first sentence above, the girl (or woman) in question is given her name: Felicity Mary Phillips. In the second sentence, her name is replaced by the pronoun 'she'. Likewise, the pronoun 'his' replaces 'John Smith's' and 'the table' becomes 'it'. In the third sentence, we even replace 'his book' by the pronoun 'it'.

Again, one could say a great deal more about pronouns and their various types, but this chapter is only intended to touch on the rudiments of grammar. Even for an older child it is probably sufficient simply to point out that pronouns can be one of four common types. These are:

Personal

I, you, he, she, it, we, they, me, him, her, us, them.

Demonstrative

If someone says, 'I like this book', the word 'this' is an adjective;

but if someone says, 'I like this', then 'this' is a demonstrative pronoun because it is a pronoun *demonstrating* (pointing to) a particular thing.

Possessive

Mine, yours, hers, his, ours, theirs. These are closely linked to possessive adjectives, for instance, 'That is my coat' becomes 'That is mine'.

Interrogative

Who, whom, whose, what, which e.g. 'To whom have you given it?' or 'Which did it?'

Adverbs

Just as an *adjective* modifies a *noun*, an *adverb* modifies a *verb*. That is, an adverb *describes* a verb. Some examples follow:

1 The girl ran fast.
2 Mr Smith drove slowly.
3 The boy easily pushed in the tent peg.
4 A young lady quickly crossed the road.

In the first sentence, the verb is 'ran' and 'fast' is the word that describes 'ran'. Hence, 'fast' is an adverb. Likewise, in the second sentence, the word 'slowly' describes the verb 'drove'. Hence, 'slowly' is an adverb. In the same way, in the third sentence, 'easily' is the adverb which modifies the verb 'pushed'. In the fourth sentence, 'quickly' is the adverb modifying the verb 'crossed'.

Make sure the child notices that many adverbs end in 'ly', but not all. For instance, some adverbs modify verbs by answering such questions as 'how?', 'when?', 'where?'.

1 The dog ate fast.	('fast' modifies 'ate')
2 The people arrived yesterday.	('yesterday modifies 'arrived')
3 I am going out.	('out' modifies 'going')

Then again, some adverbs actually *ask* questions, such as:

1 Where have you been?   ('where' modifies 'have been')
2 When did school begin?   ('when' modifies 'did begin')
3 Why are you laughing?   ('why' modifies 'are laughing')
4 How does Mary play?   ('how' modifies 'does play')

Then, as well, one sometimes finds two adverbs modifying the same verb, as in: 'He performed extremely poorly.' This can be regarded as one adverb (extremely) modifying another (poorly). Those adverbs which modify other adverbs are referred to technically as 'adverbs of degree'. Some examples are: 'minutely elegant', 'very beautiful', 'painfully slowly', 'rather difficult', 'so viciously' and 'remarkably swiftly'. Given this, we must refine the definition of adverb to: 'An adverb is a word which modifies a verb, an adjective or another adverb.

Prepositions

Preposition is one of those grammatical words that children pick up in school without giving much thought to its logical meaning, but, if you have the child separate the prefix, the word becomes 'pre-position', and this suggests what a preposition really is. It is a word which means 'placed in front of'. Thus, a preposition is usually placed in front of a noun, or a pronoun, and is said to *govern* the noun or pronoun following it. The preposition shows a relationship between its noun (or pronoun) and some other word (a verb or a noun) in the sentence. This relationship may be in *space* or in *time*.

For instance, have the child consider the sentence:

The horse climbed up the hill.

The preposition is 'up'. It indicates a relationship (in space) between the noun it governs ('hill') and the verb 'climbed'.
Consider another one:

The house down the road is empty.

The preposition is 'down'. It governs 'road' and relates it to the noun 'house'. It also is a relationship in space.
Now, show him the sentence:

He swims before breakfast.

'Before' is a preposition in time. It governs 'breakfast' and relates to the verb 'swims'.

A point that children invariably find difficult is that many words can be either adverbs or prepositions according to the way they are used. The difference is (and this may require some patient explanation) that an adverb modifies the verb *without* a noun or pronoun following it, for instance:

The sick cow began to lag behind.

The word 'behind' modifies the verb 'began to lag'. It does not govern any noun or pronoun. Therefore, in this case 'behind' is an adverb.

But consider the sentence:

I put the envelope behind the clock.

In that case, 'behind' is a preposition in space, governing 'clock' and relating it to the noun 'envelope'.

Make sure that the child can recognise the principal prepositions where he runs across them. They are:

in
out
up
down
around
about
over
under
through
across
above
below
beneath
before
between
after
until

on
during
since
throughout

Conjunctions

A *conjunction* is simply a 'joining' word in a sentence, such as 'and', 'but' or 'or'. The grammar of conjunctions becomes very complicated indeed if we start to consider what grammarians call *subordinating conjunctions*. Therefore, in this rudimentary account we shall not discuss them. It is sufficient for the child to be able to pick out the three principal conjunctions in sentences and to recognise that they are 'joining' words. The following three examples should help:

1 Acid splashed on his fingers and hurt him.
2 They will play tapes or listen to records.
3 He hates the dark but he will go through the tunnel.

Interjections

The last of our nine parts of speech are *interjections*. An interjection is a word that does not fit into what we ordinarily mean by a sentence. Consider these examples:

1 Look!
2 An abominable snowman!
3 Get away!
4 Holy smoke! I forgot the keys!

The exclamation mark at the end of each of these word groups tells us how to read them with expression. It also tells us that we are dealing with an interjection. The first one, if said in a dull voice, loses its force. The same is true of the second and the third examples. The fourth one contains the expression 'Holy smoke'. Now, if you analyse the fourth example, you can see that 'Holy smoke' cannot really be made part of any sentence, not even of the sentence following it. 'I forget the keys' is a sentence. 'Holy smoke' makes the statement that you forgot the keys somewhat surprising or alarming or annoying or whatever. It is an interjection.

Elementary Grammar of the Sentence

We shall close this rudimentary account of grammar with a more formal account of what a *sentence* is. The child already knows that a sentence is a statement of a complete thought. We now go further and explain that a sentence *must* have two parts: a *subject* and a *predicate*. Make sure that the child can pronounce each of the two words accurately.

Now, explain that the *subject* is the word (or words) that *names* the thing that the sentence is talking about. The *predicate* is the word (or words) which tells what the subject is doing or what is happening to it. The child should be able to appreciate that the *subject* of a sentence has to be a noun (or involve a noun) and that the *predicate* of a sentence has to be a verb (or involve a verb).

Some examples will make this perfectly clear:

1 Richard walked back to the house.

2 Stella baked a cake with butter icing.

3 Bullets whizzed by Steve's head.

Ask the child to notice that each of these clusters of words is, in fact, a sentence. Each one expresses a complete thought. The *subject* of the first sentence is 'Richard', the subject of the second sentence is 'Stella' and the subject of the third sentence is 'bullets'.

Now, what about the *predicates*? The predicate of the first sentence is 'walked back to the house'. It tells what the subject (Richard) did or what happened to the subject. The child should be able to pick out the main verb in the predicate. It is 'walked'.

In the second sentence, have the child pick out the predicate. It is 'baked a cake with butter icing'. Then ask *why* that is the predicate. It is the predicate because it tells what the subject (Stella) did. Can the child find the main verb in the predicate? It is 'baked'.

Similarly, in the third sentence, the predicate is 'whizzed by Steve's head' because it tells what the subject (bullets) did or what happened to the subject. The main verb in the predicate is 'whizzed'.

As well as a *subject* and a *predicate* (which every sentence *must* have), most sentences also have an *object*. An *object* is another noun (or a group of words involving a noun) on which the verb acts. The object is usually part of the predicate. The sentence introduces a 'doer' (the noun or subject) which 'does' something (the verb or predicate) and this affects a 'thing' (the object). Consider these examples:

1 The cat ate the mouse.

2 Lisa kicked the ball.

3 Stones broke the window.

In the first sentence, 'the cat' is the subject, 'ate the mouse' is the predicate and 'the mouse' is the object. Explain this carefully. Now, in each of the other two sentences, guide the child to discover the subject, predicate and object.

If the child has understood all of this, and if he is intrigued by such things, it would be of value to draw his attention to an interesting feature of pronouns. In English nouns, the spelling does not change (nor does the pronunciation) according to whether the noun is the *subject* or the *object* of the sentence. In most other European languages the spelling of a noun *does* change according to whether the noun is a subject or an object, which makes it very easy to pick out the subject and the object of a sentence. But English has no such simple system!

However, Latin is *one* of the roots of English and in Latin the nouns *do* change spelling according to whether they are subject or object. In English we do have some traces of this Latin background: some of our pronouns have different spellings according to whether they are subject or objects. For instance, consider the sentences:

1 Mary kissed Michael.
2 Henry shook hands with Mrs Smith.
3 Tom met Harry.
4 Ruth chased Helen.

In each of these, let us exchange the nouns for pronouns. In the first sentence, 'Mary' becomes 'She' and 'Michael' becomes 'him':

   1 She kissed him.

Would it have made any sense to write: 'Her kissed he.'? The child, of course, will find that ludicrous. You can then point out that the male pronoun has two forms: 'he' (if it is a subject) and 'him' (if he is an object). Likewise, the female pronoun has two forms: 'she' (if it is a subject) and 'her' (if it is an object). This all becomes clear when we substitute pronouns for nouns in the other three sentences:

   2 He shook hands with her.
   3 He met him.
   4 She chased her.

The pronoun 'it' does not change.

While considering the issue with the child, it is worthwhile to remind him that a preposition is said to *govern* a noun or a pronoun. The noun or the pronoun that it governs is called its *object*. The same rule applies when a pronoun is the object of a preposition as when it is the object of a sentence. Consider the sentences:

   1 The man went with the woman.
   2 The woman went with the man.

In the first sentence, 'with' is a preposition having 'the woman' as its *object*, the noun it governs. In the second sentence, 'with' is a preposition having 'the man' as its *object*. If we now let the child replace the nouns with pronouns in those two sentences, obviously, he should come up with:

   1 He went with her.   ('Him went with she' would be nonsense.)
   2 She went with him.   ('Her went with he' would also be nonsense.)

Congratulations! Together you have now mastered the rudiments of grammar and your child should be well on his way down the road to reading!

26

From print to cursive script

Making Script as Painless as Possible

One of the differences between the way I have always taught children to read and that used in most schools is that I try to combine reading and writing almost from the start. Anyone using this book will have noticed that already.

As far back as 1964, I found that children in school printed their written work for the first two years, if not more, before moving on to handwriting. If you think about it, you might well wonder why this is so. After all, we don't ordinarily print, unless we are writing a *very* short message, a memo or an advertisement of some sort. The reason is simple: printing is laborious and cramps the hand and finger muscles. In Britain, people tend to refer to cursive script as *joined-up writing*. However, *cursive* is a better word for it, for *cursive* means 'running', as in 'current', 'course' (a racecourse) or 'coursing'. It suggests fluency and speed, and that is an accurate suggestion, for cursive handwriting quickly becomes smooth, flowing and fast, whereas printing is always arduous. The child who is kept at the printing stage of writing for too long develops an understandable aversion to writing much. His ideas may flow, but if he has to print, putting them down on paper is tortuous.

The solution, then, is to teach him to write in cursive script as soon as possible and while he is at a comparatively early stage of learning to read. Once he has learned the letters, there is no point in him continuing to print. However, you don't want to tie it in so precisely with fixed points in the reading programme that you find you are holding back his rate of progress in reading until his cursive writing skills develop. The best way by far is to exercise flexibility!

For instance, it is probably best to begin teaching the child 'cursive' script when he starts reading complete sentences, say, at about Exercise 64. Care must be taken, though, if he finds it difficult or worrying, to let him keep on printing for a few more exercises before you broach the subject again. Even if several children of the same age begin to learn cursive writing when at Exercise 64, they develop their mechanical writing skills at quite different rates. Some may still prefer to print when they are reading at the level of Exercise 112, but eventually the need to write more and more renders the speed and smoothness of cursive script increasingly attractive. Whatever your child's disposition and level of skill, it is very important that you do not give him the impression that his pleasure in mastering reading is conditional on him mastering the skill of joined-up writing!

Changing Views on Handwriting

When I first raised this issue in 1964, it fell largely on deaf ears. Other teachers seemed surprised that my pupils were already writing in cursive script at six or seven years of age, but back then the argument was that children needed to write in a fashion as similar to the print they read in books as possible. My own research has not only indicated that such is not the case, but that children who had developed facility and speed with cursive script *enjoyed* writing. It was less of a chore for them.

In Quebec, Canada, when I was a child, we were always taught cursive script in our first year of primary school. It was done terribly mechanically, with lots of copying of Biblical passages and wise sayings – and with a very strong emphasis on writing *exactly* as the model showed. I would *not* suggest that *that* part of it was such a good idea. Certainly it was assumed that all children should be able to write in cursive script by the time they were seven. For instance, in all subjects, the teachers wrote in cursive on the board and that is what the pupils had to copy just to get the information. Today, in France, the same policy is followed.

In Britain, the view is now being strongly promoted that children should be taught to write in cursive. By the time you are doing this with your child, it may well be generally accepted in your local schools. Interested readers may like to check an article about this on page ten of *The Sunday Times* for 1 November 1997. Herne Infant School in Kent has apparently led the way in this because its Head Teacher, Fiona Thompson, was impressed by the ease with which French school children move at an early age on to cursive script.

A Method for Teaching Cursive Script

I recommend a routine, but a fairly relaxed one, for switching a child from printing to 'grown-up' writing. After all, the child is usually highly motivated to do it – and for two reasons. First of all, reading is fun and therefore the desire to write is strong. But he will quickly discover that printing is too slow and painful: writing out, say, twenty words in print makes the hand uncomfortable. If one attempts to print fast, the letters – because they are not flowing together in each word – become messy and crowded. A second motivation is, simply, that cursive has status – it is more 'grown-up' than printing.

So, how should one go about it? I tend to do it as follows. Tell the child that you are going to show him how to write like a grown-up and that it is *much* easier than what he has been doing. However, he does have to go back a bit and learn again how to form each letter.

Then, point out that the idea is to be able to write the *whole* letter without taking the pencil off the paper. For this, you want to use ordinary, lined, school exercise-book paper. To start off with, rule every second line darker than it is on the page, so that the child has twice as much letter height to work in just as you did when you were teaching him to print (see Figure 32 at the back of the book). The idea is that every letter has a lead-in stroke to start and a tail-stroke to finish. Many letters have a body *and* a tail and that is why two spaces of lined exercise-book paper are required.

Look at the cursive lower-case 'a'. Stroke 1 leads in, then stroke 2 is the 'belly' of the letter. Stroke 3 is the *upstroke* for the back and stroke 4 is the *downstroke* for the back (it retraces the upstroke) and then runs off into stroke 5, the tail. These strokes are *not* separate movements. The pencil stays on the paper throughout.

The child will have to do many 'a's – possibly a page full of them – before he gets the smooth flow of it. Once he does, of course, the other letters come more easily. Not every letter can be done with one movement. For instance, 'i' and 'j' require lifting the pencil off the page to make the dots, and 't' and 'x' require two separate strokes.

Preventing Bad Habits

What is *vital*, though, is that the child does get into the habit of putting the lead-in and tail strokes correctly on each letter. For instance, notice that on 'a' 'b', 'c', 'd', and 'e' the lead-in stroke starts in the middle of the space, while the tail comes away from the bottom of the letter. Unless you insist (gently) on the importance of these things, some very bad habits will arise and these are *very* difficult to eradicate once the child's writing becomes rapid and smooth. Indeed, I have postgraduate students whose handwriting is such that one cannot pick out their 'o's from their 'a's. A young child can easily be taught that the lead-in of 'a' starts in the middle but its tail is 'on the floor', whereas with 'o', the lead-in and the tail are both in the middle. Letters such as 'm' and 'n' likewise will cause problems later unless you are a stickler for detail at the outset. Again, 'r' must not look like 'v', and 'u' and 'v' must be quite distinct from one another.

The reason for emphasising the lead-in and the tail, of course, is because these are crucial for the development of smooth joined-up script. If, on the other hand, you are a little bit laid-back about these initial niceties, you will produce a child whose handwriting does *not* flow smoothly and whose handwriting may even be difficult to read! Indeed, he will get few of the benefits of cursive script over printing.

It is the necessity of making sure that these initial stages have been correctly mastered that makes it so important for you not to spend too much time each day on the writing. The incessant, but necessary, emphasis on detail could turn your child off the whole enterprise. Let the *reading* remain the main thing. If that is a source of steady achievement and pleasure, the motivation to master the writing will remain high enough to let the child cope with five or ten minutes of drill on it each day.

Of course, his progress in reading demands more encoding time than that each day. For instance, he has to write out spelling words and short sentences. But let him print that material until he himself decides that it is easier and quicker to do it by cursive writing. Every few days ask him if he wants to try a bit more of his written work in cursive writing instead of print.

When it comes to writing complete sentences in cursive, especially after your child has moved from using 'double-spaced' lined paper with the lines drawn in by yourself, he will not need so much space between words. If he does still need to measure it from time to time – to keep his words from running together – one finger's breadth rather than two, would be sufficient (see Figure 34).

Cursive Script Capitals

There is far more legitimate disagreement (meaning 'untested either way by good research'!) among teachers about the 'correct' way of scripting capital letters than there is about lower-case ones. What I have shown in Figure 33 is by no means universal. Many teachers approach capital letters in cursive simply by teaching the child to put a tail (if you think about it there is no need for a lead-in on a capital letter!) on the ordinary printed form of capital letters. The advantage of such an approach is that it is quicker and easier. It does not involve learning completely new shapes for the letters 'D', 'E', 'F', 'G', 'I', 'Q', 'S' and 'T'. The disadvantage is that it can become sloppy and the capitals often don't get properly joined up to the letters following.

But to summarise with respect to learning to write in cursive script, it is important that you *insist* that:

1 Capital letters use up the full height of the space, e.g. touch the line above and below.
2 In lower-case letters with stems (such as 'd' and 't'), the stems cross the whole space between lines, so that the stem is as high as a capital letter.
3 In lower-case letters with hanging tails (such as 'g' and 'y'), the tail hang below the bottom line and the body of the letter must lie right on the line.

4 The bodies of all lower-case letters occupy half the space between lines, and always lie neatly on the lower line.

His writing will take a while to measure up to these standards. Be patient and good humoured about it. Do not insist that he keep on rewriting his work to get it perfect as long as you can daily see a steady improvement tending in the right direction! Remember, you don't want to make him apprehensive about writing.

Why Be So Fussy?

You might well ask: Why all the fuss? Why not let him write as small as he likes? The reasons are straightforward:

1 It will interfere grossly with his efforts to learn cursive handwriting. Once a child has got into the habit of excessively crimping and crowding his print, it is *very* difficult for him to open it up again to learn how to join letters together and to develop an even, flowing hand.
2 It eventually tires the small muscles of the hand (and the big muscles of the shoulder, from tensing to lean forward) to the degree that writing becomes quite uncomfortable. The aim is for him to be able to write effortlessly for as long as he wishes – not to see how small he can write! (See Figure 31.)

One of the *major* problems that secondary school and university students have with writing is that they are *uncomfortable with the mechanics of it*. This can produce illegible script, poor spelling and atrocious grammar, all because the physical act of writing is so unpleasant. Even as a university professor, I have *literally* had students who chose to print rather than write in cursive script! If it were simply a matter of appearance, it would be of little consequence. But the person who cannot write fluently and effortlessly in a simple, open style, is restricted in the content of what he can write. The act of writing becomes a serious barrier between what he is thinking and what gets put down on the paper!

Don't let that fate befall your child.

List of sight words used in this book

As explained in the text, although the method relies primarily on phonics, it is occasionally necessary to introduce one or more sight words: words which either do not easily lend themselves to decoding by phonic rules or which are needed for use before the appropriate phonic rules have been learned. Learning these words has the great advantage of enabling the child to read more natural-sounding material. I recommend that for each of these words you make a flash card (an ordinary white filing card with the word printed on it in black felt-tip pen). Thus, you will end up with seventy flash cards.

It would absolutely defeat the purpose of this method to insist on forcing the child to recognise these words at a faster rate than that at which they are introduced in the book. They are only all listed here so that the parent/teacher has some insight into the order of their occurrence. They are numbered in the order in which they appear in the text.

1	the	15	shall	29	school
2	I	16	there	30	one
3	to	17	where	31	two
4	he	18	were	32	was
5	who	19	says	33	any
6	you	20	said	34	guess
7	go	21	before	35	people
8	she	22	have	36	believe
9	we	23	some	37	taught
10	me	24	come	38	put
11	no	25	could	39	pull
12	be	26	should	40	bull
13	are	27	would	41	full
14	or	28	they	42	push

43 young

44 course

45 laugh

46 go

47 so

48 to

49 do

50 sign

51 piece

52 friend

53 want

54 eight

55 because

56 four

57 hour

58 done

59 suit

60 thought

61 though

62 does

63 neighbour

64 eye

65 woman

66 women

67 their

68 know

69 knew

70 colour

Figures

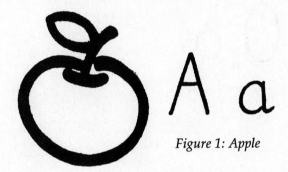

Figure 1: Apple

Figure 2: Egg

I i

Figure 3: Indian

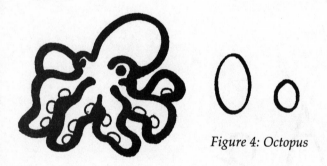

O o

Figure 4: Octopus

U u

Figure 5: Umbrella

B b

Figure 6: Bat

 C c

Figure 7: Cat

D d

Figure 8: Dog

Figure 9: Fish

Figure 10: Goat

Figure 11: Hat

J j

Figure 12: Jar

 K k

Figure 13: Kite

L l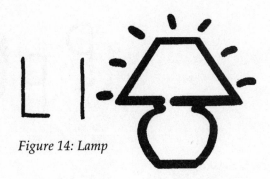

Figure 14: Lamp

Figure 15: Moon

Figure 16: Nest

Figure 17: Pig

Figure 18: Queen

Figure 19: Rabbit

Figure 20: Snake

Figure 21: Tie

Figure 22: Vacuum

Figure 23: Watch

X x

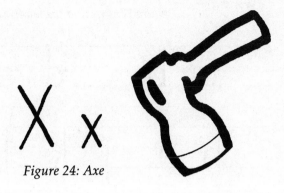

Figure 24: Axe

Y y

Figure 25: Yacht

Z z

Figure 26: Zip

Figure 27: Printing the lower-case letters

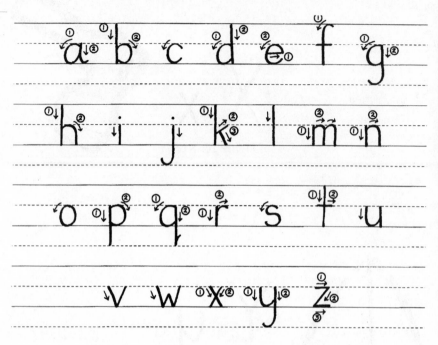

Figure 28: Printing the capital letters

Figure 29: Introductory printing of sentences

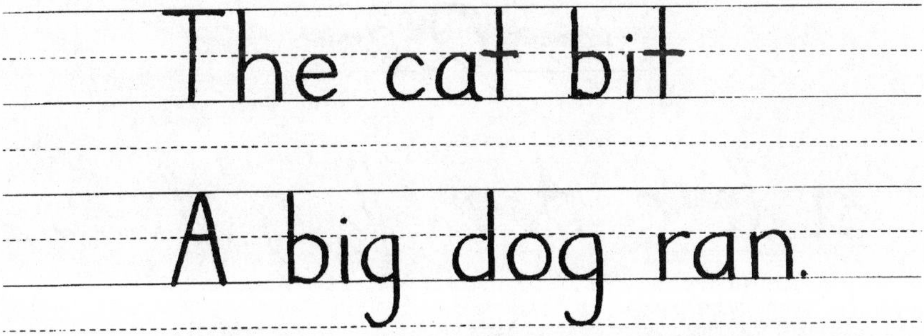

The cat bit

A big dog ran.

Figure 30: More advanced printing using one space

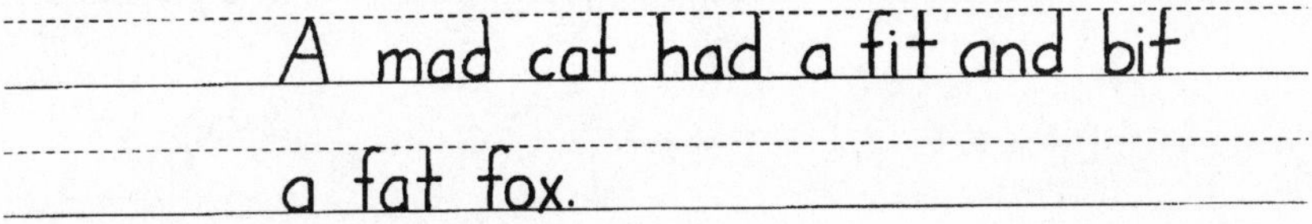

A mad cat had a fit and bit
a fat fox.

*Figure 31: The child's printing should never be allowed to become
this cramped.*

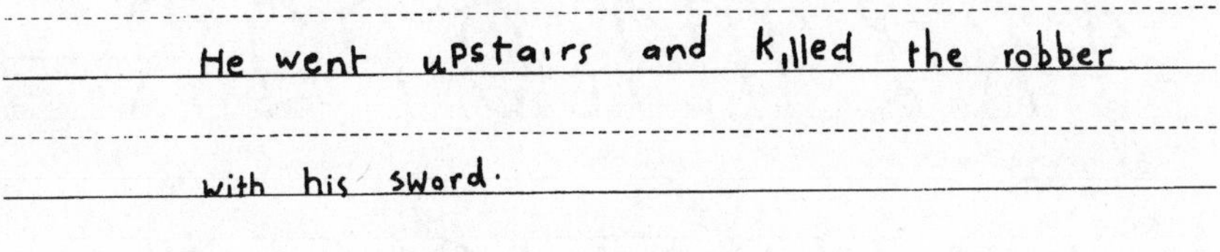

He went upstairs and killed the robber

with his sword.

Figure 32: Writing the lower-case letters in cursive script

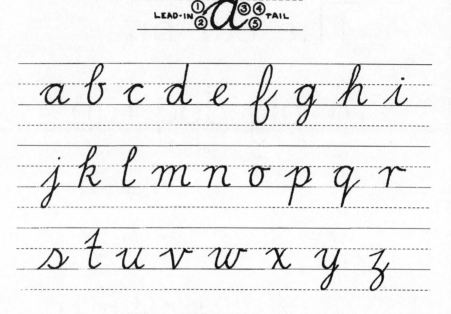

Figure 33: Writing the capital letters in cursive script. Note: the style presented here is by no means universal; see also the discussions in Lesson 32 and Chapter 26.

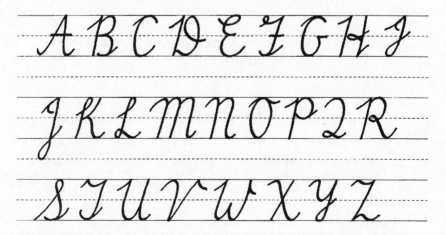

Figure 34: Writing sentences in cursive script

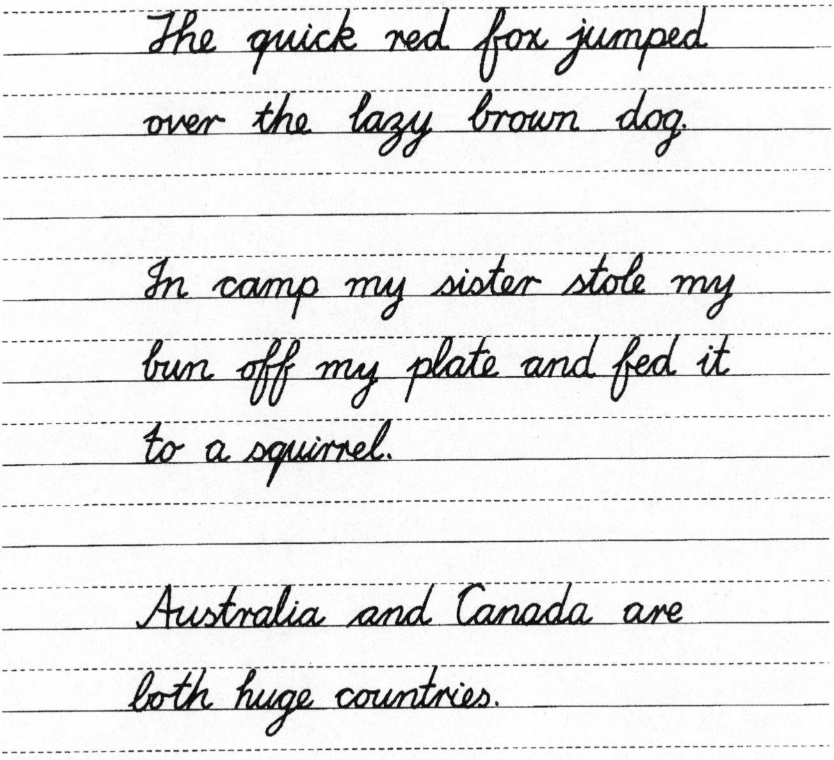

The quick red fox jumped
over the lazy brown dog.

In camp my sister stole my
bun off my plate and fed it
to a squirrel.

Australia and Canada are
both huge countries.